The Guinness Book of
CRICKET BLUNDERS

CRIS FREDDI

GUINNESS PUBLISHING

This publication © Guinness Publishing Limited (1996), 33 London Road, Enfield, Middlesex

Reprint 10 9 8 7 6 5 4 3 2 1 0

Quotes courtesy of *Private Eye*'s Colemanballs

Text design and layout by Moondisks Ltd, Cambridge

Front cover illustrations courtesy of Allsport UK Ltd. *Clockwise from top:* Ian Botham *(Adrian Murrell)*, David Gower *(Adrian Murrell)*, Michael Atherton *(Graham Chadwick)*

Cover design by Dryden Design

Printed and bound in Great Britain by The Bath Press, Bath

A catalogue record for this book is available from the British Library

ISBN 0–85112–624–3

CONTENTS

Introduction & Acknowledgments

It goes without saying that many of the best cricketing clangers went straight into the original *Guinness Book of Sporting Blunders* – but there were always going to be more than enough left over for a separate book. If a well-known error doesn't appear in this one, there's every chance of finding it in the original (shamelessly signposted *Blunders Vol. 1*).

As before, we've generally kept to mistakes that mattered (run outs that cost Test matches, stroke selection that lost cup finals, etc) while leaving space for the more harmlessly humorous. No apologies for the number of dropped catches: it's hard to think of a lapse that leaves the culprit feeling more lonely and exposed, wishing the earth would open up and start swallowing. The ultimate sporting blunder.

Anyone spotting a deliberate mistake should of course blame it on the author and not on those who helped him out, including *Private Eye* for permission to dip into their famous Colemanballs postbag.

I suppose I daydreamed of putting together a cricket book without any input from Steven Lynch, just to prove it was possible. It wasn't. His proof reading and supply of oddball snippets were invaluable, as befits the deputy editor of a leading cricket magazine, fearsome quiz league captain, and author of *The Lord's Test*, the best book of its kind. He also entered into the spirit of the book by picking England to win the last World Cup.

Above all, as always, thanks to Charles Richards, my editor at Guinness, for his unfailing patience, attention to detail, and of course sense of humour.

About the author

Cris Freddi has the right credentials for writing this, his fifth book for Guinness. His knowledge of the game has been demonstrated in national newspapers, cricket magazines, and *A Question of Sport*. More importantly, in his first representative match at any level, he didn't bowl, dropped a vital catch, and was clean bowled first ball.

Catches lose Ashes

(and assorted Ashes matches)

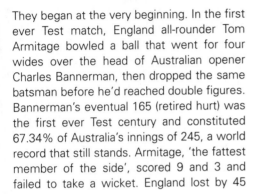

They began at the very beginning. In the first ever Test match, England all-rounder Tom Armitage bowled a ball that went for four wides over the head of Australian opener Charles Bannerman, then dropped the same batsman before he'd reached double figures. Bannerman's eventual 165 (retired hurt) was the first ever Test century and constituted 67.34% of Australia's innings of 245, a world record that still stands. Armitage, 'the fattest member of the side', scored 9 and 3 and failed to take a wicket. England lost by 45 runs.

It all went horribly wrong for Australian left-arm seamer Chris Matthews in the first Test of the 1986–87 series, his first against any country. Not only did he bowl nervously and none too well (3–106) but he also dropped David Gower at slip before he'd scored. Instead of making his third consecutive duck of the tour, Gower went on to reach 51 and help England take a 1–0 lead in a series they eventually won 2–1 to retain the Ashes.

England, going into the third Test of the 1958–59 series 2–0 down, brought Fred Trueman back in place of Peter Loader and gave a first cap to wicketkeeper Roy Swetman, who promptly dropped Colin McDonald in Fiery Fred's first over. McDonald made 40, Australia drew the match and went on to regain the Ashes.

During the next series, 1961 in England, Trueman had another Australian opener dropped, this time at slip. Bill Lawry, on 25 at the time, went on to top score with 102 and help Australia to a winning 2–1 lead.

In 1962–63, even more of the same for Fred. On the last day of the fourth Test, England were pressing to dismiss Australia early enough to give themselves a good chance of winning the match – and might well have done so if Fred Titmus hadn't dropped Australia's captain Richie Benaud at leg slip off Trueman. Benaud stayed to make an important 48 and force the draw. The series ended 1–1, which left the Ashes in Australia.

In the first Test of the 1964 series, Australia's world-class wicketkeeper Wally Grout dropped the ball when he threw it up before completing a catch off England captain Ted Dexter, whose 68, easily the highest score in the second innings, helped draw the match.

In 1985, a similar thing. Just before the end of the second day of the Lord's Test, Australia's captain Allan Border turned a ball from Phil Edmonds off his legs into the hands of Mike Gatting, who was alleged to have thrown it up in celebration before it was under control. In fact, he was trying to knock it upwards to give himself a better chance of taking it second time, but it was nevertheless a costly miss. Border, who'd been on his way back to the pavilion, went on to make 196. It was the only Test Australia won that summer. They haven't lost at Lord's since 1934.

(During the disastrous 1992–93 series in India, Gatting dropped one of the easiest catches ever seen in Test cricket, a gentle pop-up from Kiran More.)

Australia won the 1909 Lord's Test and with it the Ashes thanks to Vernon Ransford's only Test century, but only after he'd been dropped three times (*Blunders Vol. 1*) . This was typical of England's fielding in the match: 38-year-old all-rounder John King, playing in his only Test, finished with figures of 1–99 in Australia's first innings, but was unlucky in having three catches dropped off his bowling, including Ransford and the great Victor Trumper in the same over.

> ## It's his second finger, technically his third.
>
> **Christopher Martin-Jenkins**

England's narrow win in the first Test of the 1886 series owed much to Arthur Shrewsbury's stabilising innings of 31 (in a low-scoring match) after he'd been dropped at slip off the first ball he received. In the second innings, Allan G Steel, who'd been dropped during his famous 148 against Australia two years earlier (*Blunders Vol.1*), 'was missed from an easy chance' by George Bonnor, again at slip. England won all three Tests that summer.

England lost the first Test of the 1954–55 series for a number of reasons, with dropped catches near the top of the list: 12 in Australia's only innings!

England regained the Ashes in 1926 by winning the last Test by 289 runs, but only after living dangerously in the third.

After draws in the first two, Maurice Tate

dismissed the Australian captain Warren Bardsley in the very first over, then almost immediately found the edge of Charlie Macartney's bat, only for the England captain Arthur Carr to drop the catch at third slip.

Macartney made 112 before lunch, shared a second-wicket partnership of 235 with Bill Woodfull, and set Australia on the way to 494. England held out for the draw. Carr, who'd put Australia in to bat after leaving out the brilliant spinner Charlie Parker, lost the captaincy after the fourth Test.

Two low scores in the fourth Test of the 1970–71 Ashes series (including a duck in the second innings) left Ian Chappell vulnerable to the selectorial axe, especially as England won the match to take a 1–0 lead. The fifth Test may have been his last chance.

Twice in his first innings, when he'd made 0 and 14, he was put down by Colin Cowdrey, one of the great slip fielders but having a miserable tour (he dropped at least four catches in that innings alone). Chappell not only went on to score a century but was made captain from the next Test on, with dire repercussions for England in the 1970s.

The folkloric, heart-stopping Test match of 1882 was a low-scoring affair in which opener Hugh Massie's 55 was easily the highest score. Decisive, too, given that Australia won by just seven runs. But he had an important helping hand early on.

As soon as Australia wiped out their first-innings deficit of 38 (with all their wickets intact), the England captain Albert 'Monkey' Hornby brought on medium pacer Billy Barnes, whose first ball was hit by Massie straight to long-on, where Alfred 'Bunny' Lucas, 'usually so reliable a fieldsman', dropped it. After the match, the *Sporting Times* printed its famous mock obituary of English cricket.

If the morale of the Australian batsmen was at a low ebb after the first day of the 1896 series in England, it was no surprise: ten days after being all out for 18 against an MCC XI, they were now dismissed for 53 on a perfect batting strip!

Still, their undaunted, probably infuriated bowlers would have got them back into the match if some of those batsmen had redeemed themselves by holding all their catches. Instead, they dropped WG Grace at long-on, then Bobby Abel was 'palpably missed in the slips' when he'd scored only nine. Grace made 66, Abel a top score of 94 in a total of 231. Australia lost the match by six wickets and eventually the series 2–1. They might have won both if three more chances hadn't been put down off Ernie Jones alone!

David Sheppard wasn't the only England culprit in the 1962–63 series (see PRETEND IT'S SUNDAY, REVEREND). In the first innings of the fourth Test alone, Neil Harvey was reprieved off consecutive balls from Ray Illingworth. Meanwhile, there had been talk of the Australian selectors dropping Norm O'Neill, but the England fielders did it instead: four times before he'd reached 26! O'Neill scored 100, Harvey 154, Australia drew the match and the series to retain the Ashes.

It's hard to know if Australia won the 1924–25 series 4–1 because of or despite some lapses in the field: the two sides dropped 45 catches between them!

England, 1–0 down in the 1956 series, were 17–3 in their first innings of the third Test, recovering thanks to Peter May and veteran Cyril Washbrook, who hadn't played Test cricket since 1951 (now a Test selector, he'd helped pick himself!). When he'd made 44, he hit the ball hard but straight to Keith Miller, one of the great fielders. The dropped catch allowed Washbrook to go on to 98 and help win the match (remarkably, their first ever win over Australia at Headingley) and square the series, which England won 2–1.

> *Richie Richardson turned blind but had a good look.*
>
> **Bill Lawry**

England's task in the third Test of the 1928–29 series looked impossible: a winning target of 332 on one of the most vicious rain-affected wickets in memory. In that second innings, balls lifted off a length to knock Jack Hobbs' cap off and bruise Herbert Sutcliffe on the shoulder, forearm, biceps and ribs. They survived through the batting skills of one of the greatest opening partnerships of all time – but there was a little more to it than that.

Australia opened the bowling with Hunter Scott Thomas Laurie Hendry, whose extra height (he was known as 'Stork') made the ball jump as well as turn. Hobbs cut one of these 'spring-heeled spinners' into the slips, where the other opening bowler, new cap Ted A'Beckett, juggled desperately before dropping it. Hobbs was later missed by Don Bradman no less, who also dropped 'Patsy' Hendren!

Hobbs made 49, Hendren 'an invaluable 45' and Sutcliffe 135 to set up a narrow win that retained the Ashes.

England players later repaid Bradman in full, dropping him during various match-winning knocks, including the famous second innings at Headingley in 1948 (see WICKED KEEPERS) and in the final Test of the

As Bradman accumulates, Edrich (at slip) measures the one that got away

1946–47 series, when he'd scored only 2 before being dropped at slip by Bill Edrich. His 63 (top score in the innings) helped win the match by five wickets.

Whatever chance Australia had of forcing a win out of the third Test in 1905 disappeared in England's second innings when Johnny Tyldesley and George Hirst were dropped at slip off successive balls, both by Warwick Armstrong off Monty Noble. Later, the hapless Armstrong missed a caught-and-bowled chance off Tyldesley, who went on to score exactly 100 (Hirst made 40 not out)

to ensure the draw which preserved England's lead in a series they won 2–0.

The England side led by Freddie Brown in Australia in 1950–51 was so poor in the field (six dropped catches against Victoria, countless fielding errors in the Test series) that they were known as Brown's Cows!

The third Test of the 1911–12 series was dominated by Jack Hobbs' 187, the bulwark of England's total of 501 which won the match by seven wickets to give them a 2–1 lead in a series they won 4–1. It was the first time they'd avoided defeat at Adelaide for 20 years and the highest of Hobbs' 12 centuries against Australia, but not 'I must candidly admit, a perfect innings as I gave a number of chances.'

Swings and roundabouts. Hobbs was one of those on the receiving end nine years later. Australia's opening batsman Herbie Collins was forever being dropped in the 1920–21 series, especially in the third Test when he made 162. In the second innings of the same match, Australia were 22 runs behind with three second-innings wickets down, but Charles Kelleway was dropped at slip by Percy Fender before getting off the mark, then went on to make 147 and help win the match by 119. England lost all five matches in a rubber for the first time.

Australia's first innings of 346, enough to draw the second Test in 1953, would have been far lower if England hadn't put down two catches off Johnny Wardle and three off Alec Bedser, who dropped another himself!

Ian Botham might not have lost the England captaincy if a few more catches had been held in the first Test of 1981. Instead, whereas Australia dropped only one in the match, England put down six simple chances in the first innings alone, including two by Botham himself and an easy catch off Allan Border which cost wicketkeeper Paul Downton his place. Border, on 10 at the time, made 63, far and away the top score in a total of only 179 on an iffy pitch. England lost by just four wickets and Botham lasted only one more match as captain.

Keith Fletcher's relationship with Yorkshire folk wasn't especially cordial. When Fred Trueman was asked what he'd like to do to the demonstrators who'd dug up the Headingley pitch in 1975, he replied that he'd drop them off the top of the pavilion. 'But I'm not a cruel man. I'd give them a 50–50 chance. I'd have Keith Fletcher underneath trying to catch them.'

This all stemmed from Fletcher's first Test, against Australia at Headingley in 1968. When vice-captain Tom Graveney injured his thumb, the selectors sent for Yorkshire's Phil Sharpe as cover. Graveney recovered, but the crowd seemed to believe that Fletcher had been picked in Sharpe's place.

Unfortunately for the new boy, he was stationed at first slip, where he'd rarely fielded for Essex and where Sharpe was one of the all-time greats. When Fletcher dropped two chances off John Snow, one to his left, one to his right, the crowd turned on him, and their temper didn't improve when he was given out caught behind for a duck in his first Test innings despite not having hit the ball! England were held to a draw which cost them their last chance of regaining the Ashes. Poor Fletcher, verbally abused by an idiot who ran onto the pitch, was dropped from the next Test.

That strike rate, just under 40 deliveries a ball.

Jack Bannister

Geoff Boycott had his heart set on India in 1981–82. Not because he especially loved the place (he felt that it caused him all kinds of alimentary problems) but because he needed to go on the tour to break Garry Sobers' world record number of Test runs. In the event, he got there and he broke it, but before the last Test of the previous series, against Australia at home, he'd worried that his place might be in doubt. So it did his cause no harm when he scored 137 in the first innings, for which he (but not

Gooch gives Tufnell the ball to stop him fielding

Sobers) could thank Terry Alderman for dropping him at slip off Mike Whitney.

England's performance in Australia in 1990–91 won't be remembered so much for specific dropped catches as a general low standard of fielding. Well, let's not sit on the fence. Their captain Graham Gooch called it 'the worst fielding side I've ever been in. It was a total disaster. I could never have believed that any side I was in charge of could be so inept.' With the unathletic likes of Eddie Hemmings, Phil Tufnell and Devon Malcolm in the side, perhaps it wasn't so surprising. A pig with Hemmings' name painted on its side had been released during the Ashes series back in 1982–83, and he was now almost 42. Another controversial selection, Wayne Larkins, was 37. As for the truculent Tufnell, former Australian captain Ian Chappell said that 'the good thing about his bowling is that when he's doing it he's not fielding.' England lost the series 3–0.

Pick of the weak

(and other selectorial gaffes)

England selectors have had some strange reasons for picking players, but surely none more bizarre than the one for Charlie McGahey's inclusion in the 1901–02 touring team. Suffering from what appeared to be the early stages of TB, he was taken to Australia for his health!

Not surprisingly, he didn't achieve much with the bat (an average of 9.50 in his only two Tests, both of which England lost), but it was said, in all seriousness, that he came back cured!

Mike Atherton's made it well known that he didn't get precisely the tour party he wanted for the 1994–95 trip to Australia. He argued for the inclusion of Angus Fraser, but Ray Illingworth and the other selectors voted for Martin McCague instead – and he came back stressing the need to invest in youth after Illingworth, Fred Titmus and Co had picked Gatting and Gooch.

Leaving behind the dependable, economical Fraser was a decision based on the belief that McCague's greater pace would be helped by the fast Australian pitches. Well, they may have been fast when Illingworth's side regained the Ashes in 1970–71, but it was generally recognised that, with the exception of Perth, they'd slowed down considerably in the intervening 24 years.

Not that McCague ever made it to Perth for the final Test. In fact, he lasted only one,

Atherton's not impressed as Illingworth surrenders the Ashes

the first, and not all of that. Under pressure from taunts of 'traitor' (he'd learned his cricket in Australia), he took only two (tail-end) wickets, conceded 80 runs in his first 14 overs, was unable to bowl in the second innings because of an upset stomach, was out for 1 and 0 (first ball), and had to be invalided back to Britain with a stress fracture of the leg. Fraser, called up as late replacement, took 2–26 and 5–73 in the third Test.

Meanwhile, although Gatting scored a century in the fourth Test, he averaged only 8.12 in his other eight innings, which included two ducks. Gooch averaged 24.50 with only one fifty. Both announced their retirements from international cricket before others announced it for them. After England had lost the series 3–1, Atherton claimed that 'we came here with a short-term ambition which failed, and I don't think we've made any progress at all in Australia.'

> ## *His throw went absolutely nowhere near where it was going.*
>
> **Richie Benaud**

The summer before that, Illingworth and Co made a clear mistake in omitting Graham Thorpe for the first four matches of the season, despite two excellent Test innings in the West Indies (86 and 84) and the fact that a left-hander would have given some balance to the middle order. When he was eventually recalled, for the second and third Tests against South Africa, his attacking approach disrupted the seam bowlers who'd won the first by 356 runs. His scores of 72, 73, 79 and 15 not out helped draw the series.

The England selectors' defensive policy of playing six specialist batsmen plus Ian Botham in the 1979 World Cup final cost the team dear. A total of 86 runs in fact, from just 12 overs which had to be bowled by Geoff Boycott, Graham Gooch and Wayne Larkins, a kind of composite fifth bowler. They didn't take a wicket between them as the West Indies retained the trophy, which England have never won.

It often happens that when one side's being badly beaten in a series, their selectors compound the sense of panic by picking more players than are strictly good for morale. England, for instance, called up 23 against the West Indies in 1988, including the 36-year-old John Childs and four different captains, among them Chris Cowdrey who scored 0 and 5 and didn't play Test cricket again. England lost the series 4–0, and Peter May (Cowdrey's godfather) resigned as chairman of selectors.

Even these 23 didn't match the record 30 picked for England against the all-conquering Australians of 1921, including seven who won only the one cap: Tom Richmond, Alf Dipper, Jack Durston, John Evans (who scored only 217 runs all summer), Charlie Parker, football internationals Andy Ducat and Wally Hardinge – and another, Nigel Haig, who didn't win a second till almost nine years later (John Arlott called it 'a sort of Falstaff's army').

Meanwhile, while Gregory and McDonald were blasting their way through the series, the selectors (Henry Foster, Reggie Spooner and rugby international John Daniell) dropped debutant opener Percy Holmes from the rest of the series after he'd top-scored in the first Test, and left out Phil Mead, one of the best players of fast bowling in the country, until the fourth and fifth Tests, both of which were drawn, ending a record sequence of eight defeats.

Mead showed the error of their ways by scoring 47 and 182 not out. Rather than pick him, the selectors had gone right to the bottom of the barrel for Charles (CB) Fry, once a classical batsman but now 49, who mercifully turned them down.

Even Fry wasn't as old as HBG Austin, who was invited to captain the West Indies in their first official Test series, in England in 1928, but declined because he was 52.

India also picked four different captains against the West Indies in 1958–59 – 'Polly' Umrigar, Ghulam Ahmed, 'Vinoo' Mankad, Hemu Adhikari – and lost the series 3–0.

The choice of Walter Humphreys for the 1894–95 tour of Australia looks bizarre today. He was 45 by then, the last exponent of the ancient craft of lob bowling to tour Australia, and so expensive against the best batsmen that he didn't play in the Tests. It's said that he was specifically asked for by the Melbourne Club, who thought him fit for his age because he could ride a tricycle!

Have England gone into a Test with a weaker bowling attack than the one against Pakistan at Lord's in 1982? Well, their opening pair in Trinidad in 1948 didn't put anyone in fear of his life: the West Indies openers made hay against 45-year-old 'Gubby' Allen and bulky Harold Butler, Andy Ganteaume becoming the only batsman to make a century in his only Test innings, George Carew scoring one in his second Test (he'd been out first ball in the other one, 13 years earlier!).

In 1964–65 Kenny Palmer (see ONE-CAP WONDER BLUNDERS) and 36-year-old Ian Thomson opened the bowling against South Africa, Palmer taking 1–189, Thomson 3–183. Neither played for England again.

Back in 1938, Australia's opening bowlers at the Oval were Mervyn Waite, whose only Test wicket cost 190 runs, and Stan McCabe, a dazzling batsman but no terror with the ball (Test average 42.86). England scored 903–7 (a world record that still stands) and won by an innings and 579.

Against Australia in 1989, David Gower and Ted Dexter left out John Emburey and

went into the first Test with an attack made up entirely of medium-pacers – Phil DeFreitas, Neil Foster, Phil Newport, Derek Pringle – who allowed Australia to declare twice (601–7 and 230–3) and win by 210 runs.

But even all these pale into significance alongside the 1982 boys. No complaints about the one called Botham (though you wouldn't always give him the new ball) – but the rest of the seam attack didn't exactly make Imran and the lads quake at the knees: Robin Jackman, Ian Greig, and Pringle again. Say no more. Well, say that they'd won only six previous caps between them and now took only seven wickets in the match (for 414 runs), which England lost by ten wickets, their first defeat by Pakistan since 1954. Temporary captain David Gower's understatement: 'We didn't have a lot of variety in the attack.'

In 1984, more problems, England going into the first Test against the West Indies with a new opening bat (Andy Lloyd), a number 3 unsuited to the task (Derek Randall) and other players short of Test class (Geoff Miller and that man Pringle again). Joel Garner identified five potential weak links in all, not least the absence of a fast-bowling partner for Bob Willis. England, he felt, ran the risk of falling apart.

Sure enough, although Pringle did bravely and well enough (five wickets, 46 not out in the second innings), Lloyd ducked into a ball from Malcolm Marshall and didn't play Test cricket again, Randall made 0 and 1, Miller's only wicket cost 83 runs in 15 overs, Garner took nine wickets, and England lost by an innings on their way to a 5–0 'blackwash'.

When a young slow left-armer was looking for a county at the end of last century, he was turned down by Warwickshire – who lived to regret it. And regret it. They'd said thanks but no thanks to Wilfred Rhodes.

In the course of a very long career (30 years in Test cricket alone), he took 4,187 first-class wickets, still easily the world record, as well as scoring 39,802 runs (58 centuries) and taking 708 catches. Yorkshire can still hardly believe their luck – though it's worth remembering that they almost made the same blunder as Warwicks: it's said that they chose him instead of someone called Albert Cordingley on the toss of a coin! While Rhodes was helping them win the County Championship 11 times, Warwickshire managed it only once.

They didn't learn the lesson. Rhodes' ageless excellence kept other slow left-armers out of the Yorkshire team in the 1920s. The best of these, Hedley Verity, went to Warwickshire for a trial and was tried out in a net, not the ideal place for judging spinners, then turned down. He went back to Yorkshire and became very much Rhodes' successor, taking 1,956 first-class wickets in a career ended by his death in the War, including 144 for England, and helped the county to win the Championship seven times in nine seasons, while Warwickshire had to wait till 1951 to take it for the first time in 40 years.

Half a century later, it was Yorkshire's turn to ignore the gift horse, a local off-spinner who'd played for their Colts and was much admired by the likes of Dudley Nourse, the famous South African batsman.

Once his home county had turned him away, he went to Surrey, whom he helped to win the Championship seven times in a row (Yorkshire finished second three times). He took a few wickets for England too, including the little matter of 19–90 against Australia in 1956. Yorkshire had missed their chance with Jim Laker.

Wilfred Rhodes signals what he thinks of Warwickshire's decision to let him go

In 1960, Gloucestershire took the captaincy away from England batsman Tom Graveney and gave it to Tom Pugh, an Old Etonian with a career batting average of 18.43. No disrespect, said Graveney, but was he worth his place in the team?

Graveney duly packed his bag for Worcestershire, whom he helped win the County Championship in 1964 and 1965, making 4,153 runs in the two seasons. Gloucestershire haven't won it since 1877!

Maybe one day there'll be radio with pictures.

Max Walker

When Tony Lock wasn't picked for the 1962–63 tour to Australia, he promptly signed for Western Australia and took part in their win over England!

On the same tour, England led 1–0 after the second Test. Before the third, a recce of the Sydney wicket confirmed it as a spinner's paradise. It was clear to off-spinner Fred Titmus, and just about everyone else, that England would need to field two slow bowlers.

The England captain Ted Dexter didn't agree. Although England had two other quality off-spinners in Ray Illingworth and David Allen, Lord Ted went in with a trio of seamers, a formation which had won the previous Test – but that had been played on a completely different kind of wicket.

Predictably enough, although Titmus took 7–79 in the first innings without support from the other end (Dexter was reduced to using Ken Barrington's leg breaks), Australia won the match to level the series.

In the next Test, the same mistake but in reverse, Dexter going in with an extra spinner – on a seamer's wicket in Adelaide.

A rare false shot by Bradman off Wright. Note the umpire calling no-ball

This time Titmus took 2–157, Illingworth 1–108, Australia never looked like losing and drew the series 1–1 to retain the Ashes.

There were times when Doug Wright was as unplayable as anyone who ever bowled. Among his 2,056 first-class wickets were seven hat-tricks, still a world record. And he took 108 in Tests. And yet, at the very highest level …

What do we make of the view that Australia helped pick the England team for years? Brian Close, for instance, claimed that Richie Benaud said in 1964 'The only way Australia will lose this Test series is if Brian Close captains England. I am going to make sure he doesn't by writing that he should.' Benaud also 'never sang Tom Graveney's praises unless we were asked and then we said he should be in the England team. People thought that was a double bluff, so Tom missed out a lot. He'd never have been out of an Australian side during my Test career.' Close again: 'You don't have to be a genius to look through Test sides and find men who should never have set foot on a field against Australia.'

Moreover, South Africa certainly used to dictate the composition of England touring teams. In 1909–10, for example, they asked for the party to include six amateurs, who were duly picked and generally sank without trace. Jack Hobbs had to open the bowling in three of the Tests and England lost the series 3–2.

Back to Doug Wright. Don Bradman's regard for him is a matter of public record – and he knew a thing or two about leg-spinners (he had Grimmett and O'Reilly in his teams) – so it sounds like high praise indeed. But did he mean it?

In Test matches in which they both played, Bradman scored five centuries, including a double, and Wright dismissed him only twice. Furthermore, his bowling figures against Australia make glum reading: in his very first innings against them he conceded 153 runs, his 12 wickets in that 1938 series costing 35.50 each.

Worse was to come. In 1946–47, he was hit for more than a hundred runs in every completed Australian innings (and 93 in another), and although he took 23 wickets he paid 43.04 each for them. In 1948, he bowled in only one match, taking 2–123, and hit rock-bottom in 1950–51, taking just 11 wickets at 45.45 each, 'distributing runs in all directions by very, very poor bowling' according to journalist and former Australian opener Jack Fingleton, who called him 'a bowling tragedy ... He could bowl the best batsmen in the world on his day ... but when he is not on his day he is hit too freely by some of the worst.'

In Ashes matches, the bad days outnumbered the good. The truth seems to be that while Wright and the likes of 'Tich' Freeman often terrorised county batsmen, the Australians had seen better at home. Wright was on the winning side only once in 14 Ashes Tests (of which nine were lost) and that total of 108 Test wickets cost 39.11 each. He was often overbowled by his captains and suffered his fair share of dropped catches, but he probably bowled more no-balls than any other spinner in history (probably caused by that odd kangaroo-hop run-up) and John Arlott wrote that he 'bowls enough bad balls, as a rule, to play Test batsmen in.' Bradman included.

The Australian selectors must always have regretted picking Walter Giffen, whose inclusion was allegedly on the insistence of his famous brother George. In his three Test matches, Walter scored 2, 0, 1, 3, 3 and 2. When he was left out of the 1890 team to England, George refused to go. Walter might have been a better batsman if he hadn't lost the tops of two fingers in 1886!

On that 1890 tour, Ken Burn was taken as reserve wicketkeeper, and it wasn't until the team's ship reached the Red Sea that they realised he'd never done the job in his life! Picked as a batsman, he went in at number 10 and 11 in the first Test, was stumped (ironically) for a duck in his first ever Test innings, averaged only 10.25 in the two matches, both of which Australia lost, and didn't play international cricket again.

Boycott, somewhat a creature of habit, likes exactly the sort of food he himself prefers.

Don Mosey

A number of things prevented Sussex from doing well in the Championship in the 1970s (see BEYOND ALL RECOGNITION). As Tony Greig said, 'We even managed to blunder in the overseas market.'

While neighbours Hampshire were hiring the world-class likes of Barry Richards, Gordon Greenidge and Andy Roberts, Sussex brought in West Indian batsman Geoff Greenidge (no relation, no comparison), who appeared in only five Tests, and the Indian spinner Uday Joshi, who didn't play in any at all.

'Two nicer chaps you couldn't have wished to meet, but ...'

When Yorkshire at last started hiring overseas players, they got little in the way of success out of the brilliant young Indian batsman Sachin Tendulkar – and even less from his replacement.

It had been clear for some time that Yorkshire's greatest need was for a penetrative fast bowler. Yet, after thinking of Australia's Craig McDermott, the committee signed Richie Richardson instead, the West Indies captain and very much a batsman.

The chairman of the cricket committee, Brian Close, called it a 'completely illogical' move, especially as six Yorkshire batsmen had averaged over 37 the previous season. Richardson averaged less than that in the 1993 County Championship, never quite coming to terms with English conditions. The following season, he took a long sabbatical from the game, suffering from physical and mental exhaustion. Yorkshire, needless to say, won nothing.

And Ian Greig's on eight, including two fours.

Jim Laker

Before the third Test in the Caribbean in 1957–58, Pakistan's captain Abdul Kardar ignored medical advice and picked himself to play despite a broken finger in his left hand – so, when Mahmood Hussain pulled a hamstring so badly in the first over that he couldn't bowl for the rest of the tour, then Nasim-ul-Ghani broke his thumb, Pakistan were left with only two fit first-string bowlers.

They did their best, but a batsman's paradise condemned the classy Fazal Mahmood to figures of 2–247, Khan Mohammad to 0–259, and helped Garry Sobers score his maiden Test century, a little matter of 365 not out to break the world record. The West Indies amassed a Brobdingnagian 790–3 to win by an innings and go 2–0 up in a series they won 3–1.

Hard to know why India picked poor, bespectacled Pankaj Roy for the 1959 series in England, let alone made him captain when Datta Gaekwad was injured. 'Poor' looks an odd word to use for a batsman who averaged 32.56 in his 43 Tests, scoring five centuries and sharing a world Test record partnership of 413 for the first wicket – but the man's weakness against pace had been exposed by Fred Trueman in 1952, when his scores in the four Tests had been 19, 0, 35, 0, 0, 0, 0!

In 1959, again against Trueman and Co, he started well with 54 and 49, but ultimately averaged only 17.90 as India lost all five Tests by wide margins. He made eight ducks against England and 14 in all Test cricket, a remarkable number for a recognised batsman.

Before the 1977 B&H Cup final, holders Kent replaced their vice-captain Graham Johnson, man of the match in the previous year's final, with Grahame Clinton and left out Chris Cowdrey in favour of Richard Hills as an extra bowler. In the event, Clinton was out for a duck, Hills didn't bowl, and Gloucestershire won by 64 runs.

The selection of the West Indies team to tour England in 1939 was something of a hit-and-miss affair. Fast bowler Leslie Hylton, for example, wasn't originally picked but was allowed into the squad when a public subscription raised the money for his fare. The experienced wicketkeeper-batsman Ivan Barrow was picked even though he was known to have been out of first-class cricket for some time (he was living in the USA). Most eyebrow-raising of all, the uncapped John Cameron was made vice-captain on the strength of his googly bowling for Cambridge University and Somerset – this when he'd given up the googly and was now bowling off-spin!

Cameron took only three wickets in the first two Tests and Hylton's three wickets cost 55.66 each. Both were dropped after the second Test, Barrow after the first. None of them played Test cricket again. With a better selection policy, the West Indies might have done better than lose the series 1–0.

At the start of the 1953–54 series in the West Indies, Len Hutton left out his off-spinner Jim Laker and went into the first Test with four seam bowlers. England lost by 181 runs.

The following year, again in the opening Test of a series, in Australia, Hutton did it again but even more so, this time going into the match without a single spinner (Tony Lock had played against the West Indies). England's first professional captain since 1877, Hutton believed implicitly in pace. So had Douglas Jardine in 1932–33; in the second Test of that Bodyline series, he'd captained the only previous England team to take the field without a single spinner. It lost. So did this one, by an innings.

So did the third England team to go into a Test (their 596th) without a specialist spinner, against New Zealand in 1984.

Odd that Hutton should have discarded his spinners. The previous season (1953), he'd gone into the last Test with two of them, the famous Laker and Lock combination, whereas the Australians had left theirs out even though Jack Hill had taken seven in his first Test series at only 22.57 each and the Oval wicket was known to take spin: after all, it was Laker and Lock's home turf. They took nine wickets in the second innings to dismiss Australia for 162 and regain the Ashes for the first time since 1934.

Clive Lloyd went into the final Test of the 1984–85 series in Australia with the usual complement of four fast bowlers, replacing spinner Roger Harper with Michael Holding, who called it 'an obviously wrong decision' (Australia's captain Allan Border thought it 'poor judgement, perhaps brought about by complacency') on a typical turning wicket at Sydney, where the West Indies had lost to New South Wales earlier on the tour. They now lost a Test for the first time in three years and Lloyd didn't play international cricket again.

> *As so often with Achilles tendon injuries, the Achilles goes.*
>
> **Pat Pocock**

There was (still is) a fair amount of controversy when Clarrie Grimmett was left out of the tour to England in 1938. Although he was 46 by then, he'd picked up 44 wickets in a series only two years earlier, becoming the first bowler to take more than 200 in Tests. Although Australia's captain Don Bradman still defends the decision to replace Grimmett with Frank Ward, it's hard to believe the old Gnome would have done worse than a player who appeared only once in the 1938 series and finished his Test career with only 11 wickets at 52.18 apiece ...

Jack Ferris formed one of the most successful bowling partnerships in cricket history, he and Charlie Turner terrorising England on the tours of 1888 and 1890, during which he took 435 wickets (no misprint). On his Test debut in 1887 he and Turner bowled unchanged to dismiss England for 45. Small wonder that the opposition later picked him to play for them in South Africa, against whom he took 6–54 and 7–37 in his last Test.

All the more surprising, then, that the 1891 Gentlemen, woefully weak in bowling, didn't put him on to bowl till sixth change! He took five wickets but it was too late. The Gentlemen used nine bowlers in all while the Players scored 390 to win by an innings.

Bad ... timing.

After Eric Rowan had made only 7 and 16 in the first Test against England in 1948–49, then just 7 in the first innings of the second, the South African selectors dropped him from the third. Fair enough, perhaps – but they made the mistake of announcing the decision before the second was over. Rowan batted throughout the last day to score 156 not out and save the match.

Richie Benaud's rather forgotten brother John played in three Tests. Against Pakistan in 1972, after scoring 24 in the first Test and 13 in the first innings of the second, he too was dropped from the third, and again was told about it before the end of the match. His 142 helped Australia win the Test and the series.

Oh, and why did the West Indies carry on picking Keith Arthurton when his scores in the 1996 World Cup were 1, 0, 0, 1, 0? They lost their semi-final by just five runs.

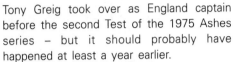

Pick of the weak (2)

Captains who shouldn't have been

Tony Greig took over as England captain before the second Test of the 1975 Ashes series – but it should probably have happened at least a year earlier.

After the crushing defeat by the West Indies in 1973, the selectors made Mike Denness captain for the winter tour to the Caribbean, even though there were doubts all round, not least about his right to a place in the side on merit.

As it happened, England were outplayed in almost every Test but drew the series thanks to some monumental batting by Amiss and Boycott and a freak bowling performance by Greig, who emerged as the personality of the tour – this while Denness (who averaged 25.66 in the Tests) had come across as someone who didn't seek advice readily (he admitted that even his own wife thought him uncommunicative). Verdict: not proven, but too close for comfort.

India, the following season, were no sort of yardstick. Badly prepared, feebly led, they lost all three Tests and were bowled out for 42 at Lord's. Added to which, they had no pace attack worthy of the name, so the England batsmen had no preparation for what was coming.

Greig should surely have captained England in Australia. A batsman who took the fight to fast bowling, he scored a gutsy and flamboyant 110 in a losing cause in the first Test, averaged 40.54 in the series, took 17 wickets and 12 catches, and kept his pecker up throughout (Australians tend to respect that kind of thing). Meanwhile Denness had to drop himself from the fourth Test after averaging only 10.83 in the first three and taking 12 innings to score his first tour fifty. The Australian captain Ian Chappell: 'I firmly believe that Denness was

thrown to the wolves as a Test player by his premature selection as captain.'

The wheels seemed to come off his tactical appreciation, too. For instance, by not bowling Fred Titmus in tandem with Derek Underwood, he allowed Australia to escape and win in Adelaide. England lost the Ashes 4–1.

Denness clung on to the job by scoring 188 in the last Test (in the absence of Lillee and Thomson) and 181 against New Zealand, a delay that helped cost England the return series: his decision to put Australia in after winning the toss (*Blunders Vol.1*) decided the first Test.

Archie MacLaren led England against Australia in more Tests than anybody else: 22, of which 11 were lost and seven drawn. England lost all five of the series in which he was captain. Neville Cardus called him 'born to rule, without despotism', but this doesn't tally with the opinions of others, who found him too authoritarian, even 'stubborn to the point of stupidity' – and several knowledgeable commentators have reported the man's underlying pessimism ('My God, Jacker, look at the team they've given me. Do they think I'm playing the blind asylum?'). Some of his decisions, too, lost Test matches.

And yet it started so well. His first match in charge, the first of the 1897–98 series, was won by nine wickets. But the second was lost by an innings, whereupon the captaincy reverted back to Drewy Stoddart for the next two, before MacLaren picked up the reins again for the fifth. If didn't help: England lost all four.

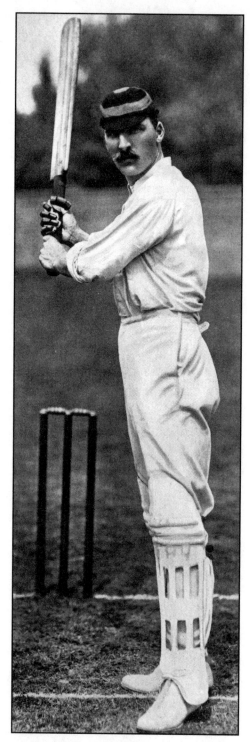

AC MacLaren defending himself against the charge of bad captaincy

In 1899, after WG Grace had led the team in the first match before retiring from Test cricket, MacLaren was something of a surprise choice as captain. Stanley Jackson was generally thought to have better credentials (especially as MacLaren hadn't played first-class cricket that season). England immediately lost the second Test and with it the series 1–0.

The real horrors took place a few years later, though again there was a good start in Australia. In the first Test of the 1901–02 series, MacLaren became the first batsman to score four Test centuries in total, and England won by an innings. But the roof just kept falling in. Again all four of the remaining matches were lost.

Back in England for the return series in 1902, MacLaren was still captain, this time of arguably the strongest England batting line-up in history (all 11 in the first Test scored first-class centuries) – but it made little difference. Australia won 2–1, losing only the irrelevant final Test. In what was effectively the decider, Fred Tate's Match at Old Trafford, MacLaren was criticised for stationing poor Fred at square leg, where he made his famous dropped catch (he was a slip fielder in county cricket and had apparently never fielded in the deep before!) and indeed for agreeing to his selection in the first place: he was 'a good bowler, but how he came to be preferred to Sydney Barnes or George Hirst passes comprehension.'

That series seemed to be the last straw for the selectors – England won their next two, in South Africa under 'Plum' Warner and at home to Australia (under Jackson at last, with MacLaren picked only for his batting) – but in 1909 Lord Hawke, who'd also been chairman in 1902, went back to Archie for yet another Ashes series even though he was 37 by then and considered himself too old.

Yet again he started well, England winning the first Test by ten wickets – but as usual it was all downhill after that, the series lost 2–1 – and this time MacLaren didn't even deserve a place in the team, averaging only 12.14. Hardly surprising, given that he'd dropped out of first-class cricket two years earlier!

Worse, some of his selections defied explanation. Responsibility for picking the team for the second Test rested entirely with him and Henry 'Shrimp' Leveson Gower; together they gave a first and only cap to John King in place of the great Wilfred Rhodes, brought in Tom Hayward 'in defiance of medical opinion' (he was lame at the time!), and went in without a fast bowler 'although Walter Brearley was at the top of his form at this part of the season. Sydney Barnes, the best bowler in England, was, it seemed, not considered.' England lost by nine wickets.

Then, although he did pick Barnes for the final Test, he again left out any bowler of real pace, a decision condemned by *Wisden* among others: 'The idea of letting England go into the field in fine weather, on a typical Oval wicket, with no fast bowler, touched the confines of lunacy.' During the match, MacLaren took Barnes off when Australia were 9–1 in the first innings, then worked googly bowler Douglas Carr 'nearly to finger paralysis for one and a half hours at a stretch.' Carr conceded 282 runs in his only Test, while Australia scored 325 and 339–5 declared and had no trouble drawing the match. Mercifully, MacLaren didn't play Test cricket again.

Talking of Leveson Gower (If you do any, pronounce it 'Loosen Gore'), he captained England in his only three Tests, all in South Africa in 1909–10. Captain of Winchester and Oxford, he was a skinny batsman short of international class (only three centuries in a first-class career spanning 27 years). The series in South Africa was lost 2–1, England's only win coming after the Shrimp had been dropped with the score 2–0.

But it was as a selector that he reached his nadir, against Australia in 1909 and again in 1924–25, when he couldn't kick his old habit, begun at Oxford University, of packing the side with batsmen.

At the Oval in 1909, England fielded only two specialist bowlers, batted all the way down to number 7, and drew the match to lose the series. In 1924–25, England batted strongly throughout but couldn't bowl the opposition out cheaply. The heroic Maurice Tate took a record 38 wickets but had little support, Cec Parkin and George Macaulay having been left at home. Australia scored 600 in the second Test, passed 400 in three other innings, and won 4–1.

Leveson Gower not only stayed on the selection committee, he was made its chairman from 1927 to 1930, when Australia won 2–1. He was knighted (Sir Henry Dudley Gresham Leveson Gower) for his services to cricket (including the game in South Africa and Australia, no doubt).

> *Everyone's enjoying this except Vic Marks, and I think he's enjoying himself.*
>
> **Don Mosey**

The Shrimp was preceded as captain by the Hon. Ivo Bligh, who led England in each of his four Tests, all in Australia in 1882–83. That England drew the series (and recaptured the Ashes) owed little to his powers as a batsman: exposed as an opener (0 and 3 in his first Test) and middle-order batsman (0 in the next), he went in at numbers 10 and 9 in each of the last two matches, boosting his average to a fraction over double figures.

Keith Fletcher missed very few matches in county cricket, which was just as well for Essex, whose temporary replacements as captain were never particularly successful, including the West Indian all-rounder Keith Boyce, a talented Test cricketer but no great tactician. Captain in a match against Leicestershire which Essex were struggling to draw, he twice charged down the pitch against Ray Illingworth, hitting the first ball for six, being stumped off the next.

When his team mates remonstrated in the changing room, Boyce explained that if he could hit the ball a long way, the opposition would use up valuable time in getting it back. Original thinking in normal circumstances, positively bizarre in this case, with another ten overs to be played, however long they took – and Boyce had been informed of that before anyone else.

> *It's now possible they could get the impossible score they first thought possible.*
>
> **Christopher Martin-Jenkins**

Cyril Walters captained England in just one Test, the first against Australia in 1934, after which he justified his over-bowling of spinner Tommy Mitchell with the explanation that he'd kept him on 'since he was a chosen member of the team.' England lost by 238 runs.

Mitchell was dropped for two Tests. When he returned, for the fourth match of the series, he took 0–117 in 23 overs, partly because his next captain Bob Wyatt insisted on talking to him after virtually every delivery. Eventually little Tommy told him in no uncertain terms what to do with his advice – and was dropped again. Australia won the series.

Despite this, Wyatt insisted on recalling Mitchell for the second Test against South Africa the following summer, despite protests from the other selectors, who wanted Walter Robins instead. 'In the end, physically and mentally exhausted, we gave way,' said Plum Warner. 'Dearly were we to pay for it, and to this day I curse myself.'

England lost the match, the only one of the series that wasn't drawn. Mitchell's three wickets cost 164 runs and he wasn't capped again.

Back in 1934–35, Wyatt had led England in the West Indies, where he won the toss in each of the first two Tests and put the opposition in to bat. It worked first time, but only just (England, batting second on a deteriorating pitch, lost six wickets in reaching the 75 they needed to win) but failed completely in the second Test, where England were again caught on a last-day pitch and were all out for 107 after Wyatt had compounded the choice of fielding first ('one of his many decisions which were baffling') by changing his batting order, sending his number 10 batsman in first, the number 11 at number 3, number 9 at number 4, and so on. Confused? They certainly were. England couldn't recover from 75–6, losing by 217 runs to set the West Indies on their way to winning a series for the very first time. In the fourth and final Test, Wyatt's jaw was broken by a bouncer. He didn't win a series as England captain.

Wyatt was replaced as captain by Gubby Allen, who insisted on including him in the touring party to Australia in 1936–37, at the expense of little Eddie Paynter, who was in fine form and had once risen from his sick bed to win a famous match for England against Australia.

Wyatt played in only two Tests, both of which were lost, averaged 23.50 with the bat, and was never picked again. Allen also left out the great Herbert Sutcliffe, with the result that slow left-armer Hedley Verity had to open the batting in the fourth Test. England became the only side to lose a series after leading 2–0. Recalled against Australia in 1938, Paynter averaged 101.75. He was a professional, Allen and Wyatt amateurs.

And one who shouldn't have been sacked.
Perhaps Mike Gatting wasn't too clever in inviting that barmaid to his hotel room – but how that could have affected his

One of Mike Gatting's last days in the sun

performance on the field is hard to imagine (no, be serious, it is). When he was sacked, England picked three new captains during the 1988 series against the West Indies, who inevitably won it 4–0.

It also ushered in the Dexter–Gower era, which lost the 1989 Ashes series 4–0, then the rather unlamented Stewart–Gooch axis. Gatting should probably have been captain right up to the time of Atherton. Although England won only two Tests under him, that was enough to retain the Ashes on the 1986–87 tour that was a triumph all round – and there were surely more to come. His county club-mate, West Indies opener Desmond Haynes, believed 'He would have done a fantastic job for England just as he has done at Middlesex.'

Instead, after a promising 1990, England muddled through one series after another. The worst thing about the whole messy, puritanical saga is that when Gooch was replaced as captain in 1989, Gatting would have been re-appointed but for the veto of the chairman of selectors, Ossie Wheatley, who'd never played Test cricket.

Even David Gower, who got the job back instead of Gatt, wondered about the point of appointing a selection committee if the likes of Wheatley could veto their selections: 'Why did he have that sort of power? Who on earth is he?' Ian Botham's view: 'Most of the players wouldn't have known Ossie Wheatley from Ossie Ardiles.'

Viz: a comic classic

Pride of place in the captains-who-shouldn't-have-been section goes without argument to the leader of India's 1936 tour of England. Before the second Test there, he was knighted, and so became Sir Gajapatairaj Vijaya Ananda, the Maharajkumar of Vizianagram (Vijaya = victory, Ananda = happiness. There was precious little of either on the tour, but more of that later). The English, who couldn't wrap their tongues round this mouthful, typically shortened it to something bite-sized. And thus a new star was born. Arise, Sir Vizzy.

This was the second Indian team to play Tests in England. The first, in 1932, had also been captained by a man of high caste and doubtful cricketing credentials, the Maharajah of Porbandar, who'd been sensible enough to step down from the match that mattered. Cottari Kanakaiya Nayudu (inevitably CK to the English) led India in the only Test, the first they'd ever played, and neither the Maharajah nor his vice-captain, the equally privileged Kumar Shri Ganshyamsinhji of Limbdi, ever played any Test cricket.

Vizzy wasn't so humble. He'd campaigned the length and breadth of the sub-continent to secure the tour captaincy, dispensing financial contributions to the Indian Board and promising different regions a player in the squad if they voted for him. Madras, for instance, got Cota Ramaswami, who was 40 and had never played in a Test. Having secured the post, Vizzy hung on to it at all costs. On tour, fulfilling his every fantasy, he was captain, sole selector, chief wise monkey.

There was no question of his stepping down from the Tests like Porbandar. He played in all three, scoring 19 not out, 6, 6, 0 not out, 1 and 1 (he averaged double that against the counties, thanks to gifts from bowlers under instructions).

Vizzy: out to lunch

To say the whole team suffered is a classic understatement. They lost two Tests and scraped a draw in the other. By the end, the only things the press could think to compliment them on were their command of English, their friendliness and a certain novelty value. Sheer condescension – but there hadn't been much to admire in their actual play. The tour made a financial loss and a motion was passed in an Indian students' union debate: 'That cricket is bad for India.'

All this was down to Vizzy. The sad thing is that the 1936 squad was quite possibly the best ever to leave India. A strong middle order (CK, Wazir Ali, Laxmidas Jai), two genuinely fast bowlers (Amar Singh, Mohammed Nissar), a wicketkeeper rated as good as any in England by *Wisden* (Dattaram Hindlekar), a pair of world-class openers (the dazzling Mushtaq Ali who walked out to fast bowlers, Vijay Merchant who was one of *Wisden*'s five cricketers of the year) and one of the great all-rounders in Lala Amarnath, whose Test career lasted exactly 19 years.

In every sense, too much talent for their captain to handle. Amarnath was India's darling; Vizzy sent him home. Merchant criticised the way the tour was being run: Vizzy told Mushtaq to run him out. Instead, the latter mentioned the conversation to Merchant before the start of the second innings at Lord's. They both scored hundreds, put on 203 for the first wicket, and saved the Test. There were no run-outs.

At one stage, the senior players demanded more consultation and an end to favouritism. CK or Wazir, they said, should be made vice-captain. Neither played Test cricket again.

Nor did Vizzy, though he flew back before the rest of the team to try to thwart a committee investigation into a tour that he'd wrecked single-handedly. Naturally the three matches in England constituted his entire Test career. A unique figure in cricket history. A pantomime giant.

One-cap wonder blunders

England

When injuries deprived England of Graham Dilley and Neil Foster before the second Test in New Zealand in 1983–84, an SOS was sent out to Tony Pigott, a Sussex seamer who was spending the winter playing for Wellington. He postponed his wedding to win his cap, but after christening his debut with the wicket of Bruce Edgar with his seventh ball, it turned into a tough baptism, his two wickets costing 75 runs in 17 overs on a bowler's wicket. With Ian Botham conceding 88 from the same number of overs, England captain Bob Willis was left to bemoan some of the worst England bowling he'd ever seen.

Mike Gatting thought Pigott 'very nervous, poor devil,' and *Wisden* mentioned the number of half-volleys bowled by 'the tiring Pigott'. Not surprising, given that he'd played a first-class match 24 hours earlier! All in all, a messy selection by the England management, who went in without a spinner for only the third time in 596 Tests. Like the other two instances, this match was lost, by an innings, helping New Zealand on the way to their first series win over England. Pigott wasn't capped again – and he needn't have cancelled the wedding: it was scheduled for the fourth day, and the match finished in three.

Is it true that Charlie Parker once grabbed an England selector by the lapels and enquired of him why he wasn't being picked more often? If so, it helps explain why he won only one cap (in 1921) despite being widely regarded as the best slow left-armer in the world.

In the quaint, preposterous early days, the England selectors picked a number of players whose appearances in Tests constituted their entire first-class experience. At best, most of them contributed little more than amusement value to Test cricket. At worst, they not only deprived good professional players of caps but sometimes helped lose Test matches.

The first of this breed, for instance, did little to prevent defeat at Melbourne in 1878–79. Leland Hone, a late choice as wicketkeeper, held a couple of catches but failed with the bat (7 and 6) as England went down by ten wickets.

The Hon. Charles Coventry batted at number 10 against South Africa in 1888–89, scoring 12 and 1 not out. One of his team mates, Joseph Emile Patrick McMaster, an Irishman like Hone, was even worse: batting at number 11 even though he didn't bowl, he made a duck in his only first-class innings! Luckily for these two, South Africa, in their first ever Test series, were so weak that they lost both matches easily, the second after being dismissed for 47 and 43.

The last to be capped by England without ever playing for a first-class county was David Townsend, who opened the batting against the West Indies in 1934–35, averaging only 12.83 in three Tests, two of which were lost to give the West Indies their first series win against England.

The bad old days of Them and Us lasted longer than some people remember. As recently as the 1953–54 visit to the West Indies, England were picking an amateur who happened to be the tour manager, Charles Palmer, instead of Ken Suttle, who'd just made 96 and 62 on the same ground in the match against Barbados. Suttle, who scored 29,375 runs for Sussex, never won a cap; Palmer scored 22 & 0 and took 0–15. England lost the Test by 181 runs.

By all accounts, Palmer wasn't the greatest of managers either. The respected journalist EW 'Jim' Swanton called his appointment just about the worst decision ever to come out of Lord's! Oh, and any career as a photographer was ruled out after he'd taken dozens of shots of the famous first Test in South Africa in 1948–49 (see DROPPING ALL OVER ENGLAND) but forgot to put film in the camera.

According to Mike Brearley, Geoff Boycott didn't do his new opening partner many favours against India in 1979, 'almost paralysing him with his account of the risks of playing shots in a Test match.' Alan Butcher didn't entirely fail 'but did not look at ease', and his 14 and 20 weren't enough to earn him a second cap.

If the England selectors were going to pick slow left-armer Cecil 'Sam' Cook at all, they might at least have given him the right kind of pitch on which to ply his trade. Instead, they chose him for the first Test against South Africa in 1947, on a Trent Bridge wicket which did him no favours. He took 0–87 and 0–40 as well as making 0 and 4 with the bat.

The 1880 Test belonged to the Grace family. WG captained the team, scored England's first ever Test century, and shared the first century partnership in Test cricket – and Edward and Fred also played: the first

instance of three brothers in the same Test team. Fred took one of the most famous catches of all time to get rid of the giant George Bonnor (it's said that the batsmen had crossed twice before the ball came down) but did little with the bat (as little as it's possible to do) – and he had one of his siblings to thank for that.

With England needing just 57 to win, WG sent in Fred and wicketkeeper Alfred Lyttelton to open the second innings. Since these two had batted at numbers 8 and 9 first time round, the Australians came to the not unreasonable conclusion that the good Doctor was taking the task insultingly lightly. As a result, George 'Joey' Palmer and Harry Boyle bowled like men possessed, firing out five England batsmen before the inevitable defeat, including Lyttelton for 13 and each of the lesser-known Graces for 0. Fred, bowled second ball in addition to his duck in the first innings, was the first batsman to play Test cricket without ever scoring a run!

> *The only possible result is a draw. The alternative is a win for England.*
>
> **Richie Benaud**

Three other brothers – Alec, George and Frank Hearne – were also capped by England, Frank also playing for South Africa. All three took part in the Test at Cape Town in 1892, Frank top-scoring for the hosts in each innings – but Alec made 9, George 0, and neither played Test cricket again. Another debutant Hearne, cousin Jack, scored 40 for England!

What criteria did the England and Indian selectors use for dropping Jack MacBryan and Rajindernath after their only Tests (1924 and 1952) when they didn't bat or bowl?

Rajindernath made four stumpings, but rain reduced MacBryan's entire Test career to less than three hours!

Surely Len Hutton wasn't having such a bad time against Lindwall and Miller in 1948 (innings of 3, 74, 20, 13) that it was necessary to drop him for the first time since his Test debut in 1937? Who could have done the job better? Certainly not little George Emmett, who was brought in for the third Test, made 10 and 0, and wasn't capped again. Ironically, it was the only match in the series that England didn't lose. The recalled Hutton scored 81 and 57 in the next.

> *Peter Sleep spent plenty of time practising his grip during the winter — running at the mirror without a ball in his hand.*
>
> **David Hookes**

Francis MacKinnon's name and title were longer than a list of his batting accomplishments: Francis Alexander MacKinnon, the 35th MacKinnon of MacKinnon. As so often in Victorian times,

he was surely chosen more for whom he knew than what he understood about batting: in a first-class career that lasted ten years, he averaged only 16.42. In his one Test, at Melbourne in 1879, England lost by ten wickets to a strong Australian team who must have wondered what he was doing playing against them. Not much, predictably enough: he was bowled for 0 and 5 and his only claim to fame was in being part of Fred Spofforth's hat-trick, the first in Test cricket.

George Vernon did little to help England at Melbourne in 1882–83. He didn't bowl, went in last, and scored 11 not out and 3. England lost by nine wickets.

A spate of injuries during the 1964–65 trip to South Africa reduced England to picking Kenny Palmer, later a Test umpire, then no more than a journeyman bowler who happened to be coaching in Johannesburg. Palmer's only Test wicket cost him 189 runs.

A number of players were surprisingly dropped after doing well in their only Test, perhaps none more so than Charles 'Father' Marriott, whose leg-breaks and googlies took 5–37 and 6–59 to win the third Test against the West Indies in 1933.

One-cap wonder blunders (2)

Other countries

At Melbourne in 1920–21, while watching the second Test of the Ashes series, a Mrs Park dropped her knitting, bent to pick it up – and therefore missed her husband Roy's entire international career as a batsman. He was bowled by the only ball he received in Test cricket!

Wicketkeeper Hammy Love was brought into the fourth Test of the 1932–33 Bodyline series after first choice Bert Oldfield had been injured by a ball from Harold Larwood. Trailing by only 16 runs after the first innings, Australia struggled in their second but were being pulled out of the fire by another Test debutant, the young left-hander Len Darling.

Love had only just come in to join him when he pushed a ball from Larwood towards mid-on and called for a run. Darling responded, but Love suddenly decided to go back, leaving his partner stranded. Larwood collected the ball, tossed it to Tommy Mitchell, 'and Darling was run out standing'. His 39 was the highest score in the innings, not nearly enough to stop Australia losing the match and the Ashes. Love, who made only 5 and 3 himself, wasn't picked again. Hard to believe there was much love and darling in the post-match chat.

During the 1953–54 home series against England, West Indies opening batsman Michael Frederick was dropped after the first Test for scoring 0 in the first innings – but he'd been a little lucky to be picked at all. Fred Trueman's first ball of the tour, against Combined Parishes in Jamaica, found the edge of Frederick's bat and went to second slip, where Alan Moss, who rarely fielded in the position, dropped it. Frederick went on to score 84.

In the first Test of the 1994 series in England, New Zealand gave a first cap to their tall strong pace bowler Heath Davis, whose second name – Te-Ihi-O-Te-Rangi – (Hail to Rangi, God of the Sky) is the broadest on the international circuit. His first ball in Test cricket went for four wides. He took 1–93 in 21 overs, no maidens, and hasn't been picked again.

Bowling for Wellington in the 1996 Shell

The fine figure of Heath Davis (his only one)

Trophy final, he conceded 35 runs in one over, the first 24 off no-balls, as Auckland won to retain the cup.

Volatile fast bowler Arthur Coningham might have played more than one Test (against England in 1894–95) if he hadn't reacted to being no-balled by throwing the next ball at the England captain Drewy Stoddart.

> *Even Downton couldn't get down high enough for that.*
>
> **Richie Benaud**

When the Australian selectors took the captaincy away from Bill Lawry for the last Test of the 1970–71 Ashes series, they threw the baby out with the bathwater, dropping him from the team as well as the leadership, this when he was still one of the most obdurate openers in world cricket (in the fourth Test, he'd carried his bat for 60 in a total of only 116).

To replace him, they brought in not a youngster to be groomed for the future but Ken Eastwood, who played under Lawry's captaincy for Victoria and was more than a year older at 35! The England players recovered from their pleasant surprise to dismiss the old newcomer for 5 and 0 on their way to winning the match and regaining the Ashes.

Australia can rarely have picked a less deserving Test batsman than Tom Groube, who went in at number 3 in the 1880 Test at the Oval (which Australia lost by five wickets) and scored 11 and 0. His lifetime record in first-class cricket: 179 runs, highest score 61, average 8.52!

If official Australian fists hadn't been so tight (they refused to increase their players' fees) they might have won the second Test of the 1884–85 Ashes series. Instead, they picked an entirely new team, including nine new caps, five of whom didn't play Test cricket again: Alf Marr, Sam Morris, Harry Musgrove, Roland Pope (who amassed a grand total of 291 first-class runs in eight seasons) and William 'Digger' Robertson. They scored 37 runs and took two wickets between them as England won by ten wickets. Reverting to their first-choice players for the third and fourth Tests, Australia won them both.

After Lennox 'Bunny' Butler had taken 5–93 for Trinidad against the touring Australians in 1955, local opinion had it that he was West Indies' answer to Ray Lindwall, despite being only medium-quick. Selected for the third Test, on his home ground, he took 2–151 and was dismissed by Lindwall in his only innings!

Although Shahid Israr held two catches in the third Test of 1976–77, he dropped so many others off New Zealand's lower order batsmen that they were able to boost the total to 468, the other wicketkeeper Warren Lees making 152, his highest Test score. The draw prevented Pakistan from winning all three Tests in the series and Shahid wasn't capped again.

In his only Test for India, against the West Indies in 1948–49, Keki Tarapore scored 2, took 0–72 and apparently fielded as badly as anyone ever has, several times allowing the ball to run between his legs before turning to give chase in vain. He later became a coach.

Captain, the ship is sinking

'The hallmark of a great captain is the ability to win the toss at the right time.' **RICHIE BENAUD**

When England lost two wickets for 34 on the third day of the second Test against Australia in 1985, David Gower sent in two nightwatchmen, John Emburey and Paul Allott. Both were capable tail-end batsmen, but the tactic always carries the threat of your last main batsman running out of partners. Sure enough, Mike Gatting was left unbeaten on 75 and England lost by four wickets.

Despite this, England regained the Ashes, so Gower, who scored a welter of runs in the series (including innings of 166, 215 and 157), stayed in the good books he'd entered by winning the previous winter's series in India. Which was just as well, because he hadn't won any of his first 11 Tests as captain – and the famously whimsical side of his nature had cost him a few brownie points against the West Indies in 1984.

On the fourth evening of the second Test, England had done well to lead by over 300 but the light was growing a dim. Nevertheless, when the umpires offered them the chance to go off, Allan Lamb and Paul Downton took it, even though England needed as many runs as possible before declaring.

Why, everyone wanted to know, hadn't they stayed out there – and why hadn't their captain appeared on the pavilion balcony to tell them to do just that? Um, because he was watching Wimbledon on TV! Then, on the last day, when it was clear that Gordon Greenidge was threatening to reach the victory target of 342, Gower didn't take the option of setting more defensive fields because 'As it was a Test match I hadn't really considered it!' England lost the match by nine wickets and the series 5–0.

In 1989, again against Australia, Gower allowed himself to be talked out of picking off-spinner John Emburey for the first Test at Headingley (listening to chairman of selectors Ted Dexter instead of groundsman Keith Boyce), and regretted it all summer ('If I could have turned the clock back and changed just one thing …'). He then compounded things by putting Australia in when he won the toss. They declared at 601–7, won by 210 runs, and went on to take the series 4–0.

Gower's first replacement as captain, Mike Gatting, once famously overslept before a tour match in Australia, and also missed the umpires' call to lead England onto the field against Pakistan in 1987 because the team were watching the racing from Ascot on TV!

Gower's second successor, Graham Gooch, captained Essex in the 1989 B&H Cup final. With Notts needing four off the last ball of the match, bowled by John Lever, Gooch put all but one of his fielders on the leg-side, whereupon Eddie Hemmings, no great batsman, found the off-side boundary. Essex lost by three wickets.

Off-spinner David Allen had taken four wickets in Australia's second innings of the fourth Test in 1961 when Alan Davidson suddenly hit 20 runs off him in a single over, which prompted the England captain Peter May to take him off immediately.

Too hasty. Before that, Allen had conceded barely one run per over and looked like breaking through at any moment. In his absence from the attack, Davidson and Graham McKenzie put on 98 for the last wicket. Australia won by 54 to take a winning lead in the series.

It would be unprintable on television.

Geoff Boycott

After South Africa had dismissed Australia for 269 in the first innings of the third and decisive Test of the 1994 series, Kepler Wessels (who'd once played 24 Tests for Australia) allowed his team to bat 11 hours for a moderate lead of 153, leaving little chance of winning the match and series. Australia held out comfortably, their captain Allan Border escaping with 42 not out in his last Test innings.

Similar sloth cost India their very real chance of winning the second Test of the 1994–95 home series against the West Indies. A first innings of 546 should have been enough, but on the fourth afternoon their captain Mohammad Azharuddin allowed Navjot Sidhu and Sachin Tendulkar, normally very brisk scorers, to make only 95 runs in 43 overs, just when quick runs were paramount. West Indies lost five wickets in surviving 70 overs to draw the match, then won the next.

At Durban in 1950, after South Africa had made 311 in the first innings of the third Test, Australia were caught on a dusty wicket and skittled by off-spinner Hugh Tayfield who took 7–23. Then, unbelievably, even though Australia had just been dismissed for 75 and the pitch was still turning square, Dudley Nourse didn't enforce the follow-on.

His batsmen didn't thank him for it. They were all out for 99, the last eight wickets falling for 14, after which Australia, on a wicket losing its spite, scored 336–5 to win the match and the series.

When Plum Warner fell ill during the 1911–12 tour of Australia, Johnny Douglas took over the England captaincy for all five Tests. In the first, he opened the bowling, alongside Frank Foster, even though the great Sydney Barnes was in the team.

Now, Douglas could be a dangerous bowler with the new ball, but when he realised it wasn't the case this time, he should have withdrawn from the attack. Unfortunately, as Jack Hobbs wrote, 'he is apt not to take himself off soon enough.' Was he trying to show Barnes, a man of strong opinions, who was boss? Or even trying to live up to a reputation (he was an Olympic gold medallist at boxing!)?

He also made the mistake of not opening the batting with Hobbs and Wilfred Rhodes, and *Wisden* felt that he didn't 'have a grip of the team on the field.'

As a result, Australia made 447 and won by 146 runs. It's said that when he finally threw the ball to Barnes, Barnes threw it back with the words 'You've bowled them in, now you bowl them out.' After post-match words with Warner, who asked the other senior players if they wanted a new captain (they didn't), Douglas didn't open the bowling again, Hobbs and Rhodes went in first throughout (putting on 323 in the fourth Test) and England won the four remaining Tests, Foster and Barnes taking another 55 wickets between them.

Not that Douglas learned everything about man management as a result. On the way to Australia in 1920, this time as England captain in his own right, he told PGH Fender he didn't think much of him as a player – then kept him out of the series till the third Test. Percy George took five wickets in an innings in the fourth and fifth, too late to

Refusing to look over his shoulder: Douglas is second from left in the middle row, Barnes fourth from left at the back in the England touring party of 1911–12

save England from becoming the first side to lose a series 5–0.

In the second innings of the first Test of the 1993–94 series in South Africa, Australia's captain Allan Border didn't give his match-winner Shane Warne a bowl until the 44th over. The leg-spinner took four wickets but it was too late: South Africa won by 197 runs, and a frustrated Warne was fined (twice) for verbal abuse after bowling opening batsman Andrew Hudson.

The Gentlemen were so far ahead in the second 1900 match that their captain Sammy Woods told his batsmen to get themselves out so that he could bowl at the Players on the penultimate evening. Despite a target of 501, the Players won by two wickets!

England, going into the fourth and final match of the 1929–30 series in the West Indies, scored 849 (Andy Sandham's 325 the first triple century in Test cricket) – then, remarkably, despite a massive first-innings lead of 563, elected to bat again.

When they eventually deigned to declare (with a preposterous lead of 835), they found they hadn't left themselves enough time to bowl the West Indies out, even though the match lasted seven days (plus two others on which no play was possible): they had to catch the boat back to England!

Their captain, picked less for his talent (Test average of 18.42 with the bat, 91.00 with the ball) than for his background (The Hon. Frederick Somerset Gough Calthorpe) didn't play for England again.

If England lose now, they'll be leaving the field with their heads between their legs.

Geoff Boycott

Although the West Indies lost the 1951–52 series in Australia 4–1, two of those defeats were by narrow margins and could have been avoided by their captain John Goddard.

In the first Test, he overbowled his spinners in the second innings (Sonny Ramadhin 40 eight-ball overs, Alf Valentine 40.7 for only one wicket), allowing Australia to win by three wickets.

In the decisive fourth, he set close fields for Australia's last-wicket pair, Doug Ring and Bill Johnston, even when they began hitting the ball over the top. For Ring's favourite hit to long-on, a fielder was placed thirty yards in from the boundary; his first attempt at the shot cleared the man's head but would have been caught by someone further back.

The last pair put on 38 runs to steal the match by one wicket. If West Indies had won, they would have levelled the series 2–2. Instead, they went 3–1 down and lost it 4–1.

Before the start of the second innings in the third Test of 1957, West Indies opener Frank Worrell was a tired man (he'd just carried his bat for 191 not out in the first innings) – which didn't stop him insisting on opening the innings again, despite a break of only a few minutes (West Indies had to follow on). Goddard allowed him to and he was bowled, 'playing the stroke of a tired man'. Nevertheless the team clung on to a draw.

In the next Test, however, Worrell again insisted on opening the batting, despite having just bowled 38.2 overs. He was out for 7, and this time the West Indies lost, a result which decided the series, after which Goddard didn't play Test cricket again.

For all his phenomenal success as West Indies captain, the feeling still persists in some quarters that all Clive Lloyd had to do was wind up his four fast bowlers, let them take their time getting through their overs, and wait for the inevitable results. Untested under pressure, it was said – a point of view which had its origins in his early days as captain, especially the Australian tour of 1975–76.

It's well documented that in the face of sustained hostile pace bowling, the West Indies batsmen disintegrated in a rash of wild strokeplay – which big Clive apparently did little to curb, instead taking the view that as professionals they should be able to work things out for themselves. Viv Richards apart, they never did.

There were question marks in the field, too. The team might have done better if Lance Gibbs had been used more often – and Lloyd's tactical appreciation looked shaky at times. In the first Test, for example, with Australia needing so few runs in their second innings, he didn't set the attacking fields that were his only hope. Moreover, he was forever plugging gaps instead of anticipating them. When Ian Chappell twice swept at Inshan Ali, he would have been caught each time if a backward short leg had been posted. Lloyd duly called one up – then sent him into the covers when Chappell hit the ball there. When he brought in a fine leg, it was only after a ball had been edged in that direction. Etc.

After the tour, Michael Holding wrote that Lloyd and manager Esmond Kentish were 'far too soft' in dealing with players who challenged their authority. West Indies lost the series 5–1.

Nine years later, West Indies had far less trouble in Australia, winning the series 3–1, but might not only have made it 4–1 but also extended their record run of 11 consecutive Test wins if Lloyd hadn't delayed his declaration until 15 minutes into the last day. Australia, 3–0 down in the series and 198–8 at the close of this fourth Test, would surely have lost if he'd sent them in earlier.

Replying to Somerset's modest 207 in the 1978 Gillette Cup final, Sussex made 93 without loss before a run of quick wickets left them on 110–4 with Somerset's most dangerous bowlers, Joel Garner and Ian Botham, operating in tandem. Then, surprisingly, their captain Brian Rose took them both off, which allowed Paul Parker and Paul Phillipson to settle in and score the runs (62 and 32) which won the match by five wickets. Some lessons are quickly learned: Somerset won the Cup the following year.

Overshadowed by Bradman throughout the 1930s despite being one of the greatest players of all time, Wally Hammond lost his final duel with the Don in 1946–47, the first post-war Ashes series, partly because of his uncommunicative captaincy and his insistence on the batsmen playing the Australian spinners from the crease.

The policy's just desserts arrived in the second Test. Winning the toss on an ideal batting wicket at Sydney, England were all out for 255 after allowing Ian Johnson and Colin McCool to bowl over after maiden over, tossing the ball higher and higher to try to tempt the English batsmen out of their crease. At one point, Johnson sent down 11 overs for three runs (three singles in 88 balls); he took 6–42 as England went down by an innings to trail 2–0 in a series they lost 3–0. Freddie Brown, who led England bravely and well in Australia four years later,

called Hammond the worst captain he ever played under.

At the time, Don Bradman's 334 at Headingley in 1930 was the highest score in Test cricket, 309 of the runs coming on the first day, another record. Looking back, it's clear (to Bradman himself, among others) that the England captain Percy Chapman erred in setting attacking fields all day, allowing 22 overs to be bowled every hour, and instructing his bowlers to try to get the little man out rather than contain him. Chapman lost the captaincy before the last match of the series, which Australia won 2–1 to regain the Ashes.

The next question has nothing to do with music or sport. On which ground did Geoffrey Boycott score his hundredth hundred?

Disc Jockey on Classic FM

Similarly, in the 1965 Gillette Cup final, Geoff Boycott scored 146, still the record for any one-day final, and Yorkshire made a prohibitive 317–4 – but they were helped by Surrey's attacking field settings: even after the score went over 200 for the loss of only one wicket, Micky Stewart kept a slip, short leg and shortish mid-wicket for Boycott. Surrey lost by the preposterous margin of 175 runs and had to wait till 1982 to win the Cup (by then the NatWest Trophy) for the first and only time.

India drew the 1985–86 series in Australia, but should have won it comfortably. The opposition, having left the Ashes in England, had just lost a series to New Zealand for the first time (at home, too). Confidence and morale were at their lowest for years.

So it was no surprise when India made 520 in a first Test shortened by rain and 445 in the second, in which their captain began to let the reins slip.

At the start of the last day, Australia were only 45 ahead with just the last two wickets left, but one of these was Allan Border – and Kapil Dev made the standard error of trying to get at the tail-enders by letting the recognised batsman take singles. Bob Willis had done this with Border in 1982–83; it hadn't worked then and Kapil Dev should have seen the script. Instead Border and Dave Gilbert used up two hours adding 77 for the last wicket, and India needed only 67 to win with seven wickets in hand when rain saved Australia again. Kapil Dev blamed the weather and the umpires, but his bowling tactics had been unimaginative and he'd let his batsmen score too slowly when the weather closed in.

Much the same problem in the third and final Test. Again Kapil Dev allowed his batsmen to crawl, and declared too late. India scored 600–4, but Sunil Gavaskar and Mohinder Amarnath, for example, made only 64 before lunch on the second day. At the end, Australia, with only four wickets left, still needed 85 to make India bat again.

The Indians had missed their best chance of winning a series in Australia (they still haven't) and Kapil Dev, after 20 attempts, still hadn't captained the winning side in a Test match.

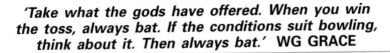

Heads you lose

'Take what the gods have offered. When you win the toss, always bat. If the conditions suit bowling, think about it. Then always bat.' **WG GRACE**

In his only overseas series as England captain, Ian Botham won the toss at the start of the first Test in 1980–81, put the West Indies in to bat, then made no attempt to get his fastest bowler, young Graham Dilley, to bowl round the wicket to aim at the damp patches on the pitch. England's chances dried up in front of their eyes, the West Indies scored 426, won the match by an innings, and took the series 2–0.

In 1954–55, Len Hutton began the defence of the Ashes by becoming the first England captain since Johnny Douglas in 1912 to put Australia in to bat. Four of his bowlers conceded more than 100 runs apiece as Australia amassed 601–8, shot England out for 190 and won by an innings.

Hutton used two slower bowlers throughout the rest of the series, which England took 3–1, the first they'd won in Australia since 1932–33.

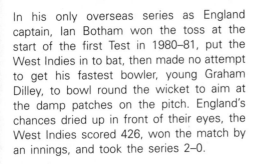

At the very start of the 1981–82 series, Javed Miandad put Australia in to bat. They scored only 180, but Pakistan collapsed to 26–8, were all out for 62, lost the match by 286 runs and the series 2–1.

In the last match of the 1980–81 series, Greg Chappell put India in, saw Dennis Lillee and Len Pascoe bowl India out for 237, then scored 76 out of Australia's 419.

In the second innings, however, he was bowled behind his legs first ball as Australia, condemned by Chappell to bat last on an untrustworthy pitch, were all out for 83 and lost by 59, allowing the Indians to draw a series in Australia for the first time.

In the third Test of the 1983–84 series, Kapil Dev should surely have seen that the newly-laid wicket would break up as the match went on. Instead he gave the West Indies first use of it. Needing 242 to win, India were all out for 103 and went two down in a series they lost 3–0.

England were 1–0 down before the third Test of the 1982–83 tour, which prompted Bob Willis to put Australia in to bat when he won the toss – even though he said he knew history was against him (other England captains who'd done this against the old enemy had been rewarded with eight defeats and only one win) and, more pertinently, the pitch, according to *Wisden* among others, 'looked a beauty'.

England didn't get a ball past the bat in the first hour, took only three wickets on the first day, were forced to follow on, and lost by eight wickets to go 2–0 down in a series they eventually lost 2–1.

After winning the toss before the one-day international against the West Indies in St Vincent in 1994, England captain Mike Atherton wasn't short of helpful suggestions. For some reason, he was more inclined to follow the advice of one G Boycott (who urged him to put the opposition in) rather than listen to a *real* expert, 'a local rastafarian with a huge spliff,' who counselled him to bat while the tide was out.

Atherton sent the West Indies in, they scored 313 and won by 165 runs, the highest total conceded and heaviest defeat suffered by England in their one-day history (this was their 222nd such match).

When Johnny Douglas won the toss before the second Gentlemen v Players of 1921, he put the opposition in, 'but his decision turned out disastrously, the Players batting the whole of the first day.' They made 302 and won by 198.

Richie Richardson invited England to bat first in the fourth Test of the 1993–94 series, probably because they'd been dismissed for only 46 in the second innings of the previous Test. However, their captain Mike Atherton thought this wicket looked 'full of runs', and so it proved. England, in their 700th Test, scored 355 and 394 to become only the second team to win one in Barbados (the first was in 1935). It was only their fifth win in the last 50 Tests against the West Indies, who'd won the last 12 to be held on the island.

Needing to win the second Test to draw the 1951–52 home series, New Zealand could only draw – after Bert Sutcliffe had won the toss, put the West Indies in, and fielded for two days while they amassed 546–6.

Much later, in 1990, one of Sutcliffe's successors made the same mistake, this time in England. A draw in each of the first two Tests sent New Zealand into the decider all square, but John Wright admitted 'I was wrong to put England in. No two ways about it, it was a bad decision.' England scored

435 and won by 114 to take a home series for the first time since 1985.

They didn't have long to wait for the next. Later that summer, they again won 1–0, this time against India, whose captain Mohammad Azharuddin invited them to bat first in the opening Test. Graham Gooch scored 333, declared at 653–4 and saw England win by 247 runs. Azza's own century was brilliant but no real atonement, and his tour manager Bishan Bedi didn't endear himself to the team by dissociating himself from the decision to put England in.

In the semi-final of the 1996 World Cup, Azharuddin put Sri Lanka in on a wicket that was turning square by the time his team batted. He was out for 0, playing a tame shot, as India were reduced to 120–8 before a riot stopped play. Sri Lanka went on to win the trophy for the first time.

After losing 5–0 at home to the West Indies in 1984, England probably thought they'd have little trouble picking up some consolation by beating little Sri Lanka in the one-off Test that followed. No doubt that's why David Gower put them in when he won the toss.

The Sri Lankans, in their first Test in England, batted for the whole of the first two days before declaring at 491–7 and drawing the match at their leisure.

Not that WG was always right, of course. You can't win ...
After winning the toss at the start of the first ever B&H Cup final (1972), Yorkshire captain Phil Sharpe thought long and hard about a wicket which heavily favoured seam bowling, of which he had plenty in the team: Tony Nicholson, Chris Old, Richard Hutton, Howard Cooper. Then, although he was without the injured Geoff Boycott, he decided to bat.

Azharuddin's Achilles heels?

His opposite number and former team mate Ray Illingworth: 'If I had been him I would have put us in.' Yorkshire were all out for 136, lost by five wickets, and had to wait fifteen years to win the Cup for the first time.

Although the Lord's pitch of 1962 was green and tailor-made for bowling, Pakistan captain Javed Burki chose to bat first. Pakistan, all out for exactly 100, lost the match by nine wickets and the series 4–0.

Nottinghamshire won the 1981 County Championship thanks mainly to their seam bowling partnership of Richard Hadlee and Clive Rice and the Trent Bridge wickets prepared for them by Ron Allsopp. Mind you, it paid to know how to use them. Notts, lucky enough to win the toss in almost every

home match, put the opposition in each time. When Leicestershire won it, they opted to bat first – and lost by eight wickets!

Australia played a single Test in New Zealand in 1990, losing it virtually from the start, when Allan Border decided to bat first, against Richard Hadlee, on a seamer's pitch. Australia were all out for 110 (Hadlee 5–39) and lost by nine wickets.

After winning the toss at the start of the third Test in India in 1993–94, Arjuna Ranatunga chose to bat first on a dodgy wicket, which contributed to Sri Lanka being all out for 119 and becoming only the second side ever to lose all three Tests in a series by an innings.

Dropping all over England

Catches lose matches (Tests against other countries)

After making only 200 in their first innings of the second Test in South Africa in 1995–96, England were left with 479 to win – or, more to the point, over ten hours to survive for the draw, which seemed out of the question when their fifth second-innings wicket fell at 232.

Soon afterwards, wicketkeeper 'Jack' Russell was on 5 when he gave a straight-forward return catch, waist high to Meyrick Pringle's right. Pringle dropped it and Russell stayed for more than four and a half hours to make 29 not out in company with his captain Mike Atherton, whose 185 not out, the highest of his Test career, owed a good deal to a dropped catch at short leg, the ball going straight into Gary Kirsten's midriff and out again. If he'd held it, Atherton would have been the first batsman to be out for 99 three times in Tests! Instead, his monumental rearguard innings saw England through to 351–5, enough to draw the match.

The following summer, Atherton helped save the third and final Test against India (and therefore win the series 1–0) with his 160, but only after being dropped before he'd scored by Saurav Ganguly – which just about evened up the ledger: earlier in the same match, Sachin Tendulkar had made 177 after also being dropped on 0 – by Atherton!

Down 1–0 after the first four Tests in 1981–82, England reduced India to 51–2 in their first innings of the fifth, then Chris Tavaré dropped catches off two of their premier batsmen, Dilip Vengsarkar and Gundappa Viswanath (Mike Gatting thought 'we might even have dropped them twice each'). Vengsarkar made 71 before retiring hurt, Viswanath a demoralising 222, India drew this match and the next to win the series.

West Indies captain Garry Sobers had made 60 in the first Test of the 1966 series in England when he offered a catch to pace bowler David Brown, who dropped it. Sobers scored another 101 runs, England were beaten by an innings and went on to lose the series. Years later, Brown felt that his miss 'probably cost Mike Smith his job as captain too.' Brown was dropped for the rest of the series, Smith for the next six years.

Early in his second innings of the second Test in 1973, Sobers played forward to England captain Ray Illingworth and gave Frank Hayes 'the easiest slip catch you've ever seen,' the ball looping so slowly that Hayes closed his hands and it hit him on the back of his fingers. Very soon afterwards, Clive Lloyd tried to sweep Illingworth, got a top edge, and was dropped by Geoff Arnold at fine leg. Lloyd scored 94, Sobers 74 (easily the highest scores in the innings) as West Indies held out for the draw on their way to winning the series 2–0.

Hayes later apologised with 'Look, there's nothing I can say. It's just one of those things that will never happen again.' It certainly didn't for Illingworth: this was his last Test series!

His cause wasn't helped in the third Test, when all-rounder Bernard Julien was dropped early in his innings by Keith Fletcher off Tony Greig. Julien went on to score his maiden first-class century as the West Indies declared at 652–8 and won by an innings and 236, which confirmed their first series win over England since 1966.

In the first Test of the 1980 series, a low-scoring affair at Trent Bridge, the West Indies were 195–7 when Andy Roberts was dropped by David Gower off Bob Willis. Gower was a world-class cover fielder and this was an easy chance. Roberts made 22 not out as the West Indies crept in by two wickets and drew the remaining four Tests.

After losing the first Test of the 1995 series against the West Indies, England's first innings of the second was repaired by a century stand between Graham Thorpe and Robin Smith, the latter knowing that he was playing for his place after a run of low form. He top-scored in each innings (61 & 90) and Thorpe made 52 & 42 – but only after both had been dropped in the first innings, Thorpe at slip, Smith twice in the same over from Ian Bishop. England won by 72 runs.

Later, in the second innings of the fifth Test, the West Indies' Sherwin Campbell took a brilliant catch to dismiss Craig White at short (very short) square leg, before being offered another chance, at short (but not that short) midwicket, by Mike Watkinson.

It was a relatively simple waist-high chance, but Campbell put it down. If he'd taken it, not only would Courtney Walsh have picked up his 300th Test wicket, but England would have been all out for 191. As it was, Watkinson went on to make his first Test fifty (82 not out, the highest score in the innings), his last-wicket partnership with Richard Illingworth adding another 78 runs (and more importantly using up a further 24 overs) as England escaped with a draw in the match and the series.

England won the second Test against West Indies in 1939 (and with it the series 1–0) thanks mainly to a partnership of 248 between their two leading young bucks, Len Hutton and Denis Compton, but only after the latter was dropped off consecutive balls.

On the same ground 14 years later, Hutton and Compton showed it can happen to anyone, each helping Australia's captain Lindsay Hassett to a century, Hutton by dropping him at second slip, Compton by going the wrong way at leg slip!

> *The Test match begins in ten minutes. That's our time, of course.*
>
> **David Coleman**

West Indies' win at Lord's in 1950, which set them on the way to taking the series, is the stuff of calypsos – but things might have been different if their top scorers in the first innings, Allan Rae (106) and Everton Weekes (63), hadn't both been dropped by Hubert Doggart at slip, each time off Alec Bedser.

In the second innings, Rae was dropped twice more – and the wretched Doggart put down Weekes (63 again) then Clyde Walcott, who made 168! England lost by 326 runs and Doggart didn't play Test cricket again.

West Indies repaid some of this in 1957, losing the series 3–0, not least because their fielding wasn't up to standard. In the second Test they dropped 12 chances, five off Godfrey Evans alone!

After the dismissal of Wes Hall, Knott and Cowdrey prepare for their long partnership

In the 1963 series against the West Indies, England did themselves no favours from the start. In the first innings of the first Test, 'Joey' Carew and Frank Worrell were dropped off Fred Trueman, who himself put down Conrad Hunte at short leg. Hunte, on 66 at the time, went on to make 182, Worrell 74 not out before declaring at 501–6. England lost by ten wickets.

They might have won the next match, the famous Lord's Test, instead of drawing when only six runs short of victory, if three catches hadn't been dropped before lunch on the first day, all off Derek Shackleton, recalled after an absence of eleven years. England levelled the series at Edgbaston before losing it 3–1.

Needing to draw the fifth and final Test to

win the 1967–68 series in the Caribbean, England were forced to struggle throughout their second innings after losing half the side for only 41. The rearguard action was led almost exclusively by their captain Colin Cowdrey and wicketkeeper Alan Knott, who made 155 between them in a total of 206–9. It was *just* enough, that wholehearted pace bowler and negligible batsman Jeff Jones surviving the final over of the series from Lance Gibbs.

Long before that, early in his innings, Knott had pushed forward to a ball from spinner David Holford and edged the ball to slip, where Rohan Kanhai dropped it. Knott's 73 not out says it all.

England won the final Test to draw the 1973–74 series in the West Indies, who should have wrapped up the whole thing much earlier, not least in the second Test, when they took a first-innings lead of 230 and were still 13 runs ahead with five England wickets down in the second. They failed to win the match, and eventually the series, when Garry Sobers, one of the greatest close fielders of all time, dropped Dennis Amiss off the second ball of the last day (in fact, he moved the wrong way for it). Amiss went on to make 262 not out, his first double century in first-class cricket and his highest ever Test score.

England also hung on to draw the third Test (they were 201 behind on first innings), thanks to an innings of 148 by Tony Greig after he'd been dropped by Sobers!

West Indies were the first side to lose by an innings in all three Tests of a series, their very first, in England in 1928 – but things might have been different if their fast bowlers, Learie Constantine, George Francis and Herman Griffith, hadn't had 'scores of catches dropped off them, which must have been discouraging'! In fact, their captain Karl Nunes went so far as to say that if he'd had England's Percy Chapman or Wally Hammond in the slips, the home team's totals in all three matches 'would have been halved'.

In the fourth Test of the 1984–85 series in India, both England openers were dropped by the close fielders: Graeme Fowler on 36 and 75, Tim Robinson on 44. Later, Mike Gatting was put down by Laxman Sivaramakrishnan (having the names of three Hindu deities in his surname didn't help). Fowler made 201, Robinson 74, Gatting 207 (the first time two batsmen had made double centuries in the same England innings) to win the match by nine wickets and the series after being 1–0 down.

Defending a first-innings total of only 136 in the third Test against Pakistan in 1987, the last thing England needed was a sequence of dropped catches, least of all in the 27 overs of Pakistan's reply on the first day. Three in all were put down, all off the luckless Neil Foster: Phil Edmonds and John Emburey missed Mansoor Akhtar twice in the slips, including his first ball, then Emburey spilled an easy chance off nightwatchman Salim Yousuf, who stayed throughout the whole of the following morning. Pakistan's 353 was enough to win the match by an innings and give them the series (the first they ever won in England) by this one Test to nil.

The first Test of the 1948–49 series between South Africa and England was famously close. Needing 128 to win a low-scoring match on rain-affected pitch, England started by throwing caution – and almost everything else – to the winds: Len Hutton thrashing the first ball to gully, where it might have been caught instead of hitting Dudley Nourse on the knee. Then, when the first ball of the next over, bowled by Lindsay Tuckett, was pitched short, Cyril Washbrook mishit it straight to a fielder.

'A close-up of Owen Wynne's face at that moment would have conveyed human despair to future generations unacquainted with such an emotion, more adequately than Marlowe's description of stricken Niobe.' In other words, he dropped the catch. The extra 25 runs made by Washbrook helped decide the match, which England won by two wickets with a leg-bye off the very last ball. One of the last two batsmen, Cliff Gladwin, had earlier been dropped by Tuckett before he'd scored!

In England's first Test after the Second World War, Joe Hardstaff was dropped when he'd made 42, which cost the opposition dear. His eventual 205 not out, his highest score in Test cricket, was five more than India's first innings total! England won by ten wickets and went on to take the series by this one Test to nil.

> ## It's physically and mentally soul-destroying.
>
> **Geoff Boycott**

It rarely pays to drop a catch off Geoff Boycott. Rick McCosker found that out in 1977 (*Blunders Vol.1*), as did New Zealand captain Geoff Howarth a year later. On his return to Test cricket, Boycott was put down by Howarth early in his innings of 131, his highest against New Zealand and the foundation stone of England's 429 which was enough to win the second Test by an innings. Meanwhile poor Howarth had to retire in the second innings after being hit on the head by a Botham bouncer. New Zealand lost all three matches in the series.

Alf Gover's eight Test wickets cost 44.87 each, but how things might have been different if two catches hadn't been dropped off his bowling on the first morning of his first match, against India in 1936.

Similar but even more 'if only' was Eric Davies' fate. His seven Test wickets for South Africa cost 68.71, but his gutsy 4–75 on his debut, in an Australian total of 439 in 1936, would have been startlingly better but for a rash of dropped catches off his bowling. South Africa lost by an innings.

Another South African, Cuan McCarthy of the great pace and dodgy action, had to pay a humbling 107.20 runs for each of his five wickets against Australia in 1949–50, but suffered 11 dropped catches in the series.

Striking it poor

A nightwatchman's job is to survive the last few balls or overs of a day, saving a more recognised batsman till the following day. No-one proved worse at this task than Robin Marlar of Essex when he came back to the pavilion after being stumped for 6 second ball!

Whether Ian Botham would ever have made a good England captain is always going to be open to doubt, but he could have done with an easier start. His first two series were against the West Indies, who won 1–0 and 2–0, scorelines England would have been grateful for in 1984, 1985–86 and 1988. When they lost the first match of his third series, against Australia in 1981, Botham was under pressure, which built up when he was lbw for 0 in the first innings of the next Test.

The first ball of his second innings, bowled by slow left-armer Ray Bright, could have been kept out with a defensive push. But that was rarely the Beefy way. Trying to score from the start, he missed with his sweep shot and was bowled round his legs, returning to a pointed silence from MCC members. He went on to write his name on the series with those two famous innings and that burst of five wickets without conceding a run – but Mike Brearley had been recalled by then, and Botham never captained England again.

Later, in 1989, again against Australia, he went for a repeat of his infamous heave-ho against the West Indies in 1980–81 (*Blunders Vol. 1*), this time when England were 140–4 and in need of what he himself called 'a modicum of discretion'. He was bowled by leg-spinner Trevor Hohns for a duck as England lost the match by nine wickets (their 100th defeat by Australia) and the series 4–0.

Just as notorious was David Gower's aberration during the 1990–91 Ashes tour, when one of his patented flicks wafted the ball straight to Merv Hughes, stationed at backward square leg precisely for that shot – and off the last ball before lunch, too. Gower was out for 11 (and out of Graham Gooch's good books for ever) and England lost their last chance of sharing the series.

Gower removes his helmet before putting his head on Gooch's chopping block

> *This was a tremendous six. The ball was still in the air as it went over the boundary.*
>
> **Fred Trueman**

Losing the England captaincy probably didn't help, but Graham Gooch's troubles in the 1989 Ashes series had more to do with a sudden problem of technique. Not that there was much sign of it when he scored 52 in the first one-day international, 136 in the third, and was made England's man of the series. But the Test matches were another matter entirely.

The Australians' tactics against him were simple. Noting his tendency to play through midwicket, they placed one or two fielders in attacking positions on the leg-side, limiting his options and forcing him to look for runs elsewhere. Worse, his front-foot movement left him vulnerable to the medium-paced ball pitched up, and Australia had the ideal bowler to produce that in Terry Alderman.

Back in 1981, his first ever Test series, Alderman had taken a record 42 wickets, helping reduce Gooch to an average of only 13.90. This time, if anything, it was worse. Time and again throughout the series, Gooch planted his front foot down the wicket, couldn't get his bat down in time, and was lbw more often than not, twice in the first Test, once in the second and in his only innings of the third. After the fourth, he asked to be dropped, came back for the sixth – and was twice dismissed by Alderman, the first time lbw for 0! Australia won the series 4–0.

Adjustments to the Gooch technique (and the restoration of the captaincy) worked wonders. England would surely have won the 1989–90 series in the Caribbean but for his broken finger, and he led them to a series win over India in 1990, scoring 333 at Lord's.

Mind you, just as a reminder, in his first innings of the next overseas series, he was dismissed early in the second Test at Melbourne: lbw to Alderman! Again England lost the series.

Needing only a draw in the final Test to win the 1991 series in England, West Indies were undone by a collective rush of blood as soon as they faced slow left-armer Phil Tufnell. His very first ball provoked Clayton Lambert into an immense agricultural heave that came down with snow on it into the hands of Mark Ramprakash. Lambert's played in only this one Test so far. Soon afterwards, having scored only 2, Viv Richards advanced from his crease to show Tufnell what he thought of slow bowling, and wicketkeeper Alec Stewart showed what he thought of the wild shot by taking the catch.

It was the pivotal moment of the match. Taking their cue from their captain, Curtly Ambrose and Courtney Walsh were out within the next four balls, both swinging mightily at Tufnell, who took six wickets for four runs in 33 balls.

In the second innings, West Indies showed how it ought to be done, leaving Tufnell with figures of 1–150, but it was too late by then: England won by five wickets to level the series.

The 1975–76 series in Australia was regarded as an unofficial world championship decider. In the first Test, West Indies won the toss and batted. By lunch, they'd scored a quickfire 125 – but at the cost of six wickets. They lost by eight, and although they took the second Test by an innings, they did it with more of the same extravagant stroke-making, which was repeated in the third, leading to a first innings of only 224 and another defeat by eight wickets. More of the same in the fourth, Fredericks, Rowe, Richards, Murray and Lloyd throwing their wickets away after making 30s and 40s. In the series as a whole, 14 West Indian wickets fell to the hook shot, countless others to catches at the wicket and in the slips as the pace attack of Lillee, Thomson, Gilmour and Walker won the 'world title' 5–1.

Three seasons later, it was Australia's turn to catch the disease. Denuded of their best players by Packer, the first thing they needed in the Ashes series at home was a good start. Instead, one by one their batsmen threw away their wickets in a spate of aggressive shots (Kim Hughes driving at Ian Botham, Trevor Laughlin hooking Bob Willis, etc). They were an eyebrow-raising 26–6 on the very first morning of the series, then 53–7 and 116 all out, beaten by seven wickets. Like the West Indies in 1975–76, they lost the series 5–1.

Needing only 127 to win the second Test and take a 1–0 lead in the 1985 Ashes series, Australia were reduced to 9–2 and 22–3 but inched their way to a win by four wickets. Their second-innings jitters had been started by opener Andrew Hilditch, who hooked Ian Botham to Allan Lamb, costing Australia their first wicket without a run on the board. Before this match, he hadn't been a persistent hooker; now, almost overnight, he seemed to become obsessed with the shot, which cost him his wicket more than once and according to his captain Allan Border 'forced him out of international cricket'.

In the first Test of the 1985–86 series against New Zealand, he fell for it again. In the first innings, he swung Richard Hadlee to fine leg, where Ewen Chatfield held the catch to take Australia's first wicket with the fifth ball of the series. In the second, he hooked Hadlee and was again caught in the deep by Chatfield, this time off the very first ball after a break. Australia lost at home to New Zealand for the first time ever and Hilditch didn't play Test cricket again.

Botham provides the bait, Hilditch the hook

Hilditch's team-mate Kim Hughes was another classic compulsive hooker, one who announced that he was giving up the shot before the first Test against the West Indies in 1984–85. Famous last words. Hooking a bouncer from Michael Holding, he was caught by Malcolm Marshall for 4. Australia lost by an innings.

In the second Test, again the hook, again the catch by Marshall, again a heavy defeat, after which Hughes resigned the captaincy in a famously tearful press conference. The Australian selectors kept him in the side for the next two Tests, in which he scored 0, 2, 0, 0 before his Test career was brought to an end.

> *No captain with all the hindsight in the world can predict how the wicket is going to play.*
>
> **Trevor Bailey**

Faced with a first-innings deficit of 419, England were left with a long rearguard action to save the third Test against the West Indies in 1973, normally the kind of situation Geoff Boycott revels in.

This time, however, he was riled by a request from his partner, Brian Luckhurst, who asked him to take the brunt of Keith Boyce's bowling towards the end of the fourth day. Boycott (and team-mate Keith Fletcher, among others) felt that Luckhurst, an established opener, should have taken his share of the flak.

When Luckhurst refused an easy single, Boycott lost his rag, hooked the very next ball, from Boyce, to deep square leg – and was caught by Alvin Kallicharran in the last over of the day ('the only time I have ever surrendered my wicket through pure hotheadedness'). Boycott was so agitated afterwards that he suffered a nosebleed (there's no substance to the rumour that his captain Ray Illingworth had a hand, or something, in it). The catch reduced England to 42–3 and they lost by an innings and 226.

In the famous, highly charged Test of 1882, England were 75–9, still ten runs short of victory, when last man Edmund Peate came to the wicket. The first of Yorkshire's sequence of great slow left-armers, but nothing very special with the bat, Peate's orders from his captain Albert 'Monkey' Hornby seem to have been predictable: try to stay there while Charles Studd at the other end looks for the winning runs.

Studd, one of the best batting all-rounders in England, had scored two centuries against the Australians that summer but was held back till number 10 and now could only watch from the non-striker's end as Harry Boyle bowled to Peate, who took a great swing and picked up two runs. One ball left in the over. All Peate had to do was keep it out, leaving Studd to take over. Instead, he took another enormous swipe at the ball, missed it, and was bowled for 2. England lost by seven runs, Studd didn't face a ball.

Bernard James Tindal Bosanquet patented, perhaps even invented, the googly (the Australians named it 'bosie' after him). It decided the Ashes series of 1903–04 and 1905. But it might never have seen the light of day in Test matches if it had been dealt with when it first appeared.

Bosanquet tried it for the first time in a county match in 1900, for Middlesex against Leicestershire, possibly as a last resort: Sammy Coe had hit the bowling to all parts on his way to 98.

He should probably have done the same to that historic first ball. Instead, he missed and was stumped, quite a feat against a ball which bounced four times before it reached him!

Against Gloucestershire in 1966, Yorkshire were trying to consolidate on the last day when David Allen bowled the last ball before lunch to Fred Trueman, who gave it an almighty thump and was caught on the boundary, then explained that he was only pushing it for a single! His captain, Brian Close, wasn't amused, at least not till much later.

Perhaps, though, Closey saw something of his own past in that shot. The decisive match of the 1961 Ashes series was the fourth, played at Old Trafford. After England had led by 177 on first innings and held Australia to a lead of only 157 with nine wickets down, Peter May's removal of David Allen from the attack [see CAPTAIN, THE SHIP IS SINKING] helped the last-wicket pair to add 98 crucial runs, leaving England with 256 to win, a target that looked well within reach when they were 150–1 with Ted Dexter sailing along on 76. Then Richie Benaud dismissed Dexter and May (first ball) and suddenly the match was a crossroads, with England's hopes resting mainly on Raman Subba Row and DB Close.

While Subba Row closed up one end, Close decided to hit, specifically to try to hit Benaud out of the attack. What followed was a series of leg-side shots that looked like hybrid sweeps, one of which went for six. It looked odd (some said ugly) and possibly dangerous, especially as Benaud had posted Norm O'Neill at fine leg.

Before long, the inevitable: Close had made only 8 when he was caught by O'Neill off Benaud, who then ran through the England tail, taking 6–70 in all, including 5–12 in 25 balls. Australia won by 54 runs to take a winning lead in the series and retain the Ashes.

That Close dismissal remains one of the most discussed incidents in a career packed with them. His own apologia sounds feasible enough: O'Neill hadn't gone back to his correct position after fielding the previous ball, so there was an element of luck about the catch; at least Close (unlike Subba Row?) was trying to do something towards actually winning the match; May's dismissal was just as culpable (he was bowled behind his legs) but nothing much was said about it whereas Close was dropped.

Fair comment perhaps, but you can't help thinking that those leg-side swings were likely to find the fielder sooner or later – and anyway Close had done the same kind of thing twelve years earlier, on his first tour, to Australia in 1950–51.

England had been in all kinds of trouble then. After losing the first Test, they faced an Australian first innings total of only 194 in the second – but were struggling at 54–4 when the 19-year-old Close came to the wicket. The third ball he received, in the last over before lunch, was hit straight up in the air for backward short leg to take an easy catch. Close was out for 0 and made only a single in the second innings as England lost the match by just 28 runs and the series 4–1. He wasn't capped again till 1955.

> *South Africa came and took a large slice of the cream.*
>
> **Tony Lewis**

Seymour Clark, who kept wicket for Somerset in 1930, was such a negligible batsman that opposition bowlers did their best to let him get off the mark. They never succeeded, at least not in the County Championship. In the nine innings of his only Championship season, he didn't score a single run! Typical of his batting prowess was a ball courteously offered up by Peter Smith of Essex, which bounced twice before Clark took a swing and was bowled. It's said that the only dents in his bat were the result of it being dropped twice on its way out to face fast bowler Bill Bowes!

The first Test of the 1991–92 series in New Zealand was effectively decided in England's favour by a single stroke. In the face of their first innings total of 580, the host team were battling to avoid an innings defeat after following-on. Although their last pair were at the wicket, one of those was captain and leading batsman Martin Crowe, who was on 48 – and they were within four runs of saving the game, so close to the end of the match that England wouldn't have time to chase any total at all.

His partner, last man Chris Pringle, had hung on well enough for five runs, but Crowe seemed to suddenly decide that he couldn't trust him to hold out. Either that or he simply backed his talent to hit those four runs in one go, even though he was facing Phil Tufnell, who'd taken 6–14 in the last two hours.

Launching into the big hit, Crowe mishit the ball to extra cover, where Derek Pringle took the catch. New Zealand lost by an innings and four runs in virtually the last minute to go 1–0 down in the series. They lost it 2–0 when Crowe put England in to bat after winning the toss in the second Test.

Going only three halves of the way to the boundary.

Doug Walters

England lost the first Test against the West Indies in 1995 when their last eight first-innings wickets went down for 57 runs, often as the result of, shall we say, ambitious shots, typified by the dismissal of the latest golden boy Darren Gough, who hooked his first ball into the hands of Curtly Ambrose at long leg. Peter Johnson's description was one of the greats: 'They

died by their own hand while the balance of the side was disturbed.'

Having won the first match of the 1984–85 series against England, India had only to bat normally on a slow pitch to draw the second. Instead, they lost their last six second-innings wickets for only 28 runs, a collapse epitomised by Kapil Dev, who drove Pat Pocock for six, then tried the same shot (the opposite of what was required) and was caught by Allan Lamb at long-off. England stopped a run of 13 matches without a win, Kapil Dev was dropped from the next match, ending a run of 66 consecutive Tests, and India lost the series 2–1.

Opening batsman Peter Richardson played a full part in England's retention of the Ashes in 1956, scoring 363 runs at an average of 45.38, figures which might have been even better but for his habit of snicking the ball to the wicketkeeper. He was out that way in all eight of his innings in the series!

Few batsmen can have make such a distinguished duck in their first Test as Doug Insole against the West Indies in 1950: stumped down the leg side in the last over of the day. England lost by ten wickets and Insole was left out for five years.

During the match against the 1946 Indians, Glamorgan number 11 batsman Peter Judge was bowled by Chandra Sarwate, which forced Glamorgan to follow on. Since there was no chance of any result, the Glamorgan captain told the two batsmen to carry on without coming off the field. Judge, facing the first ball, took a swing at it ...

He was dismissed in the same fashion, by the same bowler, off consecutive balls, the only two he faced in the match!

Jim Higgs was such a negligible batsman that he averaged only 5.55 in his 22 Tests for Australia and was bowled by the only ball he faced on the 1975 tour of England!

If you're going to make a duck, make it in style. In 1948, one Gerald Pedder was dismissed for 0 while playing in Ditchling, Sussex – having travelled from Nicaragua for the match! He once played a match in Sussex after setting off from Fiji.

West Indies' chances of saving the third Test at home to Australia in 1954–55 disappeared when two of their premier batsmen were dismissed in unusual, self-destructive fashion after putting on 125 for the fourth wicket, Clyde Walcott treading on his stumps, Frank Worrell hitting them with his bat. West Indies lost the match by eight wickets to go 2–0 down in a series they lost 3–0, despite a record five centuries from Walcott.

Sri Lanka should have won the first Test of their 1992 home series against Australia. Replying to a first innings of 256, they declared at 547–8 and eventually needed just 54 to win with eight wickets left and plenty of overs to go.

Then their best batsman Aravinda de Silva, with no need to hurry, swung a ball from Craig McDermott high to mid-on, where the Australian captain Allan Border threw off his hat and sunglasses and ran to take the catch.

There were still plenty more batsmen to come, but they all seemed to catch De Silva's mood, collapsing to 164 all out, the

last eight wickets falling in 17.4 overs, to hand Australia victory by 16 runs and eventually the series 1–0. Border called it 'the greatest heist since the Great Train Robbery'. Sri Lanka have never beaten Australia in a Test match.

> *David Boon is now completely clean-shaven, except for his moustache.*
>
> **Graham Dawson**

Still, perhaps they can take heart from the fact that it happens to the best of 'em, including the best Australian.

Having lost the first Test of the 1932–33 series, Australia were looking for the return of Don Bradman from illness to revive them. The first ball he received in the series, a short one from fast bowler Bill Bowes, pitched well outside the off stump, yet the Don stepped across and tried to hook it to leg, succeeding only in dragging it onto his stumps. He himself called it 'a rotten shot, that's all that can be said about it.' It was the first ball the bespectacled Bowes had bowled to Bradman in a Test, and the only Test wicket he ever took in Australia!

The Don recovered to score a century in the second innings, and Australia won the match, but his way of dealing with the Bodyline tactic designed specifically for him, resulted in his lowest batting average in any series and couldn't stop Australia losing this one 4–1.

Bodyline had been outlawed by the time Bradman came back to England in 1934. In the second Test, Australia trailed by 156 runs after the first innings and were 57–2 in the second when the Don tried to hit Hedley Verity against the spin, 'a most unguarded stroke at a critical time' wrote Plum Warner.

The ball went straight up in the air (*The Times* called it 'the worst shot he has ever made in his life') for wicketkeeper Les Ames to take an easy catch. Bradman was out for 13, Verity took 15 wickets in the match and England won by an innings, their last win over Australia at Lord's to date.

In the second Test of the 1936–37 series, Bradman tried to hook Verity, took his eye off the ball, and was bowled by a long-hop. CB Fry announced that 'The greatest run-getter in the history of cricket has made the worst stroke in the history of cricket,' which is stretching it a bit, but it certainly contributed to Australia's defeat by an innings.

Not striking it at all

The perils of shouldering arms.

The last Test of the 1968 rubber couldn't affect the destination of the Ashes (Australia had already retained them) but England, who felt they were unlucky not to be ahead, still wanted to win it and square the series. After reducing Australia to 65–5 in the second innings, they were hindered by torrential rain, but the Oval crowd helped mop the water off the outfield in time for Derek Underwood to get at the Australian batsmen on a drying pitch.

The left-armer was nicknamed Deadly for his prowess on this kind of wicket – but even so Australia might well have survived if two of their batsmen hadn't shouldered arms at the wrong time. First wicketkeeper Barry Jarman played no shot at a ball from Basil D'Oliveira (a partnership breaker of some repute) and was bowled off his pad.

Then, right at the death, with nine wickets down, the last lapse. John Inverarity, still there on 56 (out of a total of 125) after opening the innings, had shielded Alan Connolly so skilfully that the number 11 had had to face only three balls. Now, with only five minutes of his vigil left, Inverarity made one of his few mistakes in the innings, padding up to Underwood. The lbw decision gave England the match by 226 runs (Underwood 7–50).

At one stage in his career, Mike Gatting was particularly prone to this kind of thing. He was out 'shouldering arms' in three, very nearly four, consecutive Test innings at Lord's.

Against the West Indies in 1984, after twice falling lbw to Malcolm Marshall, for 1 and 29, he was dropped for the next Test.

Against Australia the following year, he padded up to Geoff Lawson and was lbw for 14. In the second innings, he did it again, this time to his very first ball, but survived the appeal. England lost both matches.

In 1989, again against Australia at Lord's, he played no stroke to a ball from Terry Alderman, who picked up yet another lbw in the series. Gatting, who'd made a first-ball duck in the first innings, was out for 22 as England lost by six wickets.

Two years earlier, against Pakistan, he'd played no stroke to Wasim Akram and was lbw for 8. (Later in the same innings, Jack Richards left a Waqar Younis inswinger and was lbw for 6.) England's defeat cost them the series 1–0.

England's tour of New Zealand in 1983–84 was one they wanted to forget: accusations of drug-taking made by elements of the press covering something other than the actual cricket, a 1–0 defeat in the series. In the second Test, replying to the hosts' 307 on a poor pitch, England lost their first two wickets for nine runs, the second when David Gower played no stroke to Richard Hadlee. Gower, who admitted the ball was 'so straight that it had to be lbw even in New Zealand,' made 2 and 8 and Hadlee took 8–44 in the match, which England lost by an innings.

The following summer, in the third Test against the West Indies, Gower again played no shot, this time to Joel Garner, and was lbw for 2. Opening batsman Graeme Fowler had already done the same (lbw Garner 10). England didn't recover from 53–3, losing by eight wickets to go 3–0 down in a series they lost 5–0.

I always wanted to bat like you – and now I do. FW de Klerk meets AR Border

There's more. In the decisive third Test against Pakistan in 1987, Gower shouldered arms against Imran Khan, and was bowled for 10 (Imran also bowled him in the second innings). Again England lost by an innings.

In the third Test against the West Indies in 1991, England captain Graham Gooch was out for the second successive innings without playing a shot, this time lbw to Malcolm Marshall. England lost their 1–0 lead in the series by nine wickets.

At the start of the last day, Australia were favourites to win the second Test of the 1993–94 home series against South Africa, needing only another 54 with six wickets still to go.

Then their captain Allan Border played no stroke to the fourth ball of the day and was clean bowled for 7 by Allan Donald, yet another bowler it doesn't pay to leave alone. The rot set in and Australia lost by only five runs, the third time Border had been on the receiving end of such a narrow Test defeat.

Faced with India's mediocre total of 183 in the 1983 World Cup final, the West Indies looked certain to win the trophy for the third successive time. But their world-class opener Gordon Greenidge had scored only a single when he shouldered arms against Balwinder Sandhu and was bowled: West Indies' first wicket down with only five runs on the board, the chink of light the Indians needed. Their 43-run victory gave them the Cup for the first and only time.

In the third Test of the 1909 Ashes series, Jack Hobbs was helping Johnny Tyldesley rebuild England's first innings after the very early loss of CB Fry when some bad feeling after a run-out incident left him not knowing 'whether I was standing on my head or my heels; with the consequence that two balls later, I let one go, never even attempting to play it.' Clean bowled by Albert 'Tibby' Cotter for 12, he had to watch England slump from 86–1 to 182 all out and defeat by 126 runs to give Australia a winning lead in the series.

Although Australia were asked to score a world record 429 to win the first Test in 1930, the England fast bowler Harold Larwood was injured and Don Bradman was going well. Anything was possible.

The Don had reached 131, the highest score of the match, when he played no stroke to a Walter Robins googly and was bowled. Australia lost by 93 runs.

A generation later, in his very last Test innings, Bradman misread another googly, from Eric Hollies, and was bowled second ball for 0, which left him four runs short of 7,000 runs in Tests and an average of 100.

England, 134 behind on first innings, were struggling to save the second Test of the 1961 Ashes series, Ken Barrington leading from the front as always. But his 66, easily the highest score of the second innings, was ended when he padded up to a ball from Alan Davidson and was lbw. The last of England's resistance went with him. All out for 202, they lost the match by five wickets and the series 2–1.

Their only win, in the third Test, came about after Australia had made 65 for the first wicket, whereupon Bill Lawry was lbw to Tony Lock without playing a shot. Australia slumped to 237 all out and lost by eight wickets.

England lost the first Test of the 1979–80 series in Australia because a) the pitch was a shocker, and b) some of their batsmen got out to bad shots. Ian Botham, for instance ('showing scant regard for the trouble we were in,' according to Geoff Boycott) lofted the ball straight to cover point – and both Derek Randall and Peter Willey played no stroke to balls from Geoff Dymock.

In the third Test, Boycott himself, of all people, did the same against Dennis Lillee, of all other people, and was bowled for seven. England lost all three Tests, Mike Brearley's only series as captain against a really strong team.

Boycott had done much the same against South Africa in 1965. In the second innings of the second Test, at Trent Bridge, he read slow left-armer Atholl McKinnon's arm ball

Bowled by Hollies, Bradman looks back on that Test average of 99.94

from the moment it left his hand, then froze and allowed it to bowl him for 16. South Africa's victory by 94 runs was enough to win them their last series against England before their ban from international cricket.

Australia's batsmen had to find what ways they could of playing England's Bodyline bowling in 1932–33. The prolific Bill Ponsford, still the only batsman to twice score over 400 in a first-class innings, adopted the technique of simply turning his back on anything aimed at his body, taking those fearsome deliveries on his ample frame. It was brave, in a way, but he was out four times 'through his besetting batting sin'. Bowled each time behind his legs without offering a stroke, he was dropped from the final Test after making a duck in the fourth.

The 1870 University Match was probably the most exciting of all. Needing 179 to win, Oxford were 175–7 when FC Cobden began his famous over. The first ball was hit for a single by FH Hill, the second had SE Butler caught at mid-off, the third bowled TH Belcher. Only one wicket left, and still three runs needed.

WH Stewart, Oxford's number 11, was a natural member of the species, who 'did not profess to be a good bat, and his friends did not claim so much for him.' His captain B Pauncefote attempted some last-minute coaching, urging the nervous one to put his bat in the block-hole and not move it until the missile had passed safely by. This was 'a piece of counsel not likely to be offered to WG Grace or Stoddart, but it might not have been inexpedient to offer it to Mr Stewart'. Thus armed, he prepared to face the last ball of the over.

When it approached, he kept his bat where it was until the last moment – then 'instead of following his captain's exhortation, just lifted it: fly went the bails and Cambridge had won the match by two runs.' Instead of levelling the series, Oxford went two behind.

The penalties of not getting on with it.

Although Ken Barrington's 137 at Lord's in 1965 helped England beat New Zealand by seven wickets, the selectors didn't like the fact that he took over seven hours to compile it, and dropped him from the next Test.

Two years later, Geoff Boycott's 246 not out (his highest Test score) contributed to a six-wicket win over India in but used up more than nine hours. During this marathon, chairman of selectors Doug Insole had suggested that proceedings might perhaps be livened up a trifle. It's said that when Boycott left the changing-room, his captain Brian Close told him to take no notice and play his natural game – whereupon Sir Geoffrey was dropped from the next Test! What England wouldn't do now for a Barrington or a Boycott at their slowest …

Replying to the West Indies' formidable 286–9 in the 1979 World Cup final, the first thing England needed was a solid base to their innings, which they were given by Boycott and Mike Brearley – but they rather overdid it. It's true that scoring quickly against the Roberts–Holding–Croft–Garner axis was never easy, but they shouldn't have allowed ten overs of Viv Richards' non-spinning off-spinners to cost only 35 runs. Taking two hours to score 129 was simply too slow (Boycott was almost perverse in taking 17 overs to reach double figures), the pressure on the subsequent England batsmen too great (they needed 158 from the last 22 overs) and they collapsed to 194, losing by 92 runs.

Bowling them in

Warwickshire had to drop their England seamer Gladstone Small when he was having such problems with his run-up that he once bowled 11 no-balls in a single over. Almost as bad was an over by Lancashire's West Indian pace bowler Patrick Patterson, who was no-balled so often that umpire 'Dickie' Bird says he became hoarse through calling them!

When David Gower declared, leaving the West Indies 342 to win the second Test of the 1984 home series, he thought he was at least safe from defeat – and probably would have been if his bowlers had produced the goods. Instead, Ian Botham in particular lapsed into his standard procedure against high-class batsmen: bounce them, and if they hit you for four, bounce them harder next time.

By his own admission, 'I overdid the delivery so much against Gordon Greenidge' that he was able to score 214 not out to win the match by nine wickets, Botham conceding 117 runs in 20.1 overs. England lost the series 5–0.

Pakistan might well have beaten England in 1982 instead of losing 2–1 if their bowlers hadn't given away 42 extras in the second innings of the third and last Test, which England won by just three wickets. Pakistan conceded a total of 221 extras in the series, five runs more than England's highest scorer!

In 1987–88, Pakistan were themselves the recipients of such generosity, gratefully accepting a world record 71 extras in their first innings of the first Test in the West Indies, including 53 no-balls, as well as another 15 that were scored from. West Indies lost by nine wickets, gave away a mere 61 extras in the second innings of the second Test, and eventually had to settle for a drawn series.

If their spinners had bowled even remotely well, the West Indies would surely have won the third Test of 1975–76. Instead, Imtiaz Ali, Albert Padmore and Raphick Jumadeen took only four wickets as India scored 406, still the highest winning score ever achieved by a side batting last in a Test (*Blunders Vol. 1*). This was the match that persuaded Clive Lloyd to use four fast bowlers every time, an attack that carried the West Indies to almost two decades of dominance.

It was 19 years, in fact, before a player picked entirely for his leg-spin (and seen as a long-term prospect) was included in a West Indies Test team.

Rajindra Dhanraj's two matches against Australia in 1994–95 didn't make the earth move (six wickets at 39.83 each) but the selectors saw enough promise to take him to England later in the year. There, in the fifth Test, his first of the series, he was brought on as early as the 19th over of the match.

It's hard to remember a bowler sending down so many bad balls in one Test, his 55 overs costing 191 runs without the consolation of a wicket. Dropped for the final Test, he was brought back for only a single match against New Zealand in 1996 (2–165), has taken only eight Test wickets to date at an average of 74.38, and may have ushered in another spell of undiluted West Indian pace, though it can't last another 19 years, can it?

Three balls left in this over and then two more.

Jim Maxwell

After comfortably drawing the first two Tests of the 1964 tour, Australia dismissed England for 268 at Headingley, only to subside from 124–1 to 178–7 with only big Peter Burge of the recognised batsmen left.

What followed can be put down, as John Arlott did, to 'the most unrelievedly disastrous' Test of Fred Trueman's career. Even FST himself said 'maybe I shouldn't have persisted in dropping the ball short,' which is the closest he ever came to admitting any mistake, so enjoy it while it's there.

His captain has to share some of the blame. When Australia reached 187, the new ball became available, and Ted Dexter took it: his first mistake (Australia had been struggling against the spin of Norman Gifford and Fred Titmus). Then, when Trueman began bowling his string of long hops, Dexter should either have taken him off or given him a man at deep square leg. He did neither.

Even so, Trueman was an experienced bowler and a grown man. He saw what was happening to his short-pitched stuff but kept on bowling it. As a result, Burge and Neil Hawke changed the tone of the match by hitting 40 off six overs from Trueman and Jack Flavell; 105 were added for the eighth wicket; Burge scored 160 before being caught off Trueman when Dexter at last posted a square leg; Australia took a lead of 121 and won by seven wickets.

Trueman was left out of the next Test, came back to take his 300th Test wicket in the last, but couldn't rescue the series,

Dexter's last as captain, which Australia won 1–0 to retain the Ashes.

In 1962–63, also against Australia, he'd made what opposition batsman Norm O'Neill called 'one of Dexter's biggest tactical blunders of the series' (exactly how many were there?) by bringing on Ken Barrington to bowl his occasional leg-breaks at debutant batsman Barry Shepherd, who scored 71 not out to help Australia win the third Test and, again, retain the series.

In the final of the 1995 MCC Trophy, the minor counties' cup final, Hertfordshire made 226–4 then restricted Cambridgeshire to 182–7 with only five of their 55 overs left – only for Kevin Jarvis, who'd played for Kent and Gloucestershire, to suddenly bowl four byes down the leg-side followed by a half-volley which Ajaz Akhtar hit for six. A grateful Cambridgeshire, who'd lost their previous five finals, won one for the first time.

The West Indies may have taken their game against the Minor Counties in 1995 rather lightly. Certainly their bowlers bowled 15 wides and 46 no-balls, major contributions to their defeat by four wickets.

West Indian seamer Uton Dowe sprayed them around so wildly against Australia in 1973 that a wag in the Kingston crowd wondered aloud if his captain Rohan Kanhai had ever heard of the 11th commandment: Dowe shalt not bowl! Bowling figures of 1–168 made sure he didn't do it again in Test cricket.

John Warr was, to be kind, a surprise choice for the 1950–51 tour: a Cambridge undergraduate whose tearaway style of fast-medium

bowling was unlikely to trouble the Australians. Sure enough, in the only two Tests he ever played (both of which England lost), his one wicket cost 281 runs. The story goes that when he appealed almost frantically for a catch at the wicket against Ian Johnson, umpire Cocks paused to enquire as to the state of his health before mercifully raising his finger.

Australian fast bowler Ernie McCormick didn't quite do the job required in his last Test series, in England in 1938, his ten Test wickets costing 34.50 each. He probably guessed it wasn't going to be his summer when he was no-balled 35 times in his first match of the tour!

Italian cricket was very much in an embryonic state in the 1980s. The standard of their bowling was summed up by an injury to their captain, who was hit by a wide while fielding at gully!

Having drawn the first four Tests of the 1926 series, Australia needed to do the same in the last to retain the Ashes. After taking a first-innings lead, they caught the England batsmen on a sticky pitch ('I think the rain's done us,' said Jack Hobbs). With world-class leg-spinners Arthur Mailey and Clarrie Grimmett backed by off-spinner Arthur Richardson and slow left-armer Charlie Macartney, they were expected to run through the Pom batting, and so they did, eventually, England's third highest score being tail-ender Maurice Tate's 33 not out.

Before that, however, the Australians had allowed the famous opening pair of Hobbs and Herbert Sutcliffe to put on 172, a stand that effectively decided the match. 'Allowed' isn't quite fair (this was one of the great partnerships in Ashes history), but it was generally accepted that Richardson, who had

limited experience of bowling round the wicket, and the other Australian spinners sent down too many deliveries which the batsmen could leave alone. It took them 164.5 overs to take eight wickets, England scored 436 to win the match and the Ashes by 289 runs, and Mailey and Richardson weren't capped again.

Defending a moderate total of 223 in the 1994 NatWest Trophy final, Warwickshire reduced Worcestershire to 29–2 and were still in the game until tea, but then bowled downright badly. The first over after the interval, by Roger Twose, went for 12 runs, and Paul Smith persisted in dropping the ball short against batsmen of the destructive quality of Graeme Hick and Tom Moody, who cut (and hooked) him to pieces. Moody hit him over the Lord's grandstand then scored three consecutive fours off another over. Smith was taken off with figures of 0–54 from just seven overs, and Worcestershire won by eight wickets (Hick 93, Moody 88, both not out). It was the only one of the four domestic trophies that Warwickshire didn't win that season.

> *They should have been selling their wickets cheaply and dearly.*
>
> **Geoff Boycott**

After drawing the first four matches of the 1995–96 series in South Africa, England won an important toss in the last Test, only to squander it with a first innings of only 153. Then their bowlers dragged them back into the game by reducing the hosts to 171–9, a lead of just 18 with only last man Paul Adams to come.

Still not quite 19, the youngest player ever capped by South Africa, Adams unveiled perhaps the strangest looking bowling action

> *He'll certainly want to start*
> *by getting off the mark.*
>
> **Don Mosey**

in history, but one that was good enough to have taken six wickets in three Test innings so far. As a batsman, on the other hand, he was in the Devon Malcolm class. He came in to face Malcolm and Co with a highest first-class score of 4 behind him.

Before long, he'd surpassed that with a single stroke, which brought him five runs (his first in Test cricket) thanks to a poor piece of fielding by Dominic Cork. He went on to reach the giddy heights of 29 before being caught by Graeme Hick, by which time the damage had been done.

Throughout the youngster's innings, the England players had been exhorting Malcolm to sort him out with something short-pitched and none too friendly. Not only did the big fast bowler ignore their pleas, he conceded 12 runs from a single over, including four leg-byes from each of two wayward deliveries. Typical Malcolm, you might say.

Adams and wicketkeeper Dave Richardson put on a demoralising 73 for the last wicket, so that when England failed again in the second innings (157) they left South Africa with only 67 to win instead of something in the region of 150. Malcolm, who took 0–68 in the match, later made some heartfelt comments about his treatment at the hands of the England management and probably won't be capped again while Ray Illingworth remains chairman of selectors.

We shouldn't have lost to this shower: Devon Malcolm on his knees in South Africa

Chucking it down

The throwing controversy

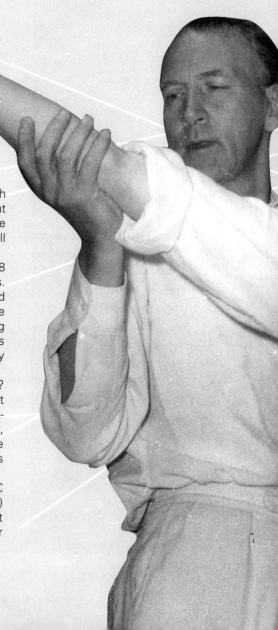

On Boxing Day 1995, during the second Test in Australia, Sri Lankan off-spinner Muttiah Muralitharan was no-balled by home umpire Darrell Hair for throwing the fourth and sixth balls of his fourth over, the second, fourth and sixth of his fifth, and the second and sixth of his sixth. Seven times in all, after which his captain Arjuna Ranatunga put him on at the other end, where New Zealand umpire Steve Dunne didn't no-ball him at all throughout 12 overs.

Muralitharan finished the day with 1–58 (the wicket of Mark Waugh) from 18 overs. The second recognised bowler to be called for throwing in a Test match in 32 years, he was left out of the third after again being no-balled seven times in three overs, this time by Ross Emerson in a one-day international against the West Indies.

Whose blunder are we talking about? Hair's, for no-balling a player who hadn't been called in 22 previous Tests and 59 first-class matches in Australia, England, Pakistan, South Africa, you name it? Or the powers-that-be, for not having sorted things out earlier?

There had been serious misgivings (an ICC statement mentioned umpires' concern) about Muralitharan's action since at least 1993, when he'd helped Sri Lanka to their

Even a famous coach like Alf Gover couldn't straighten Geoff Griffin out

only Test win over England. Meanwhile Sri Lanka's coach, former Australian Test player Dav Whatmore, had filmed him from six different angles, admitting that 'some of them looked suspicious' but deciding that the action was legal.

It turns out that a defect from birth prevented Muralitharan from straightening his elbow – which left the authorities with a problem that they'd failed to address.

Muralitharan should either have been banned very early on or publicly exonerated, as happened with England pace bowler Graham Dilley. Instead, nothing was done, or officially said, leaving an undercurrent of suspicion and resentment. Bolting the door after the defective horse had caused havoc, the ICC advised Muralitharan to modify his action. Whether he did or not,

within three months he was Sri Lanka's most economical bowler in the World Cup final – so who knows how much had actually been resolved?

Someone somewhere, much earlier, should have cleared up a very obvious mess.

Oh well, 'twas ever thus. In 1960, when South African pace bowler Geoff Griffin took the wickets of MJK Smith with the last ball of one over and Peter Walker with the first ball of his next, he'd done the hard part of his hat-trick: Smith had scored 99, Walker 52, and the next man in was Fred Trueman, an effective hitter at times but whose eventual Test average was 13.81.

FST, who could never believe that any other seamer was fit to tie his bootlaces, took an almighty swipe at his first ball and lost his middle stump. It was the only Test hat-trick ever taken at Lord's and the first for South Africa in Test cricket – but should never have been allowed to happen.

Before this match, Griffin had already been called for throwing 17 times in matches against the counties. During it, he became the first player ever to be called during a Lord's Test, five times on the first day – and someone, either the umpires or his captain Jackie McGlew, should surely have taken him off before he had any chance of taking a hat-trick.

After England had won by an innings, an exhibition match was played, during which Griffin was no-balled for throwing four times in one over, then once more because he hadn't informed the batsman when he changed to bowling underarm! He didn't play in another Test.

Griffin was just one of the bowlers of his day whose action should have been sorted out once and for all. Another South African, Cuan McCarthy, played in 15 Tests (1948–51) despite being called for throwing. There were accusations about Australian Test players like Jimmy Burke (whose action was compared to a policeman hitting a small offender on the head with a truncheon), Keith Slater, and especially Ian Meckiff during the 1958–59 tour.

Fred Trueman considered Meckiff's action 'totally illegal and he should never have been allowed to play', but when the England management mentioned this to Don Bradman, he told them to look at two of their own bowlers, Peter Loader and Tony Lock, the latter having been no-balled as far back as the 1953–54 series in the West Indies, immediately after dismissing the venerable George Headley with his infamous faster ball. Trevor Bailey once called 'no-ball' when another one flashed towards him, and after being bowled by a similar delivery in 1955 Doug Insole asked the umpire if he'd just been run out! Lock later went away to remodel his action after watching, horrified, a film of his bowling.

Meckiff, meanwhile, was belatedly no-balled for throwing against South Africa in 1963 (the last before 1995). His second, third, fifth and ninth deliveries were called by Australian umpire Col Egar, he bowled only that one over in the match, and retired from all levels of cricket.

Haseeb Ahsan, later Pakistan's tour manager, had been no-balled while playing against India in 1960–61. Later, there were rumblings (from Ken Barrington, Fred Trueman, John Snow, Bill Lawry and Richie Benaud, among others) about the fast and hostile West Indian Charlie Griffith. To the 1965 Australians, 'the unanimous verdict was that Griffith was a chucker.' He was twice called for throwing, and in 1963 the chairman of the England selectors, Walter Robins, instructed two English umpires not to no-ball him for fear of sparking racial tension in London.

Another West Indian, 'Charlie' Stayers, played against India in 1961–62 despite having been called three years earlier. Before him, England pace bowlers David 'Butch' White and Harold 'Dusty' Rhodes were no-balled in 1960 (Rhodes six times in one match). Later, off-spinner Geoff Cope was capped three times by England in 1977–78 after rebuilding his action, only to be banned

The long arm and the law. Meckiff's bent on controversy

from bowling in county cricket the following season! New Zealand Test player David O'Sullivan was called in Australia in 1973–74.

Later still, there were noises off about Kharsan Ghavri and Chetan Sharma of India, Wayne 'Fang' Clark of Australia and Sylvester Clarke of the West Indies, especially when they threw in a bouncer. Even Curtly Ambrose was no-balled for throwing in 1988, and Mushtaq Mohammad once cast doubts about Joel Garner, whose action had been remodelled by Griffith! And when Graham Gooch performed one of his well-known impersonations of another player's action, he was no-balled from square leg!

More recently, there was some brief New Zealander grumbling about Phil Tufnell and strong reservations about Muralitharan's team-mate Jayananda Warnaweera, who was not only branded a chucker by Martin Crowe in 1992–93 and queried by England players later that season, but had been under suspicion 16 years earlier!

As recently as February 1995, Zimbabwe's youngest ever international, 18-year-old pace bowler Henry Olonga, was no-balled for throwing in his very first Test.

These are the exception nowadays, which hasn't always been the case. At the turn of the century, Test and especially county cricket was positively infested with dodgy actions. The finger was regularly pointed at Test players like Arthur Mold, who played for England in 1893 but wasn't called for throwing till 1900; the equally fast and aggressive Ernie Jones, he who once bowled through WG Grace's beard ('Sorry, doc, she slipped') and was the first bowler to be no-balled for throwing in a Test (1898); and Tom McKibbin, of whom *Wisden* wrote that 'there can be little doubt that he continually threw when he put in his off-break.' An Aborigine called Henry, who played for Queensland around 1900, once accused an umpire of knowing nothing about cricket because he no-balled his good balls and not the ones he did throw!

Some 30 years later, another Aborigine, the very fast, very iffy Eddie Gilbert, dismissed Don Bradman for a duck. Incidentally, by reversing and slowing down a film, Bradman (who had an obvious interest in this) cast doubts on even Harold Larwood's action. Meanwhile, one of the Don's team-mates, Bert 'Dainty' Ironmonger, was never chosen for a tour despite being a regular at home, allegedly because it was felt that his action wouldn't pass muster in England.

The bad old days were largely ended by bans from first-class cricket for Mold, ER Bradford, FJ Hopkins, Arthur Paish, the famous CB Fry (who thought Mold's action was fair!), the Test left-armer Edwin Tyler, etc – but it took 20 years to start happening, and between them, and the players who followed, they took thousands of wickets, helped win several county championships (Lock seven in a row with Surrey) and broke the odd bone here and there, including one in the finger of the great Australian bowler Fred Spofforth, cracked by a blatant thrower in 1880, keeping him out of the subsequent Test, which Australia lost.

It could all have been prevented with more courage and determination, but the problem's rarely been taken seriously enough. Indeed the first England bowler to be called in a home Test was David Gower, of all people, who jocularly threw the last ball of the match to give New Zealand victory in the second Test of 1986. Too much apathy, not enough umpires like Jim Phillips (who no-balled Mold [16 times in one match], Ernie Jones and Fry) and Darrell Hair.

Having said that, another thought raises its mischievous head: perhaps the original blunder lies with those who decided on bowling being the only legal way of propelling the ball; it seems so difficult to police. According to one well-known player, whose action has been described as model, 'I reckon everyone throws the ball at one time or another. I know I have. But I've never been questioned or called.'

Men in white coats

'It was a great error of misjudgment.' **HENRY BLOFELD**

The second Test of the 1967–68 series against England was so tense that it affected Douglas Sang Hue, the best of the West Indian umpires. Having moved from square leg to square on the off side because so many fielders were crowding round the bat, he found the ball rolling towards him, sent there by batsman Fred Titmus, who was trying to buy time by pushing the ball into the unguarded outfield – and wasn't best pleased to see Sang Hue pick the ball up and throw it back to the bowler! 'Whose side are you on, umpire?' asked Titmus. Luckily England held out for a draw.

> *England were beaten in the sense that they lost.*
>
> **Dickie Davies**

England batsman Arthur Fagg, still the only player to score two double hundreds in the same first-class match, later became a Test umpire, the one who refused to officiate when the West Indies objected to one of his decisions in 1973. They weren't the only ones to harbour dark thoughts about Fagg; Bill Lawry of Australia once asked why he'd given him out. Lbw, said the umpire. But I hit the bloody ball, said the Australian captain. 'I know, that's why I gave you out caught behind.'

During an MCC match at Lord's, the Notts wicketkeeper Tommy Oates was drafted in as emergency umpire. When Essex bowler Bill Reeves appeared to induce a catch behind the wicket, Oates forgot he was officiating and instinctively appealed for the catch, whereupon the opportunist Reeves gave him out. And the batsman walked!

In one of the Tests in India in 1963–64, England pace bowler John Price flicked Vijay Manjrekar's glove to give Micky Stewart a catch in the gully. Not out, said the umpire, touching his sleeve to say that the ball had hit the batsman high on his arm. As a crestfallen Price began to walk back to his mark, he noticed Manjrekar returning to the pavilion.

What was this? A rare example of a Test batsman deciding to walk? No, explained the umpire, he's going off for treatment. He thinks the ball may have broken his finger! All five Tests were drawn.

Just as thankfully, England won the 1984–85 series in India, despite some, er, interesting decisions by the well-known Swaroop Kishen, who weighed about 20 stone and made some heavyweight mistakes, which Tim Robinson was able to smile about even at the time. England lost the first Test (Robinson's first, too) after he'd been given out lbw despite hitting the ball with his bat, then caught when he didn't touch it.

When Dean Jones was bowled during his second innings of the second Test of the 1990–91 series in the Caribbean, he set off for the pavilion and was given out by the square-leg umpire – run out, not bowled. It had been a no-ball.

Jones made only 3. A normal contribution from him (he eventually averaged 46.55 in 52 Tests with a highest score of 216) might have saved the match and kept the series level after two Tests. Instead Australia lost it (West Indies' first win in Georgetown since 1965) and the series 2–1.

A simple aberration by Jones? Undoubtedly – but it shouldn't have been costly. Part of Law 38 makes it clear that 'the striker cannot be given out unless he attempts to run' (which Jones clearly hadn't) and a section of Law 27 adds 'The umpires shall intervene if satisfied that a batsman, not having been given out, has left his wicket under a misapprehension that he has been dismissed.' The decision by umpire Clyde Cumberbatch was a costly one for Australia.

The 1980 Test held in Bombay to mark the Indian cricket board's golden jubilee is best known for Ian Botham's feat of scoring a century and taking ten wickets, the first double of its kind in international cricket, and for Bob Taylor's ten catches, another Test best. But umpires JD Ghosh and SN Hanumantha Rao had a finger or two in it.

The latter first gave Taylor out caught behind the wicket, only for the Indian captain Gundappa Viswanath to confirm that he hadn't got a touch (see TOO GOOD FOR THEIR OWN GOOD). Then John Lever turned a ball off his legs for two runs, got back to his crease to discover that he'd knocked a bail off, replaced it without the umpires' knowledge, and carried on batting.

Most glaring of all, Geoff Boycott edged a catch to wicketkeeper Syed Kirmani and was correctly given out. Instead of walking back to the pavilion, he didn't look at the umpire and instead began preparing to receive the next ball. The Indian fielders appealed again and this time the umpire gave him not out! England won by ten wickets.

David Gower admitted doing the same thing against Pakistan in 1987, edging Abdul Qadir to the wicketkeeper and carrying on as if nothing had happened. Small wonder that the visitors were unimpressed by the standard of English umpiring in this series. Nothing had changed, they said, since they'd complained about David Constant in 1982.

Some thought this a bit rich, visiting teams having queried the umpiring in Pakistan since time immemorial. It all came to an explosive head during the 1987–88 tour, which the England players, not least their captain Mike Gatting, believed to be a kind of Revenge Of The Umpires for what had happened in England. The famous flashpoint took place during the second Test.

When Shakoor Rana came striding across from square leg, accusing Gatting of cheating and using some fluent Anglo-Saxon terminology to do so, he was under the impression that the England captain had moved a fielder without the batsman's knowledge. Leaving aside the fact that it's traditionally the non-striker's job to keep his partner informed about such wiles, in this case Shakoor had simply made a mistake: Gatting had already informed the batsman, Salim Malik, of his intentions.

The affair still rankles today (England haven't played a Test in Pakistan since) and Gatting eventually suffered its consequences: he was forced to pen an apology to Shakoor, and the fracas was surely held against him when an excuse arrived for his removal as captain the following year. At the time, though, the TCCB showed what they thought of the whole business by awarding each of their players in Pakistan a £1,000 bonus.

Cricketers from other countries had had their problems with Shakoor. He earned poor marks when he stood in County Championship matches in 1981; New Zealand threatened to walk off in protest against one of his decisions in 1984; he once held up a

You know what you can do with this. Shakoor Rana shows Gatting the new ball

Test match because he'd left his clothing at his hotel; and the last time Dickie Bird saw him he made off with two of his white caps!

Australia, below strength without their Packer players, lost the first Test of the 1978–79 Ashes series and were struggling to save the second when the linchpin of their second innings, opener Graeme Wood, was given out caught behind off John Lever.

He was furious with the decision, which slow-motion replays confirmed as wrong. Wood's departure for 64 (highest score in the innings) hurried Australia to a defeat which left them 2–0 down in the series. Criticism of veteran umpire Tom Brooks was so great that he retired from first-class cricket immediately after the match.

He may well have allowed himself a wry smile during the sixth and last Test, when Andrew Hilditch was also given out caught behind by Bob Taylor, who wasn't sure that the catch had carried. Sure enough, a puff of dust on the TV replay proved that the ball had hit the ground about a foot in front of the wicketkeeper. Hilditch, the first to fall in Australia's second innings, had made only a single. Australia lost the match by nine wickets and the series 5–1.

In his last first-class match (1970) South African Test all-rounder Trevor Goddard did the hat-trick without taking a wicket! The first ball hit Duncan Fletcher's boot and he was adjudged caught behind, the second hit Errol Laughlin's pad and he was given out caught at slip, the third had Jackie du Preez lbw even though he'd lunged a long way forward. It was said, in jest of course, that the umpire was the first to congratulate Goddard after the match.

In 1874 the Grace family won the third Gentlemen v Players encounter virtually on their own, Gilbert (WG) scoring 110, more than half the side's total in the second innings, after which he and his brother Fred took all ten wickets to win the match by 60 runs.

The good doctor had contributed in other ways too. It seems he was up to his famous tricks in this one, and the umpires, not for the first or last time, let him get away with them. *Wisden* maintained 'that every appeal by a Gentleman was decided affirmatively, and the Players' appeals were mainly met with Not Out.' The worst incident came when he and Fred were building their match-winning partnership in the second innings, the latter hitting the ball tamely back to Jim Lillywhite, who would have taken a very simple caught-and-bowled if WG hadn't stood in front of him! 'To run round him involved too great a detour,' and both umpires, G Keeble and A Luff, turned down appeals for obstruction.

In a match in Sri Lanka, Wilfred Rhodes appealed for a stumping, only for the umpire to give the batsman not out because he'd regained his crease before the appeal was made!

Viv Richards scored 24 Test centuries, which might well have been 25 if he hadn't been given out lbw to Ian Botham at Lord's in 1984 when he'd made 72. The ball seemed to have been going down the leg side, so clearly that umpire Barrie Meyer apologised to Richards afterwards.

> *West Indies have got to dig deep to get out of this hole they're in.*
>
> **Anon**

England, in particular their captain Ray Illingworth and leading fast bowler John Snow, weren't best pleased with the umpiring of the 1970–71 series in Australia. For a start, they didn't win a single lbw decision in any of the six Tests – and the three officials used, Tom Brooks, Lou Rowan and Max O'Connell, made a number of identifiable errors.

Australian opening batsman Keith Stackpole benefited from two of the most glaring. In the first Test, he'd made 18 when Rowan gave him not out (photographs and TV replays proved he'd been clearly run out), then went on to make 207, his highest Test score. In the first over of the fifth, Snow had him caught behind the wicket, only for O'Connell to give him not out because he hadn't seen the catch being taken: he'd started walking towards square leg to prepare for the next over!

In the sixth and final Test, Stackpole again edged to the keeper (Ray Illingworth called it 'a real thick one to Alan Knott') before going on to make another 54 runs after being reprieved by Rowan. Illingworth again: 'It was really unbelievable.'

After winning the toss at the start of the second Test, Illingworth demanded the use of a roller, which was turned down even though it's a captain's right. Rowan apologised at lunch.

During the fourth Test between the West Indies and Australia in 1995, David Boon was given out caught behind (wicketkeeper Courtney Browne's first dismissal in Test cricket) by West Indian umpire Steve Bucknor after missing the ball with his bat but flicking it with his helmet. Not the way he'd have chosen to celebrate his 100th Test.

England, needing to win the last Test to draw the 1982–83 series, seemed to have got the start they wanted when their captain Bob Willis ran out John Dyson in the first over of the match. Photographs and replays showed the Australian opener to be two feet out, but umpire Mel Johnson gave him the benefit of the doubt. What *Wisden* called 'this unhappy decision' affected England materially as well as psychologically: Dyson went on to score 79, Australia to draw the match and regain the Ashes.

Oxford, strong favourites to win the 1895 University Match, were undermined by the umpires on the first day, losing six wickets for 67 runs because James Phillips and William West refused to end play for the day despite the light being 'indeed so poor that from the pitch one could see the gas-jets burning in the bar under the grandstand!' Cambridge won by 134 runs.

The umpiring in the 1958–59 Ashes series, especially by Mel McInnes, who'd had a very good series four years earlier, upset both teams but mainly England. The last straw came in the fourth Test, which they needed to win to have any chance of retaining the Ashes. First McInnes hesitated for several seconds before giving Ken Mackay out caught behind off a blatant snick, then he moved the wrong way to judge a run-out, with the result that Jimmy Burke, acting as runner for Colin McDonald, went behind his back. He was so far out of his crease when the stumps were flattened (McInnes gave him not out) that McDonald lost patience and told Fred Trueman to bowl him a straight one, which he deliberately missed to give Fred 'the easiest Test wicket I've ever taken.' England, demoralised throughout a controversial series, lost it 4–0.

In his first Test innings after the War, against England in 1946–47, Don Bradman made 187 after famously being given not out on 28 when caught by Jack Ikin at slip (*Blunders Vol.1*). Not the least amazing aspect of this horror was that it repeated itself in the very next match of the series.

This time the Don had made only 20 when he swung a short ball from Alec Bedser to square leg, where the unfortunate Ikin again took the catch. After umpire Jack Scott had turned down the appeal, Bradman went on to make 234 and share a world record partnership of 405 for the fifth wicket! Again Australia won, taking a 2–0 lead on the way to a 3–0 win. It wasn't Ikin's series: he made a duck in his first innings and another in each of his last two.

Later, Scott further infuriated the English by giving Bill Edrich and Denis Compton out lbw, Edrich when he'd hit the ball so hard with his bat that it left a red mark on the blade, Compton when the ball pitched well outside the leg stump ('I have never been more amazed in the whole of my cricket career').

The third Test was the critical match of the 1972–73 series. India, needing a paltry 86 to win, struggled to 51–4 and 67–5 on a turning wicket, and England might have won if Salim Durani had been given out when he was caught at the wicket off Pat Pocock. The ball hit the shoulder of the bat and everyone except the umpire knew Durani was out, including Durani himself. Later, he told his team-mate Mansur Ali Khan that he hadn't exactly nicked the ball. 'I hit it very hard. I am sorry but I am playing for my life.' After the incident, Durani hit out at everything, slogging two sixes on his way to a vital 38 to give India a winning 2–1 lead.

Of the two official England sides playing Test cricket in the winter of 1929–30, the Dad's Army in the Caribbean (two players over 50, several others over 40) probably acquitted itself better, against stronger opposition, taking a 1–0 lead after the first two matches.

In the third Test, however, they began their second innings 616 runs behind and were emphatically up the creek when their ninth wicket went down at 327. Even so, they still had 'Patsy' Hendren's redoubtable paddle at their disposal, and it had made 123 (on top of 56 in the first innings, the only English blade to score a half-century in the match) with only four minutes to go.

Then it put its edge to a delivery from medium-pacer Edwin St Hill, whose two Test wickets so far had cost 110.50 runs each. The noise of bat on ball was apparently audible all round the wicket. Unfortunately for England, it didn't percolate as far as the umpire, who gave Hendren out lbw. It was the West Indies' first ever win and St Hill had taken a wicket with his last ball in Test cricket.

During the second Test of the 1956 Ashes series, Fred Trueman had Keith Miller caught

behind then did the same with his next delivery to Richie Benaud, the ball taking the edge and carrying to wicketkeeper Godfrey Evans. The appeal from Trueman and the slips was loud and confident, but umpire Emrys Davies turned it down when Benaud rubbed his sleeve. After the match, he admitted getting an edge. By the time he was out, ironically caught Evans bowled Trueman, he'd made 97, helping Australia win by 185 runs. England haven't beaten them at Lord's since 1934.

Then there was that dark horse with the golden arm, Mudassar Nazar.

Trevor Bailey

The following winter, in Johannesburg, Trevor Bailey took his bat away from a ball from off-spinner Hugh Tayfield and let it hit his pad – so he was somewhat aggrieved ('unquestionably the worst decision I have experienced') to be given out caught at forward short leg. He was Tayfield's (and the umpire's) first victim of the second innings; another eight followed, to make him the only South African to take nine in a Test innings. England lost the match by just 17 runs.

In the sixth and last Test of the 1983–84 home series, India were 92–5 in reply to the West Indies' 313 when their great opener Sunil Gavaskar, down at number 4 after a run of low scores, edged Malcolm Marshall's second ball of the fourth day to third slip, where that excellent fielder Roger Harper held a good low catch. The umpire gave Gavaskar not out.

The West Indies were so furious that they refused to acknowledge Gavaskar's subsequent landmarks: his 30th Test century (breaking Don Bradman's world record) and eventual score of 236 not out, still the highest individual Test score for India!

England win by a solitary nine runs.

Frank Bough

In New Zealand's only innings of the third and final Test in Australia in 1985–86, the very tall left-arm seamer Bruce Reid found the edge of Richard Hadlee's bat to give Tim Zoehrer an easy catch behind the stumps. Hadlee, given not out by the umpire, knew full well that he'd nicked the ball but stayed where he was ('I know it's not right; it was a case of double standards on my part') to

make 26, an important part of New Zealand's first-innings lead of 96 which helped them win the match and the series.

Ricky Ponting's one of the great bright hopes of Australian batting, fulfilling some of them as soon as he made his Test debut, at the age of 21 against Sri Lanka in December 1995. His 96 helped Australia win by an innings, but he was deprived of a century in his first Test innings by an lbw decision from Pakistani umpire Khizar Hayat so controversial that the Sri Lankan captain Arjuna Ranatunga wanted to recall the batsman.

It wasn't Khizar's match. He gave David Boon out caught at slip when the ball seemed to hit only the pad, and Chandika Hathurusinghe was given not out when he appeared to be caught by Mark Waugh.

Who's counting?

India, needing to win the fifth Test to draw the 1948–49 series, dismissed the West Indies for less than 300 (for the first time in the series) then did it again to leave themselves needing 361 to win at a run a minute: a slim chance of winning a Test against the West Indies for the first time.

Despite the leg theory and time-wasting tactics John Goddard used against them, they reduced the target to 11 with two overs left. The first ball of the twelve went, like so many others, defensively down the leg side. The second Dattu Phadkar hit for four, the third for a single: six to win, nine balls left. He refused a single off the fourth, and the fifth was a bouncer over his head.

There was no sixth. Not only did umpire AR Joshi miscount and therefore end the over a ball too soon, he also removed the bails and walked off even though there were another ninety seconds to play. He ended the Test, and his country's chance of winning, seven balls early. India didn't win a Test against the West Indies until 1971.

The record for most runs taken from a six-ball over in first class cricket is the maximum 36 – six sixes – by Garry Sobers off Malcolm Nash in 1968 and Ravi Shastri off Tilak Raj in 1985. Or is it?

During their Shell Trophy match against Canterbury in 1990, Wellington tried to keep the home side interested in going for a definite result by offering some easy runs.

Easy? Babies bowling sweets. In the penultimate over of Canterbury's second innings, Robert Vance bowled 17 no-balls, allowing Lee Germon to score 69 runs, including 8 sixes. Altogether, 77 runs were taken from the over, then another 17 from the last, leaving Canterbury to score a single off the final ball to win the match. They didn't try and the match was drawn.

And the blunder? Well, Vance somehow included five legitimate balls in that monumental over, including two in a row twice. In the welter of no-balls, the umpire lost count and ended the over before a sixth legal ball could be bowled, thereby depriving Vance and Germon of a record worthy of the name instead of that piffling 77!

In 1995, Germon captained New Zealand in his first ever Test match, but hadn't always looked obvious leadership material: he described his most embarrassing moment as joining in the mirth at an official function when asides were being made about someone's undone fly, 'then realising the comments were directed at me.'

No scores below single figures.

Richie Benaud

In 1921 the umpires allowed Australia's captain Warwick Armstrong to bowl two consecutive overs in the Old Trafford Test: the teams had to be recalled to the middle after umpires J Moss and AE Street had allowed the England captain Lionel Tennyson to illegally declare the innings closed.

Almost thirty years later, MF Pengelly and J McLellan didn't notice that Alec Moir of New Zealand had bowled two overs in a row against England, either side of a break in play.

Steve Bucknor counting a few chickens

In the fourth Test of the 1995–96 series between South Africa and England, West Indian umpire Steve Bucknor allowed both Paul Adams and Gary Kirsten to bowl seven-ball overs.

Worse, during the 1994 series between New Zealand and Pakistan, the umpires miscounted the number of balls six times in a single Test. Dickie Bird ended an over after only five balls, but couldn't match the feat of local boy Steve Dunne, who allowed two of those five-ball overs as well as two seven-ballers and an eight!

And two extremes, both in New Zealand v England Tests at Eden Park, Auckland. In 1963 local off-spinner John Sparling bowled 11 balls in a row after umpire Dick Shortt had problems with his hand counter and simply started the over from scratch! In the second Test of the 1991–92 series, Phil DeFreitas bowled an over of only four balls.

By dismissing the Gentlemen for 111, the dreaded Nelson, the Players won the 1881 match by a single run. Except that they didn't. A scorer's mistake, subsequently discovered, had deprived the Gents of an extra run, and the result was in fact a tie. Remarkably, each team scored 204 in their first innings and 112 in the second. Equally surprisingly, the original result has never been altered.

Foot in mouth

In January 1982, Lynton Taylor, managing director of one of Kerry Packer's companies, announced that he doubted whether Test cricket could be saved!

When Essex spinner David Acfield was recounting his experiences while fencing at international level, he mentioned to team mate Alan Lilley that he'd competed in Budapest. 'Oh yes?' said Lill. 'Was that in the Commonwealth Games?'

It's said that when one of his Worcestershire team-mates asked him who Sherlock Holmes' partner was, Graeme Hick protested that 'We didn't do Shakespeare in Zimbabwe.'

On the same literary theme, an old England captain once took a bet that he couldn't name ten poems by Alfred, Lord Tennyson, managed seven, then suggested the famous 'If', which was penned by Rudyard Kipling. A surprising error, considering that the England captain in question was Lionel Tennyson, the poet's grandson.

Ken Barrington, rugged and world-class mainstay of so many England middle orders (6,806 Test runs at 58.67), was also cricket's unchallenged master of the malapropism, creator of such gems as 'The press went through the food like a swarm of lotuses' and 'them high-philosophy bullets'.

Too late by now to dispute the veracity of the old one about Fred Trueman after his first match for Yorkshire, against Cambridge University in 1949. Presented with a menu written in French, he's said to have pointed at the date on the bottom of the page and said 'Aye, I'll have that for sweet.'

The joke wasn't always on Fred. Yorkshire's match against Hampshire at Portsmouth in 1960 was heading for a tame draw on a plumb pitch when suddenly Trueman, who'd had no more joy than any other bowler, took the new ball and bowled the home team out twice: six wickets for 11 in ten overs to reduce them from 166–2 to 191 all out, followed by 6–28 in 19.3 overs to win the match by an innings – and all because some of the Hampshire players, with bravery bordering on recklessness, had dared to enjoy themselves at his expense when he suffered a temporary bout of diarrhoea!

At the start of Australia's first innings in the fifth Test of the 1981 Ashes series, Trueman was his usual retiring self on Radio 3, describing Bob Willis' first two overs as 'The worst bowling with the new ball I've ever seen. I'd be ashamed to draw my pay if I bowled like this in a Test.'

With his next six balls, Willis took three wickets. Australia, suddenly 24–3, were all out for 130 and lost the match (which decided the Ashes) by 103.

BBC commentator Henry Blofeld once wondered, aloud and on air, if anyone had ever played the off-drive better than Greg Chappell. At the end of the over, co-commentator Trevor Bailey announced what most people knew, that Chappell was best known for the on-drive.

Blofeld's rarely been slow in coming forward with an opinion, notably before the 1984–85 tour of India, when he wrote that it was 'a disgrace' for Mike Gatting to be selected at all, let alone as vice-captain, when his Test record was poor and his place could have gone to a younger man. Gatting scored his first Test century, followed it with 207 in the fourth Test, and averaged 95.83 in the series, which England won 2–1 after losing the first match. By the following summer, when he again topped the Test averages (87.83, this time in the 3–1 win over Australia), Gatting claimed that Blofeld was saying he'd always been a fan of his 'and other such rubbish'.

A year later, after having his nose broken during the 1985–86 tour of the West Indies, Gatting's next ordeal was a press conference, where he had to field a famously inane, televised query. Sitting there with his nose splattered over his face, two black eyes, several stitches, and strips of plaster across the whole mess, he was asked 'Where did the ball actually hit you?' It cheers you up, said Gatt, listening to really stupid questions.

Mind you, it cuts both ways. Asked if he felt he'd been vindicated by a certain result, Gatt replied that no he didn't think the press were vindictive!

When Ian Botham said that Pakistan was a place to send your mother-in-law on an extended vacation, he was only articulating more colourfully the views already expressed by several other Test cricketers, including Tom Graveney, Keith Fletcher, Allan Border, Joel Garner, Graham Gooch (who called the umpiring there 'a joke') and Brian Lara (who thought it 'a dangerous place to play cricket').

Nevertheless, as well as raising the eyebrows of his own wife's blameless mother, it cost him a hefty fine. Worse, when he was given out caught behind for 0 in the 1992 World Cup final despite not having touched the ball, he had to endure

Aamir Sohail's jibe on the way back to the pavilion: 'Why don't you send in your mother-in-law? She couldn't do any worse.' England lost by 22 runs.

While working as guest summariser for BBC Radio's *Test Match Special*, former Pakistan captain Mushtaq Mohammad was forced to squeeze into a chair next to commentator Mike Carey's labrador dog. When Christopher Martin-Jenkins asked Mushtaq something about Javed Miandad, millions of listeners were surprised to learn that 'He's licking my leg.'

Since Ian Chappell had had a rather mixed series with the bat in India in 1969–70 (one century, one 99, but also 0, 4 and 5), it's hard to understand why Australia's captain Bill Lawry should have decided to publicly refer to him as 'the best batsman in the world.'

This was the last thing Chappell needed (he called it 'an extraordinary statement') just before the series in South Africa the following month. Faced with the pace and hostility of Mike Procter and Peter Pollock, he averaged 11.50 (highest score 34, a duck in each of the first three Tests) as Australia lost all four matches.

During the run-up to the 1986–87 Ashes series, Martin Johnson wrote in the *Independent* that there were only three things wrong with the England team: 'They can't bat, they can't bowl and they can't field.' England won the first Test by seven wickets and the series more easily than the 2–1 scoreline suggests.

In a radio interview during the 1978–79 trip to Australia, England seamer Mike Hendrick

had just told the world that he wasn't at all homesick when he was put through, in a surprise hook-up, to his wife back in England!

When Chris Cowdrey was chosen to captain England against the West Indies in 1988, despite not having played in a Test since 1985, many thought they detected the sound of vats being scraped – but chairman of selectors Peter May was quick to rationalise the choice: 'We believe that Chris Cowdrey's dynamic style of leadership is what is now required.'

It's true that Cowdrey had taken a limited Kent side to the top of the Championship table, but the Windies were a different story altogether. He did nothing very wrong tactically, but couldn't justify his place in the team, making 0 and 5 and never playing for England again. Needless to say, England lost this match too.

After Jim Laker had taken eight wickets for two runs in a Test trial in 1950, someone from the *Daily Express* famously asked him if these were his best first-class figures!

Against Gloucestershire in 1921, Australia's giant captain Warwick Armstrong, who wasn't doing too well with the ball, tossed it to his talented, whimsical leg-spinner Arthur Mailey, telling him to bowl at the good batsmen for once, rather than wiping out the tail – whereupon Mailey took all ten wickets in the innings, then used them as a title for his autobiography: *Ten for 66 and all that!*

Even John Arlott didn't always get it right. He once referred to Bill Frindall doing some mental arithmetic on a calculator – and when

a naked spectator first ran onto the field during a Lord's Test (v Australia 1975), the famous commentator referred to him as a 'freaker.'

After England's defeat in the second Test of the 1993–94 series, former West Indian fast bowler Colin Croft wasn't especially complimentary about England seamer Angus Fraser, who'd taken 2–85 and reminded him 'of my favourite things: aeroplanes. His bowling is like shooting down F-16s with slingshots. Even if they hit, no damage is done. Like an old horse, he should be put out to pasture.'

When Fraser had taken 8–75, his best international figures, to help win the fourth Test, he was able to respond to these mixed metaphors: 'I'm just pleased to have bowled as well as Colin Croft did every day of his life.'

> *Unless something happens that we can't predict, I don't think a lot will happen.*
>
> **Fred Trueman**

England opening batsman and squadron leader Bill Edrich (he won the DFC) once accused writer and editor David Frith of having done very little towards winning the Second World War, something Frith couldn't deny: he'd been only eight when it ended!

After scoring a century in the Lord's Test of 1994, veteran South African batsman Peter Kirsten listed some of the injuries he'd received during the innings: bruised fingers, head and chest, and a sore calf muscle. 'Cricket has been good to me,' he said.

Especially for Asif Masood: a picture of Giant Bronson

The BBC's Brian Johnston swore he never said 'The bowler's Holding, the batsman's Willey' (though sometimes he said he did) – but he did come out with 'Harvey, standing there at leg slip with his legs apart, waiting for a tickle'; he referred to Pakistani pace bowler Asif Masood as Massif Arsood; told listeners that Fred Titmus had two short legs, one of them square; meant to mention a dark cloud during an England–India match, which came out as 'There's a dirty black crowd here;' and once tried to say 'sitting on a shooting stick' and got it wrong.

Best of all, perhaps, Johnners watched New Zealand opener Glenn Turner take a fearful blow in the nether regions, collapse, rise gingerly, and prepare to resume his innings – then informed his audience of millions that 'Turner looks a bit shaky and unsteady but I think he's going to bat on. One ball left.'

Clarrie Grimmett and Bill O'Reilly were Australia's great match-winning leg-spinners of the 1930s (360 Test wickets between them) – and friendly rivals when bowling together. In South Africa in 1936, all-rounder Chud Langton hit O'Reilly for such a huge six that it provoked a rare smile from Grimmett (actually O'Reilly remembered him 'laughing like a hyena'). Bill, he said, I do believe that's the biggest hit I've ever seen. O'Reilly, through clenched teeth, was inclined to agree.

Almost immediately afterwards, Langton found his way to Grimmett's end, and hit him for two sixes, the second into the nearby railway yard. A new ball had to be called for, and Grimmett kept well away from his spin twin for the rest of the afternoon.

During a visit by the Australians in 1990–91, West Indies' captain Viv Richards waxed

lyrical about his 'African' team, thereby managing to alienate virtually the entire Caribbean Asian population, which had produced the likes of Ramadhin, Kanhai and Kallicharran. Richards later explained that 'African Caribbean people include all the different nationalities of the Caribbean.' If there was any logic in that, those of Asian descent in the crowd at Georgetown failed to spot it, loudly supporting the Australians.

Martin, Lord Hawke, often expressed his fervent hope that England, 'pray God,' would never be captained by a professional. They already had, by Jim Lillywhite, in 1877, the first two Tests ever played!

For several years, Hawke captained Yorkshire, the county that fielded only players born within its boundaries, even though he was born in Lincolnshire.

> *Well, Wally, I've been watching this game both visually and on TV.*
>
> **Ken Barrington**

Who said the chairmen of the England selectors were out of touch? When Alec Bedser passed Test hopefuls Ray East and John Lever, he called one Roy and confused the other with Peter Lever. When Bedser's successor Peter May heard the accusation that he was out of touch, he's quoted as having said 'Oh really? I haven't heard that one.' And of course Ted Dexter, referring to England's new fast bowler, asked 'Who can forget Malcolm Devon?'

During lunch on the third day of the match against Western India States in 1948, the Maharashtra captain informed his opponents that he wasn't going to declare, even though his team led by 588 runs! This was too much in every sense for the lowly Western States, who immediately abandoned the match. By spilling the beans when he did, the captain had deprived one of his batsmen of the chance of breaking Don Bradman's world record score for a single first-class innings: BB Nimbalkar was on 443 not out at the time, only nine runs short.

Talking of Bradman, when Australia went 2–0 in the Ashes series of 1936–37, his first as Australia's captain, former international team mate Alan Fairfax was quoted by the *Daily Express* as saying that 'Some of the trouble is caused by Bradman being captain. He can't give the time to the other players. You have to mother a cricket team, and Bradman is no mother.'

He learned his maternal duties spectacularly fast, scoring 270, 212 and 169 to win the next three Tests (the only time a rubber's been won from 2–0 down) and never lost a series as captain!

After Yorkshire wicketkeeper Jimmy Binks had dropped two catches and missed a stumping, all off Ray Illingworth, the latter repaired to a local hostelry to drown whatever he felt the need to drown. There, one of Illy's acquaintances approached him with commiserations: 'Bad luck, Raymond lad. We'd have had that match won by now but for that silly bugger Binks.' Illingworth, 'with a certain amount of delight,' then introduced his other drinking partner: 'Meet Jimmy Binks.'

Before the second Test against the West Indies in 1995, Illingworth (by now England manager) was as unequivocal as ever: 'Steve Rhodes will definitely play.' Rhodes didn't take part in any Tests that summer.

When he arrived to play for South Australia, much was expected of South African opener Barry Richards, already regarded as one of the great batsmen. At Perth in 1970–71, the first ball he received, delivered by Test pace bowler Graham McKenzie, swung away and beat him, which tempted the Western Australia wicketkeeper Rod Marsh to venture a few words on the subject (something he was rarely loath to do): 'Jeez,' he said to slip fielder John Inverarity, 'I thought this bloke was supposed to be able to play a bit.'

Richards scored 356! At the end of the first day, Inverarity turned to Marsh as they trudged off: 'I suppose he *can* play a bit.'

At an England team meeting before the 1978 series against Pakistan, Geoff Boycott gave the rest of the team the benefit of his experience (he'd captained the team in Pakistan the previous winter) by letting them know that Shafiq Ahmed sometimes played the hook shot badly. According to Bob Willis, this piece of information brought the house down: Shafiq wasn't in the touring team.

The young girl playing in the street with her brother and friends ('my first cricket memory') was furious when a passing policeman took their names but not hers because 'Girls don't play cricket.' This one, Rachael Heyhoe Flint, went on to captain England.

Assorted injuries led to the 41-year-old Colin Cowdrey being called out to Australia in 1974–75 to face the Lillee and Thomson onslaught, which he met bravely and withsome success. During the second innings of the second Test, Cowdrey walked down the pitch to his captain Mike Denness and ventured the opinion that they'd just about seen Thomson off. Almost immediately, Thomson dismissed Cowdrey for the second time in the match.

After a Test match in which Cowdrey had received what commentator Brian Johnston thought a bad umpiring decision, the latter mentioned the fact to Don Bradman at a post-match function, adding that he didn't think the official could have had much experience of actually playing the game. The Don defended the umpire fervently: 'How dare you talk about him like that? He used to open the innings for South Australia before his eyesight failed.'

Because 'Buns' Cartwright's fingers were so arthritic, *The Cricketer* magazine arranged for him to make the draw for their annual competition by picking table tennis balls (rather than fiddly pieces of paper) from a jug held by Belinda Brocklehurst, wife of the magazine's owner. After the function, the publication's office was graced by a postcard from the colonel thanking them for having asked him to do the honours 'and please thank Belinda for holding my balls.' One of *The Cricketer*'s own writers swears it's true.

After half an hour of a Championship match in May 1982, one of the Warwickshire fielders, former England batsman Dennis Amiss, sidled up to Worcestershire's New Zealand opener Glenn Turner and bet him he couldn't score 300 in the day. Worcestershire's declaration stopped Turner from breaking Charlie Macartney's world record for most runs in a day and he had to settle for 311 not out. Not a bad way to score the 100th hundred of your first-class career. Amiss' team-mates 'weren't too pleased with me, but I didn't think he could carry on in the same vein.'

That same season, Sunil Gavaskar bet Ian Botham that he didn't have the patience to score a double century in the Test at the Oval, where the wicket was so good that Botham felt 'I should have said 400.' He was annoyed to be out for 208: 'of all my dismissals this was the one I most regret.' The draw cost India the series 1–0.

West Indies have scored 244 for 7, all out.

Frank Bough

In the dramatic 1996 World Cup semi-final against Australia, West Indies' captain hit a four off the first ball of the final over, which prompted TV commentator Tony Greig to announce in his inimitable way that 'Richie Richardson's going to win this match for the West Indies.' They lost by five runs and haven't reached the final since 1983.

Prophets and their losses

When Jan Waller met her daughter's new boyfriend in 1974, she was impressed: 'What a nice quiet young man.' Within three months, Kath Waller was on her way to being Mrs IT Botham.

Before the 1995–96 series, Jack Bannister wrote that there was no way England could lose. After the 1–0 defeat, he tore up the offending article and ate his words in public, washed down with a bottle of South African wine.

In 1992, England's newly appointed team manager Keith Fletcher flew to Johannesburg at considerable expense to watch India play South Africa, returning with the opinion that leg-spinner Anil Kumble was unlikely to be a threat: 'I didn't see him turn a single ball from leg to off. I don't believe we will have much problem with him.'

Kumble turned a few in the next series, taking more wickets than anyone else on either side (21, at 19.80) as England lost all three Tests and came home in disgrace [*Blunders Vol.1*].

Before the 1975–76 tour of Australia, West Indies captain Clive Lloyd felt there was so little to choose between the teams that 'you don't need a crystal ball to predict the outcome could hang on a slender thread.' West Indies lost the series 5–1.

One of Lloyd's nemeses that year, Dennis Lillee, prophesied in 1989 that 'England will win a tight series by one game.' Australia won 4–0.

One of Lloyd's predecessors as captain, Garry Sobers, wrote in a 1988 autobiography that his world record Test score of 365 not out 'would never be beaten'. Six years later, he was walking across the field to shake Brian Lara's hand after his 375 against England.

Basil D'Oliveira came to England late in his career and was already in his thirties (he won't say how far into them) by the time he tried his hand in county cricket. Since he was playing in the Central Lancashire League, he hoped to be signed up at Old Trafford, but was turned down. Official reason: Lancashire had just signed Sonny Ramadhin, and another overseas player would restrict the opportunities for the county's younger players. Real reason: apparently that Cyril Washbrook, the former Lancashire and England batsman, had deemed D'Oliveira to be 'just a Saturday afternoon slogger'.

Not only did Dolly slog 2,484 runs for England at an average of 40.06 (some of them on afternoons other than Saturday) as well as taking 47 Test wickets, he also helped Worcestershire win the Championship in 1965 and 1974 while Lancashire haven't won it since 1950.

Fifteen years after the slogger verdict, D'Oliveira was 'particularly delighted' to receive one of his six Gillette Cup man of the match awards from adjudicator C Washbrook!

Keith Fletcher dealing with the idea that Anil Kumble might be a match-winner

In the first Test of the 1928–29 Ashes series, after Australia's latest bright young hope had gone in at number 7 and scored only 18 and 1, his team-mate Charles Kelleway's verdict was nothing if not succinct: 'Not up to Test match standard.' The selectors seemed to agree, dropping the newcomer from the next match.

Even when he scored 79 and 112 on his recall in the third Test, English pundits weren't entirely carried away. The great medium-fast bowler Maurice Tate is said to have told him to his face that 'You'll have to keep that bat a bit straighter when you come to England, or you won't have much luck there,' a view shared by Test all-rounder and Surrey captain Percy George Fender.

To begin with, i.e. at the start of the 1930 series in England, they seemed to have got it right – in his first Test innings in England, the young man was first embarrassed then clean bowled by Tate for 8 – but from then on, a few opinions needed some revision. In the second innings of that Test, Donald George Bradman scored 131, in the series 974 (still the world record), on the whole tour 2,522 at an average of 100.88. Australia regained the Ashes, and at the end of the second Test, Fender believed that 'His 254 was as perfect an example of real batting in its best sense as anyone could wish to see.'

It happened with many of the great batsmen. For instance, after WG Grace had made 344 and 177 in consecutive county matches in 1876, the Notts players, who'd just lost the second of those games, met the Yorkshire team coming down to play Grace's Gloucestershire, and warned them about the great man's form – only for Tom Emmett to reply that 'the big 'un can't do it three times running.' Grace batted eight hours for 318 not out, still the highest individual score ever made against Yorkshire!'

Nineteen years later, after WG had knocked a slow long-hop from Sammy

Woods to the boundary to become the first player to score a hundred first-class hundreds, Woods thought that now the feat had been accomplished, at least 'Now we'll get the old devil out.' Instead, Grace stayed to make 288. Oh well, thought Sam, at least I'll drink him under the table tonight (WG was 46). He was wrong about that too.

Jack Hobbs recalled that at the start of his first visit to South Africa (1909–10), a local paper suggested that he 'might as well go back. He will never be any good on matting wickets.' Hobbs scored 539 runs in the series at an average of 67.37. On his second trip to South Africa (1913–14), he averaged 63.29.

Before a match against Hampshire, Hobbs received a crank letter which assured him that 'You won't come off so grand with Jaques and Kennedy's bowling. I hate your dam swank.' Hobbs scored 167.

> *The batting side find it easier to bat in bad light than the fielding side do.*
>
> **Trevor Bailey**

During a match at Adelaide in 1950–51, a local journalist wrote that 'If South Australia doesn't pass the MCC score by tea today, then the State batting is weaker, the English attack stronger, and the pitch more responsive than I think they are – and you can call me a poor judge right out loud.' By tea, South Australia were all out for 126.

When he was nine, a young Australian was told by a doctor that his eyes were malformed, he'd be blind before he was 21, 'and not to worry too much about my schooling, all I could become was a strong-arm farmer.'

The boy, William Joseph O'Reilly, grew into one of the greatest leg-spinners of all time, taking 144 wickets at 22.59 each (1932–46), then one of the most respected sports journalists in the country. He lived, and saw things more clearly than most, till he was 86.

After watching Australian opening batsmen Arthur Morris in 1946–47, in particular his habit of flicking the ball off his leg stump, England captain Wally Hammond predicted that he wouldn't be a success on English pitches.

In the 1948 series, which Australia won 4–0, Morris scored three centuries in a total of 696 runs at an average of 87.00. His last two innings in the rubber were 182 and 196.

The squad for the 1958–59 Ashes series was widely regarded as one of the very strongest England had ever sent abroad: May, Cowdrey, Graveney, Evans, Laker, Lock, Statham, Trueman, Tyson. It lost 4–0.

On the other side of the coin, who knows how many sides have been written off as 'the worst to leave such-and-such a country'? Australia in 1995, for one (*after* winning a series in the West Indies!); Australia in 1964, for another, following the retirements of their best batsman Neil Harvey, their best bowler Alan Davidson, and their great captain Richie Benaud. One English critic described them as 'the faceless ones, athletes anonymous, whose names escape the memory.' They won 1–0 and retained the Ashes.

In 1970–71, Neil Harvey apparently described England as 'rubbish.' They won the series 2–0 to win the Ashes for the first time since 1959. In 1986–87, England were written off by journalists from both sides before retaining the Ashes with a match to spare.

During the second Test of the 1979 series, after England had scored 419 in reply to India's pitiful 96, the *Daily Mirror* felt it safe to begin their report with 'As England's cricketers prepare for the formality of their second successive thrashing of India today ... ' The Indians scored 318–4 to force an honourable draw.

Australia's great all-rounder Keith Miller thought that the first Test of the 1950–51 series would be 'the dullest in history'. What, even with the possibility of rain, and therefore the threat of an infamous Brisbane 'sticky dog' pitch?

The storm broke after Australia's first innings of 228. England declared at 68–7, Australia at 32–7, then England were all out for 122 to go 1–0 down in a series they lost 4–1. The last 24 wickets had fallen for 222 runs, Miller making 15 and 8!

In the *Sydney Daily Mirror* in January 1966, Miller wrote that opening batsman Bill Lawry should be dropped from the fourth Test: 'Australia can never hope to win a Test against this new-look zipalong English batting line-up as long as slow-coach Lawry is there.' Lawry scored 119, Australia won by an innings!

During the 1962–63 tour, some England players made no secret of the fact that they didn't rate Barry Shepherd, the burly batsman who captained Western Australia. It's even said that they tried to play him into the Test team (when he was bowled by David Larter in the state match, another played felt this 'was bad luck for us, wasn't it?'). If the story's true, they got their wish: Shepherd made his Test debut in the third

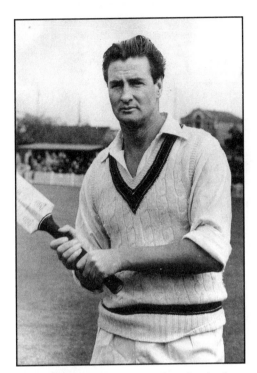

Keith Miller in the days when he had a grip on things

match of the series – and scored 71 not out to help beat England by eight wickets. Australia retained the Ashes by drawing the series 1–1.

Before the 1981 Ashes series, Ian Botham said of the bowler called Lillee 'You can forget about Dennis being quick. He's not well. He's medium-paced.' That's as may have been, but it didn't stop the great man taking 39 wickets in the series, including Botham's five times.

Before the West Indies match against Surrey in 1933, their fierce little fast bowler Manny Martindale announced that Jack Hobbs was finished as a major batting force. Fair comment, you might think (Hobbs was now

50 and this was his first match of the season) but unwise to let the Master get to hear of it; he still had a few shots in the locker, using them to score 221, after which the chastened Martindale came to him and admitted 'Mr Hobbs, you're a great player.'

> *It makes you realise he's probably a better batsman than you realise.*
>
> **Ian Botham**

The return of Viv Richards and Joel Garner (missing during the tour by the West Indies the previous year) made Somerset many people's favourites for the 1985 County Championship, especially as they also fielded Ian Botham, Peter Roebuck and Brian Rose. They finished bottom.

Before the 1928–29 series in Australia, the old England captain Plum Warner, writing in the *Morning Post*, criticised the team for intending to use Maurice Tate as an opening bowler now that he was 33. Tate took 17 wickets in the first four Tests, all of which England won to retain the Ashes.

Before the next tour Down Under (1932–33), another former England captain Arthur Gilligan, writing for the *News Chronicle*, was adamant that Percy Chapman 'is the man to skipper in Australia and no-one else.' Under Douglas Jardine, England regained the Ashes 4–1.

Pride cometh ...

At the end of the second day of the third Test in 1995, although England still trailed West Indies by almost 100 with seven second-innings wickets left, their pugnacious new seamer Dominic Cork declared publicly that 'We won't lose this.'

Perhaps he meant 'won't lose this before lunch'. Within 77 minutes, England were all out for 89 (Cork gone in the second over of the day) and had lost by an innings and 64.

After taking 15 wickets in the first two Tests of the 1989–90 series in the Caribbean, helping England win the first and come close to taking the third (the second was washed out), Devon Malcolm was quoted by the English press as having said that he now had Viv Richards' number.

It's true that the West Indies captain was 37, hadn't played first-class cricket for a month after missing the third Test, and had been dismissed by Malcolm in the first – but even so, the comments seemed a trifle premature (not that accuracy has ever been a feature of Devon's participation in Test cricket) and just desserts seemed to be in the offing.

Sure enough, in the third Test Viv's dander came up and smote Malcolm to all parts, hitting him out of the attack and leaving him with figures of 0–188 from 43 overs. Richards' furious first innings of 70 drove the West Indies to a win that squared the series which they eventually won 2–1.

Malcolm wasn't the only pace bowler to treat minor victories over the great man with an inordinate swagger. Playing for Glamorgan against Somerset, after beating Richards several times outside the off stump, England opening bowler Greg

Put me in front of a firing squad if I'm wrong. Dominic pops his cork

Thomas called down the wicket 'Viv, it's red and it's round.' His very next ball was hit back over his head into a nearby pond. 'Since you know what it looks like,' said Richards, 'you go and fetch it.'

Mind you, neither Malcolm nor Thomas nor any other cricketer was ever as proud as Richards himself. In macho land, the rules are pinned up in full view: no crash helmets, no ducking when you can hook, impose yourself from the start, all spinners and medium-pacers are fodder.

The Indian bowlers in the 1983 World Cup final looked the tastiest of feed: with the exception of Kapil Dev and perhaps Balwinder Sandhu, nothing but up-and-down trundlers (Mohinder Amarnath, Madan Lal, Roger Binny) to take on Richards, Greenidge, Haynes and Lloyd. When India scored only 183, that seemed to be that.

Although West Indies' reply got off to a bad start – Greenidge lbw for 5 – Richards, the next man in, was expected to win it on his own. In the last World Cup final, he'd scored 138. Earlier in this tournament, he'd made 119 against the same Indian attack. Now he began by casually pulling Sandhu for four through midwicket then hitting Kapil Dev past mid-off and midwicket. He scored at least one boundary in each over.

Even when Haynes was caught at extra cover, West Indies were still in charge at 50–2 with Clive Lloyd at the crease. Madan Lal, a private on jankers in the world of military medium, sent down another innocuous offering. Richards sent it back. It flew over midwicket like so many others – and fell into Kapil Dev's trap (and hands): 57–3.

Even Richards' walk back to the pavilion bristles with defiance – but he'd set a flawed precedent. Lloyd, who scored a century in the 1975 final and was trying to win the Cup for the third time as captain, was made of the same haughty stuff. Trying to dominate too early, he gave a catch to mid-on: 57–3 became 66–5, then 76–6, finally 140 all out (Madan Lal 3–31, Amarnath 3–12), the lowest total in any World Cup final. India, complete outsiders before the tournament, won by 43 runs.

'We got carried away,' said Lloyd. 'It was an amateurish performance.' The West Indies, some of whose supporters arrived at Lord's with placards proclaiming 'The Cup Is Ours,' haven't reached the final since.

Lloyd and especially Richards were entitled to a spot of hubris: they were batsmen of the highest class. So too was another West Indian captain, Garry Sobers, who proved it most of all in the 1966 series England: 722 runs at an average of 103.14 as well as 20 wickets, in a series well won before the final Test.

The latter, at the Oval, saw England's third captain of the series, Brian Close – and some success at last for the home side, a last-wicket partnership of 128 between Ken Higgs and John Snow completing a first innings total of 527. When West Indies were reduced to 137–5 in their second innings, they were still 122 runs away from making England bat again – but there was still Sobers to come.

The first ball he received was a short one, bowled by Snow on orders from Close, who was sure the great batsman would attack it rather than duck like any mere mortal. Sure enough, Sobers went for the hook, didn't get the entire bat on it, and gave a catch to Close himself, standing (and typically not flinching) only a couple of yards away at short leg. Sobers out first ball, West Indies all out 225, losing by an innings, England's only win of the series.

Before a cup semi-final against Enfield Under–17s, the Brondesbury (and future England) captain Mike Gatting told his opposite number that he hoped 'we can get this over quickly as my school-mate Ashok Patel and I have to go and play for England Schools.' Gatting was out cheaply, Brondesbury lost the match.

After scoring a century in his first Championship innings for Sussex, Tony

Greig was pleased that Chris Danziger, his old cricket teacher, was in the crowd to watch his second match, against lowly Cambridge University: 'it gave me another chance to relate the story of my century.'

The come-uppance came early. Reasoning that if he could score 156 against Lancashire's Test bowlers, a university off-spinner would be even easier meat ('an awful approach to an innings'), Greig aimed a 'brash cover drive' at David Acfield and was bowled first ball. Back in the pavilion, he had to pay a fair chunk of his wages to pay for his Primary Club tie, presented to county players on the occasion of their first duck!

During the 1976–77 home matches against Pakistan, Dennis Lillee took such a fancy to Majid Khan's bush hat that he made public his intention of knocking it off the opening batsman's head with a bouncer. Majid averaged 49.40 in the series and ended the third and final Test (which Pakistan won to draw the series) by hooking Lillee to the boundary – then presenting him with his hat.

Although not in the same class (or intended in the same spirit) as Greig's infamous 'grovel' remark about a forthcoming series against the West Indies [Blunders Vol.1], David Gower's forecast for the winter trip to the Caribbean in 1985–86 rebounded on him even more spectacularly. From the Oval pavilion after the 3–1 win over Australia in 1985, the England captain told the assembled masses that the Windies were probably 'quaking in their boots' at the prospect of facing this resurgent England team. Coming from Gower, it was meant partly in jest of course, but he admitted to being a little drunk with success at the time: 'We were guilty of overrating ourselves when we arrived in the West Indies.'

As a result, it was English batsmen who did most of the quaking, blasted out by hostile bowlers on spiteful pitches. Mike Gatting had his nose broken and England lost all five Tests by emphatic margins: 10 wickets (twice), 7 wickets, an innings and 30, 240 runs. Gower bravely topped the England averages, but that wasn't saying much: only three others managed more than 17.00. A humbling experience ...

... especially perhaps for Ian Botham, who Gower thought was more 'physically under-prepared' than anyone else in the team. The consequences for the celebrated all-rounder, whose record against the West Indies is anything but Beefy, were Test averages of 16.80 with the bat (highest score 38) and 48.63 with the ball.

Botham once stuck one on Ian Chappell's chin, chased him out of a bar, and boasted that he'd score more Test runs than him. Close but no cigar. He finished 145 runs short despite playing 102 Tests to Chappell's 75.

> *So that's 57 runs needed by Hampshire in 11 overs, and it doesn't need a calculator to tell us that the run rate required is 5.18 recurring.*
>
> **Norman de Mesquita**

After winning the toss at the start of the last Test of the 1984–85 series, Australia's captain Allan Border heard laughter coming from the West Indies dressing-room at his decision to bat first. He chuckled last and loudest as Australia scored 471 and won by an innings.

The following winter, it was Border's turn to put his foot in it. After Richard Hadlee had taken 9–52 and 6–71 to win the first Test in Brisbane, Australia won the second by four wickets, somehow a wide enough margin for AB to believe that they'd come to terms with the great seamer – 'and I made the mistake of saying so publicly.'

Hadlee responded by saying he'd take 12 wickets in the third and final Test. He didn't – but 11 were quite enough (5–65 and 6–90) to bowl New Zealand to their first ever series win against Australia.

When Rohan Kanhai and John Snow met over a few drinks at the end of the 1967 season, the West Indian batsman cordially informed the English bowler that 'We'll smash you all over the park when we get you on those wickets in the Caribbean.'

Snow found those wickets to his liking, taking 27 wickets in four Tests to help England win the series.

> *Australia must now climb to the top diving board for a last desperate throw of the dice.*
>
> **Bob Willis**

Australia went into the decisive fifth Test of the 1993 series against the West Indies with a new fast bowler, the 6ft 6in Jo Angel, who was short on experience (only 13 first-class matches) but not confidence: he announced that he was going to give the Windies 'some of their own medicine.'

While Curtly Ambrose was bowling like the devil himself to take 7–25 and win the match by an innings, Angel managed only 1–72 and was dropped for more than a year.

Part of the problem may have been his height. An Australian newspaper's misprint made him 200 metres tall!

During the fourth Test of the home series against Australia, the prime minister of Guyana, Forbes Burnham, adjourned a

meeting with the heads of the other West Indian countries so that they could watch their team bat in their second innings.

The West Indies were all out for 109 and lost by 10 wickets to give Australia a winning 2–0 lead in the series.

After winning their last match of the 1962 Championship, Worcestershire's players though they'd won the title, but Yorkshire pipped them to it.

The same thing had happened to Lancashire in 1920. Despite winning their last match, against Worcestershire, they were edged into second place by Middlesex's dramatic win over Surrey.

It's reliably reported that both Worcs and Lancs were drinking champagne in the changing-room when news of their near misses broke.

The same libation was on ice in the Australian changing-room towards the end of the famous Headingley Test of 1981, but stayed unopened after the heroics of Botham and Willis. When the England team sent their changing-room attendant round to ask if they could borrow a few bottles, he received a typically pithy reply. It was Peter Willey's 19th Test and the first time he'd touched the bubbly as a winner.

The following year, more of the same for the Aussies. Against the West Indies at home in 1981–82, they led 1–0 in the series and began the last day of the third and final Test 190 runs ahead with six wickets still in hand. Bottles and cans lay ready in the changing-room. Then those last six batsmen fell for 24 runs in little more than an hour, Australia lost by five wickets, and didn't win a series against the West Indies until 1995.

The story may be apocryphal but it illustrates a few things. Before his first visit to Australia, WG Grace accepted a bet that he wouldn't be bowled in any of his matches there. In his first, he had his leg stump knocked back by Harry Boyle!

Before the 1950–51 series, there had been rumours about Australia's new mystery spinner, the uncapped 35-year-old Jack Iverson – so when Denis Compton had a good look at him during his long innings against Victoria, he felt confident enough to declare that 'I think I've got this fellow now.'

Well, it's true that Iverson didn't once take Compton's wicket in the Tests, but there wasn't much need to: while 'Wrong Grip Jake' was heading the averages with 21 wickets at only 15.23 to win the series (the only one he ever played), Compton scored a total of 53 runs at an average of 7.57.

Before the 1962–63 Ashes series, the Rev. David Sheppard hadn't thought of Richie Benaud as a great bowler ('He must prove this to me himself'). Almost as soon as he came on to bowl in the first Test, the Australian captain had the English chaplain caught at short leg. 'He certainly succeeded in winning my respect.'

In a match against Notts at Clacton, 'when I was a young and very naive cricketer,' Essex all-rounder Trevor Bailey 'had the foolishness to announce during the tea interval that I had never had a hundred runs scored off me' in an innings. His captain Tom Pearce put him on to bowl immediately after tea and 'every run was counted by my colleagues.' When he'd conceded a hundred, Pearce took him off!

Who was the member of the Australian team who celebrated winning the first Test of the 1911–12 series by offering odds of 4–1 that England wouldn't win a single Test?

His name has been concealed to protect the poor innocent. As for those odds, they were exactly right: England won the series 4–1!

Back in 1903–04, another England team had been written off by the Australian press: 'When they return beaten five-love they will be more than ever the laughing stock of cricketing England.' Australia lost 3–2.

Jon Fellows-Smith played in four Tests for South Africa on their 1960 tour of England. It's hard to believe that anyone used his nickname ('Pom-Pom') to his face: he played rugby for Northampton. In the front row, too.

His approach to cricket was cast from the same mould. Captaining Northants on one occasion, he insisted on going ahead with the match even though the rain had been hammering down. When his team had to field first, their leading pace bowler wasn't keen on running in over that sodden outfield – so Pom-Pom typically took the ball instead.

Pounding up to the wicket, he slipped before he reached it, fell, broke his ankle, and had to be stretchered off virtually before the match had begun!

Waiting to bat in the fifth match of the 1958–59 Ashes series, Norm O'Neill felt confident. He'd scored 56 in his last Test innings and this 'was a good day for batting and with an appreciative crowd in attendance I felt like a million.' He was caught at gully off the only ball he received in the match!

Four years later, he was caught in the same fielding position by the same fielder (Colin Cowdrey) off the same bowler (Fred Trueman) on the same ground for the same score.

Although South Africa's opening bowler George Bissett had bowled him for just a single in the first innings of the fourth Test

DR Jardine's overjoyed at the thought of facing Morris Leyland. Honest.

in 1927–28, England's 41-year-old opener Percy Holmes was confident before the start of the fifth: 'I can play bloody Bissett with a broom handle.' Bissett dismissed him for a duck in each innings!

England sent a virtual 2nd XI on that trip (no Hobbs, Woolley, Larwood, etc), apparently ignoring the fact that the hosts had improved immeasurably since their first excursions into Test cricket. This time England were held to a 2–2 draw after winning the first two Tests.

England sent another weak team to the West Indies in 1947–48 (recalling 45-year-old Gubby Allen, leaving out Hutton, Washbrook, Bedser and the like) and paid for it by losing the series 2–0 and becoming the first England side not to win a single first-class match on tour.

Batting for Surrey on an excellent Oval wicket in 1932, England captain Douglas Jardine spent almost three hours making 35 in his stubborn determination to subdue the Yorkshire attack. It seemed complete exasperation on the part of their captain Brian Sellers to call up Morris Leyland, who averaged 46.06 with the bat for England but was very much a part-time bowler. 'What, me?' he said. One of his team-mates, fast bowler Bill Bowes, was less polite ('Nay, the hell, skipper') and another, slow left-armer Hedley Verity, accused Sellers of ruining three hours' work.

Jardine, meanwhile, was so delighted with what he saw as a triumph that he could be heard muttering 'Beaten 'em. I've done Yorkshire, ah ah!' Untypical of the man to show so much of himself – or to come charging out of his crease to Leyland's first ball. He would have been stumped by yards if he hadn't been bowled!

Plum Warner felt he had a good season in 1904, especially his innings of 48, in a

Middlesex total of only 87, against Yorkshire 'on very false turf at Bradford.' He might have made that half-century, too, if he hadn't listened to wicketkeeper David Hunter: 'Ah, Mr Warner, you play Wilfred Rhodes better than anyone else.' Within minutes, he was out, caught Hunter, bowled Rhodes!

Warner captained England in the 1903–04 Ashes series. At lunch on the last day of the fourth Test, his opposite number Clem Hill told him 'in his pleasant manner' that Australia were going to win – even though they'd lost three wickets, including the great Victor Trumper, for 59. England won by 157 runs.

Yorkshire were left needing to score 86 in 45 minutes to beat Essex in 1959, a task the Essex and England all-rounder Trevor Bailey believed to be impossible, especially if the right fields were set for himself and fellow seamer Barry Knight. He went as far as drawing diagrams to prove it. Yorkshire got the runs, won the match, and went on to take the Championship for the first time in ten years. Bailey conceded 40 runs in 4.5 overs, Knight 44 in 4!

Eighty years after his death in 1915, Victor Trumper's still regarded by many as the most brilliant batsman of all time, though one of his old club colleagues in Australia didn't always think so.

Tommy Rose was a young spinner who could bowl with either hand. Having played with Trumper for the Paddington club in Sydney, he told his new Waverley teammates that he knew how to get the great man out. Unfortunately for him, Victor got to hear of it. Rose's first ball to him went for four, the next five for six. Trumper reached fifty in nine out of ten balls in five minutes and 'Needless to say, Rose was taken off, a sadder and wiser man.'

Before the 1992–93 series in the Caribbean, former Pakistan captain Imran Khan announced that his country were about to prove their right to be considered world champions. True, they'd won the 1992 World Cup, but that was a tournament composed of one-day matches and this was the real thing. Pakistan lost two of the three Tests (by 204 runs and 10 wickets) and drew the other, after which Imran's silence was positively deafening.

Those who live by the sword ...

Bouncing back

Devon Malcolm celebrates as South Africa's Craig Matthews plays his part in history

Why have fast bowlers persisted in bowling bouncers at Devon Malcolm (Courtney Walsh being just the most infamous example)? It really does look like a case of throwing a hammer at a nut: he's one of nature's natural number 11s.

In times gone by, the fast bowlers' union existed as much through a sense of self-preservation as respect; you didn't bounce Tyson or Thomson because they'd bounce you back and then some. Perhaps Malcolm's fellow quicks weren't too concerned by the threat of retaliation, reasoning that he didn't get too many on target. Whatever, the 1994 South Africans thought they'd probably better get in on the act, and a few chuckles were raised when Fanie de Villiers made Devon's

helmet ring with a bouncer during the third and final Test at the Oval.

It didn't turn out to be such a good idea. Whether or not Malcolm made his 'you guys are history' speech, he certainly bowled as fast as he's ever done, this time with the radar working consistently. His 9–57 in the second innings, including Jonty Rhodes whom he'd hospitalised in the first, won the match by 8 wickets and squared the series. He was the first England bowler to take nine in a Test innings since Jim Laker in 1956.

Starting these bouncer wars has always been a risky business, especially if your guns aren't as big as theirs. When England took a battery of fast-medium bowlers to Australia in 1974–75, the intention seemed obvious: do to them what John Snow had done four years earlier – especially as the Australian pace attack was thought to be no more dangerous than in 1970–71. Dennis Lillee had lost a yard of pace and surely hadn't recovered from the crippling back trouble that broke him down a couple of years earlier. As for this new tearaway Jeff Thomson, wasn't he just a beach boy who'd taken 0–110 in his only Test so far?

No surprise then, when the England attack began plying their opponents with bouncers in the very first innings of the series. Bob Willis hit opener Wally Edwards on the head in each innings, but the ones that really lit the touch paper were aimed by Tony Greig's very medium pace at Lillee himself, who made it quite clear that reciprocation was imminent. Greig just laughed.

He seemed to have some justification – a brave and talented batsman, he made a century in England's first innings – but he hadn't done his team-mates any favours. If Lillee had lost a little pace, he was as rebarbative as ever – and Thomson's poor first Test had been due to a foot injury he'd kept quiet. Now fully fit, his slingshot action in working order, he traumatised the English batsmen, taking nine wickets in the match and 33 in the series, almost breaking a record and certainly breaking a few bones and hearts. Although Greig stood up well to the bombardment throughout the series, England lost it 4–1, their only win coming in the final Test, when Thomson was absent and Lillee injured.

Twenty years earlier, the boot, or something, had been on the other side. Although Frank Tyson had bowled a bouncer at Ray Lindwall, Lindwall was probably ill-advised to bowl one back at Tyson. The Australian, still a world-class bowler, wasn't quite as fast as in 1948 (he was 33 now) whereas Tyson was at his typhonic peak. Besides which, Lindwall's mistake lay not so much in

bowling the bouncer as in hitting Tyson with it. It's said that the bump on Frank's sparsely thatched dome was visible from the other end of the ground.

A thoroughly galvanised Tyson took 6–85 to snatch this low-scoring second Test by 38 runs and level the series, which his extreme pace helped win 3–1.

Lindwall had been tempting this kind of fate for some time. In the final Test of the 1953 Ashes series, he'd broken the fast bowlers' golden rule by letting Fred Trueman have a short one, which hit him in the shoulder 'so hard I thought someone had stuck a knife in it.'

Revenge, a dish eaten cold by Fred, took more than five years. In the last Test of the 1958–59 series, a Trueman bouncer reared up onto Lindwall's bat handle, thence into the hands of Colin Cowdrey at slip via the Australian's noble brow. Lindwall was out for 0. His old partner Keith Miller also bounced Trueman 'and he was another who got paid back in the end.'

In a B&H Cup match in 1974, a bouncer from Hampshire's formidable West Indian fast bowler Andy Roberts hit a young Somerset all-rounder in the face, flattening him and knocking out a couple of teeth. 'It was the worst thing Andy could have done,' recalled the youngster, one Ian Terence Botham. 'It made me all the keener.' He went on to smash 44 runs which won the man of the match award, brought him widespread fame for the first time, and took Somerset to a famous win.

Big John Jackson (6ft 1in, 15 stone) never took all ten wickets in a first-class innings, which was his own fault. While bowling for the North of England against the South, he took nine wickets but also injured little John Wisden (later founder of the yearbook) so badly that he couldn't bat.

Those who live by the sword ... (2)

Reginald Wood made only 6 and 0 and didn't bowl in his only Test for England, at Sydney in 1887 – but he was lucky to win even this one cap, coming in as replacement for Billy Barnes, right-handed batsman and famous imbiber with either hand, who'd injured one of them by trying to punch the opposition captain Percy McDonnell – and hitting a wall instead!

> *Parker, literally fighting for a place on an overcrowded plane to India.*
>
> **Trevor Bailey**

Despite a crude grip and stance, Clem Hill was one of the great left-handed batsmen, scorer of 3,412 Test runs (1896–1912), a world record at the time, which might have been considerably more but for his involvement in a fracas with former Test team-mate Peter McAlister during an Australian team selection meeting in 1912.

'Involvement' in this case went something like this. McAlister: You're the worst captain I've ever seen. Hill: Call me that again and I'll punch your nose. McAlister: You're the worst captain I've ever – you hit me when my hands were down. Hill: Well, *my* hands are down now.

McAlister was a six-footer, Hill seven years younger and more strongly built. It's said that their blood dripped on fellow selectors Frank Iredale and Syd Smith. Several senior players were already in dispute with the newly formed Australian Board, and this little contretemps didn't help

matters. Hill and several others, including Victor Trumper, didn't play Test cricket again.

1876 was a vintage year for schemes and schemers. When an innkeeper called Brown bet an auctioneer named Piers that he couldn't bowl him out even once within 12 hours, he thought he was onto some easy money: he appeared with a bat whose blade was almost a foot across. Unfortunately for him, his opponent proved to be of the same nefarious mind, marching out to do battle with a ball that weighed nearly two stone!

Piers proceeded to whittle away at Brown's broad blade until so many slivers had been chipped off it that it was very thin indeed, leaving enough space for the great boulder to knock down the uncovered stumps at its leisure. Instead of 12 hours, the auctioneer won the wager within ten minutes.

Keith Fletcher had been touted as a possible England captain for quite a while (his sustained success at Essex was genuinely exceptional) and was the obvious choice to lead the tour to India in 1981–82 after Mike Brearley's last retirement.

When he got there, however, things turned sour, England losing the first Test before being dragged into a sequence of very dull, ill-tempered draws, Fletcher showing 'lack of flexibility' according to *Wisden* and allowing the standard of umpiring to get to him. This after telling the rest of the team to accept it and get on with it. Given out caught behind in the second Test, sure that he hadn't touched the ball, he flicked the stumps with his bat on his way back to the pavilion. He was stripped of the captaincy immediately after the tour.

When one of their league matches had to be cancelled in 1994, the Horton Print club saw it as an opportunity, not a calamity: their captain Mohammed Isaq sent in an imaginary score! The fantasy win would have earned them promotion if some of the other players hadn't turned up to watch matches being played at the same time as their own! Isaq moved south after being banned for three years from playing any level of cricket anywhere in Yorkshire.

Brian Close had no problem carrying over his imaginative, attacking captaincy of Yorkshire into the international arena, leading England in seven Tests, all in 1966 and 1967, of which six were won and none lost. He would certainly have led England on the 1967–68 tour to the West Indies but for a single match played at the end of the season before it.

Yorkshire were in the process of grinding out a draw against Warwickshire on their way to retaining the Championship when someone in the Edgbaston members' enclosure passed comment on the Yorkshire captain's antecedents and lack of cranial hair as the teams were coming off the field at the lunch interval.

Close walked along a row of seats, put his hand on someone's shoulder, and asked him if he'd like to repeat that opinion. No he wouldn't, said the someone; he hadn't said it in the first place. Close had laid hands on the wrong man!

It wasn't much of an incident in itself (Close apologised and the man handled said 'There was nothing for me to complain about') but there seems little doubt that some powers-that-be were looking for any excuse to take the England captaincy away and give it back to a thoroughly nice chap like Colin Cowdrey. Close knew this, too: he remembers being told so by at least one journalist. Under scrutiny as he was, he should have been more careful. Besides, he'd doubtless been called worse things in the past.

Sure enough, using the alleged time-wasting tactic against Warwickshire as a pretext, the selectors invited Cowdrey to lead England in the Caribbean. Close was never made captain again.

That slow motion doesn't show how fast the ball was travelling.

Richie Benaud

When little Sunil Gavaskar ran a sharp single in the 1971 Lord's Test, he also ran into John Snow. Or rather, big John ran into him. Although the fast bowler later protested at length that he'd only been going for the ball, ref, that's not how the camera, or the selectors, saw it. Nor did he, being honest; after watching the TV replay in the changing room, he knew the game was up: 'Oh well, the scene's been far too quiet without me anyway.' He was banned from the next Test as England lost a series at home to India for the first time.

Side wagers on matches made Ted Pooley some useful extra money on the 1877 tour to Australia, but it cost him a Test career. On one occasion, going to collect his winnings, he was involved in a difference of opinion and found himself in jail for assault and destruction of property, this while England were losing the first ever Test match. Pooley, their first-choice wicket-keeper, never played international cricket.

When Cleethorpes wended their way through a traffic jam to play Harrogate in a Yorkshire League match in 1991, the home club insisted on starting on time – even though the visitors had only three men and were forced to declare at 11–2! Harrogate had 12 points deducted for 'not playing in the proper spirit of the game,' though their captain Austin Jelfs insisted that 'If I'd been really unsporting, I'd have batted first!'

> *I don't think he expected it, and that's what caught him unawares.*
>
> **Trevor Bailey**

Batting against Leicestershire in 1968, Hampshire's great South African opener Barry Richards edged a ball from John Pember to wicketkeeper Ray Julian – and 'did not walk for the only time in my career in England'.

Richards regretted his action, in more ways than one. He apologised to the Leicestershire captain Maurice Hallam at the end of the day – and Julian went on to become an umpire 'and I'm sure he has enjoyed giving me out on several occasions since then!'

When that ebullient wicketkeeper David Bairstow had been behaving even more boisterously than usual in the Yorkshire changing room, his captain Geoff Boycott decided to teach him a lesson by immersing him in a bath full of ice. Having organised the filling of the tub by other members of the team, Boycs stood by in readiness – only for the others to push him in instead of Bairstow. The water, he noted rather superfluously, was 'freezing cold'.

When Viv Richards bent the rules a little by switching balls during a round of golf, he was quickly found out by his opponent Desmond Haynes. He'd made the mistake of trying to con a man who'd once worked as a caddie!

Why did Douglas Jardine dislike Australians so? Well, when he played against them for Oxford University in 1921, he'd scored 94 not out and might well have become the first batsman to make a century against them that summer if they'd bowled another over or two at the end of the second day, especially as Oxford had forfeited a day to allow them to rest before the next Test. Instead they left him high and dry.

More than a decade later, by now England captain, Jardine unleashed the horrors of Bodyline on them without compunction.

It's an oft-told tale but still just about worth it. WG Grace once insisted on measuring the bat of his Australian equivalent as an all-rounder, George Giffen. Sure enough, the implement was found to be slightly too wide and had to be replaced (some say filed down). Giffen then asked for the good doctor's bat to undergo the same examination, and a red-faced WG discovered that it was just as wide as Giffen's.

When the well-known broadcaster Gilbert Harding was at school, a teacher forced him to umpire a cricket match. Vengeance wasn't long in coming. The teacher had reached 99 when Harding gave him out lbw. On the way back to the pavilion, the batsman fumed 'Harding, you weren't paying attention. I wasn't out.'

'On the contrary, sir,' came the reply, 'I *was* paying attention and you weren't out.'

Those who live by the sword ... (3)

Violence of the tongue (and pen)

Although they'd beaten England in the first ever Test match, at home in 1877, the Australians were still something of an unknown quantity when they toured the old country the following year, so much so that a certain Arthur Ward remarked to Allan G Steel, the England batsman, 'I hear you are going to play against the niggers on Monday.' And this from a man of the church!

Steel then introduced his neighbour in the pavilion. Reverend, meet Mr Spofforth, 'the demon nigger bowler'.

Fred Spofforth was one of the greatest bowlers of all time. In the match against the MCC, an England XI in everything but name, he took 6–4 (six wickets for four runs) in the first innings, including a hat-trick, and 5–16 in the second to dismiss the hosts (WG Grace and all) for 33 and 19 in a single day.

That should have persuaded a few people that Spofforth's ire was something best left unaroused (he wasn't called The Demon for nothing), but four years later WG didn't seem to have learned the lesson.

Although England needed only 85 to win the only Test at the Oval, the Australians had been galvanised by a typical piece of Grace gamesmanship: he'd run out Sammy Jones by removing the bails without a warning when the batsman left his crease to pat the pitch in the second innings.

Wisden's 'several of the team spoke angrily of Grace's action' was the understatement of the season. Spofforth, his dander up again, took 7–44 (14 wickets in the match), England were all out for 77, lost by seven runs and the Ashes (of 'the body of English cricket') were invented.

The Demon eyes the vicar

In Colombo in 1993, Alec Stewart's ploy of using combative speech as well as strokes wasn't an unqualified success. His verbal assault on spinner Jayananda Warnaweera (see CHUCKING IT DOWN) was criticised by Sri Lanka's captain Arjuna Ranatunga – and didn't work anyway. Stewart was caught off Warnaweera for 3 as England lost a Test to Sri Lanka for the first time.

The losers of the 1965 Gillette Cup final would play in the following Scarborough

Festival. Just before the match, Surrey captain John Edrich wished his opposite number Brian Close well 'when you get to Scarborough'.

Close scored 79 in Yorkshire's record total of 317–4 which won them the Cup by 175 runs, another record.

Cec Pepper lived up to his name as a batsman, leg-spinner and especially talker, one of the most unforgettable personalities in county cricket. Back in 1945–46, after having three appeals rejected against Don Bradman, he gave umpire Jack Scott a piece of his mind, presumably the one where he kept his most manly vocabulary. He always believed this cost him any chance of playing Test cricket, even though he sent the Australian board a written apology.

> *You join us at a very appropriate time: Ray Illingworth has just relieved himself at the pavilion end.*
>
> **Brian Johnston**

Journalist Charles Finlason was a savage critic of the England team during the 1888–89 tour, which rebounded on him in interesting fashion: invited to put his bat where his pen was, he played in South Africa's first ever Test team, which lost by eight wickets. Finlason was out for 0 and 6 and didn't take a wicket despite opening the bowling. Back to the writing board after that: he wasn't capped again.

By the time the third Test in India in 1958–59 came round, Rohan Kanhai had played 12 matches for the West Indies without scoring a century. After the match, he claimed he'd been taunted by Subhash 'Fergie' Gupte, who'd dismissed him in each of his last three innings, once for a duck. Kanhai retaliated by turning his maiden Test hundred into a mammoth 256, including 42 fours, and contributing to Gupte's figures of 1–119. India lost the match by the humbling margin of an innings and 336 runs, and the series 3–0.

Chasing India's 287 in the quarter-final of the 1996 World Cup, Pakistan's openers Aamir Sohail and Saeed Anwar set off at a cracking rate, putting on 84 in 61 balls. The score was 113–1 in the 15th over when Sohail hit Venkatesh Prasad for yet another four – then took time out to say a few colourful things to the bowler – who promptly bowled him next ball then sent him on his way with a few syllables of his own. Pakistan lost the match (and the Cup they'd won in 1992) by 39 runs.

Too good for their own good

Sometimes you try to do a bit of good instead of a bit of naughty – and look where it gets you

In the Jubilee Test of 1980, in Bombay, England wicketkeeper Bob Taylor was given out caught at the wicket off Kapil Dev, only for the Indian captain Gundappa Viswanath to persuade umpire Hanumantha Rao to change his mind because he didn't think Taylor had got a touch, an opinion shared by the bowler and the slips, all consulted before the decision was made.

It backfired on Vishy in a big way. Taylor stayed to share in a partnership of 171 with Ian Botham, scoring 43 himself, as well as making a world record ten dismissals to help England win by 10 wickets. Viswanath, whose decision was criticised in many quarters, didn't captain India again.

The first match of the 1894–95 Ashes series was one of the most extraordinary, topsy-turvy Tests ever played. Replying to Australia's total of 586, England had to follow on 261 runs behind, made a vastly improved 437, but still looked sure to lose when the hosts reached 130–2 in their second innings, needing only 46 more to win with eight wickets left.

The match went into a sixth day. The night before, with defeat apparently inevitable, the England slow left-armer Bobby Peel drowned his sorrows. He was good at that, so proficient that it cost him his county career, which ended when he relieved himself on the pitch in front of his captain (*Blunders Vol.1*). The morning after the night before in Sydney, he surfaced with the mother of all hangovers and would have been unfit to bowl if the Australian captain, their veteran wicketkeeper Jack Blackham, hadn't generously allowed the start of play to be postponed for 20 minutes.

It may not sound much, but in those days of uncovered pitches it mattered enormously. After overnight rain, the longer the sun now shone on the wicket, the more difficult it became to bat on. Peel may have been handy with a glass, but he was no mug with a ball (102 Test wickets at only 16.81 each). He took 6–67 to dismiss Australia on the stroke of lunch, win the match by a mere 10 runs (those 20 minutes made all the difference) and set England on their way to taking a famous series 3–2. The chivalrous Blackham didn't play for Australia again.

Faced with an Australian first innings total of 668 in the fourth Test of the 1954–55 home series, the West Indies lost their first six wickets for 147. During his partnership with wicketkeeper Clairmonte Depeiaza, Denis Atkinson walked down the pitch for a tactical conference, thinking the ball was dead. Keith Miller picked it up and could have run him out but didn't.

Atkinson played a captain's innings of 219 and put on 347 with Depeiaza (122), still the world record for the seventh wicket in Tests and enough to draw the match.

Before the very first Gentlemen v Players match, way back in 1806, the professionals lent the amateurs 'Silver Billy' Beldham and Billy Lambert 'to balance the sides'. Since Beldham was the best batsman of his generation and Lambert the best all-rounder, the scales were rather tipped the other way. Certainly the Players seemed more gentlemanly than was strictly necessary.

So it proved. Lambert scored 57, the highest innings of the match, and made two stumpings while Beldham took three catches as the Players were dismissed for 69 and 112. 'The all-round play of Beldham and Lambert was the main factor in the victory of the Gentlemen' by an innings.

For the second match between the sides, only two weeks later, the Players again lent Lambert to the Gents. Again he top-scored in the second innings and provided two stumpings – and this time also bowled three of the Players, who lost by 82 runs.

In 1825, more generosity which backfired. This time, not only did the Players give their opponents W Mathews, they allowed them to play 16 men! In the Players' second innings, Mathews clean bowled six men and caught and bowled another to win the match for the Gentlemen by 72 runs.

Too good for their own good (2)

In the first Test of the 1973–74 series in Australia, New Zealand bowler David 'Daffy' O'Sullivan chased the ball towards the boundary, dived, reached it just before it hit the fence, got up, picked up, threw in, and saved the four. The batsmen ran five.

Fred Trueman's first Test series, against India in 1952, was the explosive success he and the English public had hoped for: 29 wickets at only 13.31, including 8–31 in the third Test, in which he helped bowl the Indians out within two days – only to find a telegram waiting for him from his commanding officer (he was on National Service) telling him to report back immediately. He'd bowled himself out of three days' leave!

Geoff Boycott made little secret of his desire and credentials to be England captain (many other cricketers made just as little of their belief that he shouldn't be). When Ray Illingworth was sacked in 1973, Sir Geoffrey believed he was next in line, but the job went to Mike Denness (see PICK OF THE WEAK), whom he regarded as the worst England captain he ever played under.

If England had lost heavily in the West Indies, Denness' first series in charge, he might have lost the job immediately after it. As it was, England drew 1–1 – by winning the final Test, thanks in no small part to Boycott's 99 and 112 (the winning margin was only 26 runs), which helped his rival keep the job till 1975! When Boycott was eventually given the captaincy (for four

AC1 Trueman jumps for joy at the thought of returning to barracks

matches in 1978), he presided over England's first ever defeat by New Zealand.

Albert Trott (1907) and Charlie Parker (1922) lost significant amounts of gate money by bowling so well that they shortened their own benefit matches (*Blunders Vol.1*). Much the same happened to Alec Bedser in 1953, when his Surrey team mate Jim Laker took 6–38 to help beat Yorkshire within two days, thereby depriving Bedser of a day's receipts. The first day of the match was big Alec's birthday!

Although his 86 runs in only 66 balls effectively won the 1979 World Cup final, West Indian all-rounder Collis King didn't achieve as much as expected in Tests – but was certainly a star in the North Wales League. In 1979 he was banned from playing in it for Ponthlyddyn because he was too good, thereby depriving himself of some useful wages. In 1978 he'd scored 283 in a single afternoon match.

> *The first time you face a googly you're going to be in trouble if you've never faced one before.*
>
> **Trevor Bailey**

In his early days with Leicestershire, David Gower twice dropped Ken McEwan in the match against Essex. Soon afterwards, against Derbyshire, he took a fine catch on the boundary from a shot by Ashley Harvey-Walker, tossed the ball up several times and bowed to the crowd, only for the bowler, his captain Ray Illingworth, to roar at him to throw 'the bloody thing back, it's a bloody no-ball.' Not only did Gower's cavortings cost an additional run, but when he returned the ball it went for an overthrow!

After being dismissed for a disappointing 186 in the County Championship match at Bradford in 1977, Northamptonshire reduced the hosts to 239–9, but struggled to finish the innings off. Their captain, the Pakistani all-rounder Mushtaq Mohammad, took 6–63, but Yorkshire's last pair of Geoff Cope and Arthur 'Rocker' Robinson added an important 38 for the last wicket, mainly because Mushtaq's leg-spinners continually beat the bat instead of finding the edge. 'Arthur,' said an exasperated Mushtaq,

'we're beginning to look silly.' It's not my fault,' countered Rocker.' All you have to do is bowl straight.' At one stage, Mushtaq beat the bat with six successive deliveries. Northamptonshire lost by six wickets.

Learie Constantine's Test figures for the West Indies were disappointing to say the least, but there was little doubt about his talent as a fielder, big hitter, and fast bowler. He was a major force in Lancashire League cricket, where one of his team-mates made the mistake of holding two hard slip catches off his bowling. Constantine was so impressed that he insisted on the same player fielding at slip throughout the rest of the season. Years later, when umpire Dickie Bird saw his hands, he thought they looked as if a horse had trampled on them.

In the first Test of the 1895–96 series, new cap Joe Willoughby didn't do himself or South Africa any favours by dismissing the great medium-pacer George Lohmann for a duck in each innings. Lohmann promptly did the same to him, finished with the incredible figures of 15 wickets for 45 runs, and won the match for England within two days.

Don Bradman's batting in the 1930 Tests in England helped Australia regain the Ashes, but he did rather overdo it: 974 runs, still the world record for a single series, at 139.14. As a result, it was the last in which England relied so much on leg-spin (300 overs from Ian Peebles, Walter Robins and Dick Tyldesley). By the next series, Down Under in 1932–33, the accent had shifted firmly towards pace, and Bradman and Co reaped the whirlwind. The Bodyline attack reduced him to something close to mortality, injured several of his team-mates, set Anglo-Oz relations back a few years, and regained the Ashes 4–1.

Dropping all over the world

Catches lose matches (Tests between other countries)

In the second Test of the 1980–81 series in Pakistan, Viv Richards had scored only 5 when he was dropped by Imran Khan, one great player's gift to another. He went on to top-score in each innings (72 and 67) of a low-scoring match which the West Indies won to take the series 1–0.

In the series between the two countries ten years later, Wasim Akram became only the third bowler to take four wickets in five balls in a Test, and missed a hat-trick only because his captain Imran Khan dropped Ian Bishop off a fairly easy chance at mid-on.

Not that Akram was immune to the habit himself. In their series against Australia in 1995–96, Pakistan dropped five catches on the very first day, allowing the hosts to reach 262–4 by close of play. Michael Slater was reprieved three times before he reached 20 (by Salim Malik, Salim Elahi and Ramiz Raja), Saqlain Mushtaq and Akram dropped caught-and-bowled chances from the Waugh twins, and Pakistan lost the match by an innings and the series 2–1.

Little more than a year earlier, the two countries had met in another series. After Pakistan had scored fewer than half their opponents' first innings total of 521 in the second Test, they seemed set to lose at home to Australia for the first time since 1959, especially when their captain Salim Malik edged Jo Angel to his opposite number Mark Taylor in the slips.

In the previous match, Taylor had become the first player to make a pair in his first Test as captain. Now his dropped catch was his seventh in three tour matches, and the most important of the lot. Malik, on 20 at the time, made 237, his highest Test score, as Pakistan scored 537 to save the match.

Mark Taylor finds something he *can* hold on to

Needing to win the third and final Test to draw the series, Australia took a first-innings lead of 82, which should have been considerably, perhaps decisively, greater.

Wicketkeeper Moin Khan, recalled after two years, had never previously scored more than 32 in a Test innings. Now he made 115 not out, but only after being dropped twice, by his opposite number Phil

Emery and Michael Bevan. Australia drew the match and lost the series.

Not the happiest of memories for Emery, making his Test debut at 30: flown in as replacement when Ian Healy broke his thumb, he had to retire himself with a badly bruised thumb!

> *It's remarkable how he can whip it out just before tea.*
>
> **Trevor Bailey**

The South Africans were very much underdogs against Australia in 1931–32, but a good start might have made a big difference. Instead, in the very first innings of the series, they persisted in dropping catches off Don Bradman, the least profitable activity in Test history.

On the first morning, the Don was missed in the slips when he'd made only 11 (by Cyril Vincent) and 15 (Bruce Mitchell), both off left-hander Neville Quinn. He didn't give another chance till he was within two runs of getting out (a missed stumping by captain Horace 'Jock' Cameron) and made 226 to help Australia win by an innings (the next highest score was 76). Bradman's subsequent scores in the series were 112, 2, 167 and 299 not out: 806 runs at an average of 201.50! Australia, unsurprisingly, won 5–0.

The Don accepted this kind of gift from all over the world, turning several of them into double centuries. Pace bowler Commandur Rangachari, who made his Test debut for India in the fourth Test of the 1947–48 series, claimed that his very first ball to the great man was dropped by his captain Lala Amarnath at slip. Bradman, who'd scored only 2 at the time, went on to make 201 and lead Australia to victory by an innings.

A whole generation earlier, against the West Indies in 1930–31, Bradman had been dropped off Learie Constantine when he'd scored only 4 in the third Test, going on to make the 223 that effectively put Australia 3–0 up in the series.

The West Indies lost the 1951–52 series in Australia 4–1 amid a welter of dropped catches, including five in 20 minutes off Alf Valentine alone!

At home against Australia three years later, the West Indies again dropped a string of catches. In the fourth Test, for instance, John (JK) Holt put down two early chances which allowed Colin McDonald and Ray Lindwall to score 46 and 118 respectively. At that time, former West Indian fast bowler Leslie Hylton had been convicted of murdering his wife, hence the cry 'Free Hylton, hang Holt'!

It didn't end there. West Indies lost the 1975–76 series in Australia for a variety of reasons (see STRIKING IT POOR), not least some important dropped catches, including a few at the very start. Opening batsman Alan Turner (81) was reprieved by Lawrence Rowe, Ian Chappell (41) by Viv Richards, both early in their innings. Second time round, Chappell (74) had made only 12 when he was put down (a comfortable return catch) by Inshan Ali. West Indies lost this first Test by eight wickets.

Worse was to come. Down 2–1, West Indies made 355 in the first innings of the fourth Test, a total overhauled by Australia but not by much, thanks to their captain Greg Chappell's typically masterly 182 not out, scored after he was dropped at fourth slip by Keith Boyce off Andy Roberts. West Indies' captain Clive Lloyd said that they might have won if Boyce had held it, and others agreed with *Wisden*: 'If ever a missed catch will go down in history as having lost a series ...'

In the third Test of the 1994–95 home series against New Zealand, South Africa's total of 440 was built round their captain Hansje Cronje's 112, compiled after he'd been dropped by Matthew Hart off Simon Doull. South Africa's win by seven wickets made them only the second side (the first since WG Grace's England in 1888) to win a three-match series after being 1–0 down.

Zimbabwe played their first Test abroad in 1993. After taking the first Indian wicket with the score at 19, they dropped a catch early in Vinod Kambli's innings, an expensive miss to say the least. Kambli went on to make 227, becoming only the third batsman to score back-to-back double centuries in Tests (the others were Hammond and Bradman). India made 536 and won by an innings.

The first Test of Australia's 1972–73 home series against Pakistan was decided by a) a controversial decision in Ian Chappell's favour when he'd made only 5 (his eventual 196 was his highest ever Test score) and b) two dropped catches off Rod Marsh soon after he'd reached double figures. His 118 was the first Test century by a wicketkeeper playing for Australia, whose 585 gave them the match by an innings and set them on the way to winning all three Tests in the series.

India won the fourth Test of the 1978–79 home series against West Indies by just three wickets after taking a narrow first-innings lead, which was built around Gundappa Viswanath's 124 out of only 255 – but they, and especially he, needed a little help. West Indies dropped several catches, including two off Viswanath and another off Anshuman Gaekwad, who stayed with him in a vital partnership of 70.

In the fifth Test, all three Indian century makers – Sunil Gavaskar, Dilip Vengsarkar and Kapil Dev – were dropped before they'd made 30. India won the six-match series 1–0.

> *Fast bowlers are quick ... Just watch this. Admittedly it's in slow motion.*
>
> **Ian Chappell**

In the second Test against Australia in 1969–70, Graeme Pollock had already scored 104 by the time he gave his only chance of the innings, edging John Gleeson to wicketkeeper Brian Taber, who dropped it. Pollock went on to score 274, still the highest individual score in any Test match for South Africa. It wasn't Taber's match: he made only 6 and 0 with the bat.

In the very next Test, Australia dropped catches all through South Africa's first innings. Trevor Goddard was missed in only the second over, Pollock (again) from easy chances at leg slip and mid-off.

In the fourth Test, Barry Richards was dropped off such a simple chance that he'd started to walk to the pavilion and was in danger of being run out! He and Eddie Barlow put on the only century opening partnership of the series. Altogether, three catches were dropped off Gleeson's bowling in the innings. In the second, Richards was dropped three times on his way to 126, including 'the easiest chance I have ever seen put down in Test cricket, a simple looper to Ian Chappell at mid-wicket.' When Ian Redpath dropped yet another chance at fine leg, the ball rolled over the boundary to give Lee Irvine his only Test century in his last international! Not surprisingly, Australia lost all four matches in the series.

On the first morning of the first Test of the 1994–95 series in India, two straightforward chances were put down at slip, by the usually reliable Carl Hooper and Brian Lara, lapses that cost West Indies dear in a low-scoring match, India winning at home for the tenth successive time, only their seventh in 63 Tests between the two countries.

> *The lights are shining quite darkly.*
>
> **Henry Blofeld**

After drawing the first match of the 1993–94 series in Australia, New Zealand had a wretched time of it in the next two. In the second Test, both Australian openers were dropped at slip early in their first innings, Mark Taylor by Blair Pocock, Michael Slater by Mark Greatbatch. They put on 65 for the first wicket, Slater going on to make 168. New Zealand's defeat, by an innings and 222 runs, was the worst in their history.

In the third Test, Mark Waugh made 68 after bring put down by Ken Rutherford and Andrew Jones, who also missed a chance off David Boon (89). Another innings defeat cost New Zealand the series 2–0. They dropped 13 catches in the three-match series, seven off their leading strike bowler Danny Morrison, who took only three wickets (one caught and bowled!) for 422 runs.

Later that winter, against South Africa, it was Waugh's turn to drop a catch, off Gary Kirsten in the second Test. Kirsten went on to top-score with 67 (and make 41 in the second innings) in a low-scoring match, which South Africa won by only five runs.

Needing just 104 to win the first Test of the 1979–80 series, New Zealand struggled to 90–8 before the visiting captain Clive Lloyd dropped a chance offered by Lance Cairns. The West Indies lost by just one wicket, eventually enough to drop the series 1–0, the last they lost until 1995.

One thing Australia needed at the start of the home series against the all-conquering West Indies in 1984–85 was a good start, which they seemed to have managed when they held them to 104–5 on the very first day of the first Test, removing Greenidge, Haynes, Richardson, Richards and Lloyd. Then they let it all slip, dropping seven catches to allow the West Indies to escape to 416, enough to win by an innings and 112 that set up a 3–1 win in the series.

Pakistan won the first Test, and with it the 1978–79 series in New Zealand, after being sent in to bat by Mark Burgess – but the decision might not have backfired if a) pace bowler Brendon Bracewell hadn't been injured in his very first over, and b) a few more catches had been taken. Instead, Sarfraz Nawaz, who scored an important 31 in the first innings, was dropped when he'd made 4 and the great Javed Miandad was let off three times.

First he lobbed the easiest catch imaginable to mid-on, where substitute fielder Robert 'Jumbo' Anderson put it down. Then he was dropped when he'd made 27. Finally, in the second innings, he was put down again when he'd made only 5. He top-scored in each innings with 81 and 160 not out!

In the third and final match of the series, Zaheer Abbas top-scored with 135 after being dropped first ball.

In the second Test of the 1968–69 series Down Under, the West Indies broke through with the Australian score on 14, Richard 'Prof' Edwards taking the wicket on his Test debut. Then they let the match slip through their fingers.

When Ian Chappell had made 10, he was dropped at gully off Edwards, who also had Bill Lawry missed off his bowling. Later, Lawry was put down by Garry Sobers off his own bowling, and Doug Walters was also reprieved early in his innings, dropped by Charlie Davis at slip.

Lawry (205) and Chappell (165) put on 298 for the second wicket, Walters made 76, the unfortunate Edwards took 1–128 in 26 overs, and Australia made 510 to win by an innings.

In the fifth Test, Lawry (on 44 at the time) and Walters (76) were given further lives, going on to score 151 and 242 respectively. West Indies went down by an inhuman 382 runs to lose the series 3–1 after winning the first Test. They dropped a total of 35 catches and Sobers called it the worst fielding side he'd ever seen!

Mind you, the great man was sometimes human himself. In the second Test of the 1970–71 series, Sobers dropped India's debut opening batsman when he'd made 12. The new boy went on to make 65 and 67

not out in India's first ever win against the West Indies, eventually made 774 in the series at an average of 154.80, and 10,122 in all Tests, including a world record 34 centuries, 13 against the West Indies. Sunil Gavaskar did most of it on his own, but he was given a good start in that first series – and not just by Sobers: in his second match, he scored his first Test century after being dropped twice before reaching 50.

New Zealand would surely have beaten India at home in 1975–76 (the series was draw 1–1) if they hadn't lost the first Test, and that thanks to several dropped catches on the first day and two more on the second. Surinder Amarnath, for instance, was missed when he'd made 8, 23 and 71, going on to score 124 and share a partnership of 204 with Gavaskar, who made 116 after being dropped on 40, 43 and 65! India won by eight wickets.

Dropped catches didn't always do Gavaskar so much good. In the very first World Cup match, at Lord's in 1975, India made a pig's ear of their innings against the hosts – a slow pig's ear at that, thanks to Gavaskar, who batted throughout the 60 overs to make 36 not out! Knowing he was in terrible form ('by far the worst I have ever played'), he decided the only remedy was to get out, but the England fielders wouldn't help: they dropped him three times (deliberately?) off simple chances. India lost by 202 runs, still a World Cup record.

With friends like these ...

CB Fry missed the first Test of the 1905 Ashes series because he'd damaged a finger while 'practising on his home ground against a small boy in short trousers.' Well, that's what it says here.

Bruce French was a talented wicketkeeper who suffered his share of injuries. First he was bitten by a dog in the West Indies, then during a practice session in Pakistan he was hit on the head by a ball thrown back by a spectator. As he walked across the hospital grounds to have his eyebrow stitched, he was knocked down by a car. When he woke up after the operation, he banged his head on an overhead light. In the circumstances, winning 16 England caps was no small feat.

In the early 1990s, 'a senior fast bowler' pulled out a handgun in the West Indies changing-room, put it in fellow pace-man Winston Benjamin's mouth, and pulled the trigger. The bullet neither of them knew was there went through Benjamin's cheek, leaving him with a permanent scar.

Garry Sobers' 102 in the fourth Test against England in 1963 was ended by Tony Lock's typically brilliant caught-and-bowled. *Playfair Cricket Monthly* wrote that Sobers 'could not believe the evidence of his own eyes and stood there dazed before he accepted he was out' – but there was more to it than that. Afterwards, he remonstrated (jokingly, he says) with his partner at the time, Joe Solomon, who'd jumped out of the way of his shot, thereby allowing Lock to make the catch!

Just before setting off for the 1987 World Cup in India, umpire Dickie Bird thought nothing could go wrong. He'd 'packed and unpacked my case until my arms ached' and the taxi arrived at the appointed hour to take him to the station.

Unfortunately, so did another vehicle, completely out of the blue, a van from Bassett's, the makers of liquorice allsorts. Hearing of Bird's anxiety about Indian food, they'd sent him a month's supply. No great substitute for a balanced diet perhaps, but welcome all the same.

By the time the box had been unloaded and various formalities completed, Bird arrived at the station with only minutes to spare. Still, no damage done – until he sampled some of Bassett's wares on the train, whereupon they pulled the crown off one of his teeth. He swallowed it, too, so the dentist he visited in India (no gentle soul with the drill, apparently) had to send out for another, adding to Bird's woes.

Soon after having the new crown fitted, he was in conversation with Geoff Boycott, another who looked askance at Indian cuisine. Boycott offered to treat his fellow Yorkshireman to something to eat. What was this, wondered Bird, a banquet based on good old-fashioned English cooking? Not exactly. A bar of fruit and nut. Oh well, if it worked for the famous batsman ...

Bird consumed it without argument – but these items of confectionery had it in for him at the time. One of the pieces of nut pulled out a filling and he was back at the dentist's within the day!

Bird wasn't immune to the tendency of all umpires to get in the way of the cricket ball when they least want to. In 1983, he was hit by a fierce pull from Essex batsman Ken McEwan (when he pulled them, they stayed pulled) and had to be carried off with a badly bruised shin. In the 1985 Ashes series, Graham Gooch drove a ball straight into his ankle bone. And he still has the lump to show where a throw by Salim Malik hit him just behind the knee in 1987.

In the second Test against India in 1952–53, West Indies' powerful middle-order batsman Clyde Walcott was given out lbw for 98 – by his uncle Harold!

Ray East was probably better known for his comic antics than for his undoubted talent as a spinner, and many of his routines lit up some dull days on the county circuit. Others, one or two, backfired.

Against the touring Indians in 1982, Essex batsman Brian Hardie had reached 161 when East pretended to go through for a single on tiptoe. Hardie made the mistake of responding, and was run out by Madan Lal – one short of his highest ever first-class score. East's apology in the changing room was just enough to save his bacon.

During the 1983–84 tour of the Caribbean, Australian batsman Dean Jones saw some of his team-mates taking their fielding practice in the sea, throwing the ball to one another while standing up to their necks in the Antiguan swell. Eager to join in (or at least to escape the heat of the beach), Jones dashed over the sand (he was one of the great cover fielders) and performed a spectacular dive, only to land face first in sand barely covered by water: the other players were kneeling in it!

Steve Waugh (left) keeping Dean Jones out of hot water

They swore they could actually feel the impact of Jones hitting the beach. After lifting him out, they took him to hospital – then spent the next two weeks contributing to his recovery from a stiff neck by calling out 'Hey Deano' and watching him turn his head sharply.

In 1947 England won the second Test against South Africa, whose captain Alan Melville did well to score a century in the first innings: he had a black eye after being hit by a throw from one of his own players while fielding.

Similarly, New Zealand captain Geoff Howarth had some excuse for being out without scoring in the second innings of the third Test in England in 1983: he'd been hit in the face during net practice that morning. New Zealand lost the match, and the series 2–1.

Just before the start of his first Test, against South Africa in 1932, Australian leg-spinner Bill O'Reilly was taken aside by one of the selectors, 'Chappie' Dwyer, and told that players and umpires were starting to say that he appealed too much for lbw. The new boy listened and nodded, and in his very first over in Test cricket, held his tongue when the ball hit Jim Christy's pad.

Two overs later, the umpire, George Hele, asked him if he ever appealed for lbws. What, said Bill, was it out then? Well, replied the official, it might have been a good idea to ask …

That was the first and last time the fiery O'Reilly didn't appeal in a Test match. He bowled Christy just to make sure, took four wickets in the match (Australia won by 10 wickets) and 144 in all Tests, quite a few by lbw.

Playing for Queensland against the England touring team in 1962–63, West Indies' famous fast bowler Wes Hall got one to rear up so savagely that it broke the jaw of his wicketkeeper, Wally Grout, who had to miss the first three Tests of the series.

During the 1972 Ashes series, England captain Ray Illingworth asked Geoff Boycott to needle John Snow a little, to stoke him into the right mood to bowl fast. Presumably he believed Boycott was particularly good at this sort of thing, and so it proved: Snow was so annoyed that he took it personally; in the next county match against Yorkshire, he reacted to Boycott's 'playful' tap on the shin by knocking him off his feet, then sent down a bouncer which broke a bone in Boycott's hand, keeping him out of the first B&H Cup final!

Yorkshire's 12th man AC Williams came on as substitute for Leicestershire in 1919 – and took four catches against his own team.

England 12th man Mike Denness came on as substitute for the Rest of the World in 1970 – and held a catch to help Eddie Barlow take a hat-trick.

Practising in the nets before the first Test of the 1911–12 Ashes series, England's Bill Hitch hit the ball so hard so often that he broke his bat, which gave him and wicketkeeper Herbert Strudwick a good laugh – until Strudwick discovered that it was his own bat, 'with which he would not have parted for a fortune.' Strudwick knew that no good could come of it, and sure enough: after scoring only 12 runs in the match, which England lost, he injured his back so badly that he missed the remaining four Tests, which England won!

Jeff Thomson's bad-boy image wasn't always entirely of his own making. In the infamous match against Sri Lanka in the 1975 World Cup, he hit Sunil Wettimuny on the chest, then almost immediately on the instep with a yorker, which made the unfortunate batsman hop about outside his crease. The ball, meanwhile, rebounded down the wicket towards Thommo, who would have left it alone but for the exhortations of his team-mates. After ignoring them to begin with, he took their advice, picked the ball up, threw down the stumps, and appealed loudly to the umpire.

'But no other bastard's moved. They all stood there with their arms folded! They'd done me stone cold on purpose.'

George Dawkes kept wicket in County Championship matches from 1937 to 1961. His first match was for Leicestershire at Old Trafford when he was only 16. As the team reached the changing room, senior professional George Geary found that he'd left his case back at the hotel and sent the team junior to fetch it. When he returned, the gateman didn't believe anyone so young could be playing in the match, and refused him entry, so Dawkes climbed the gate, only to be apprehended by the local plod.

After explaining that this was George Geary's case, he was made to open it. There were sandwiches inside. The team had played its initiation prank on the new boy. Dawkes had to pay part of his match fee to go in and watch himself play. And it rained all day.

When Dennis Lillee was a new boy in the Western Australia side, he travelled from Brisbane to Sydney by train, sharing a sleeper compartment with John Inverarity, who informed him that as the junior player he'd have to take the top bunk, which to Lillee's horror looked barely wide enough for a suitcase. Bravely, he hauled himself up onto it, much to the amusement of Inverarity. The top bunk, of course, had to be pulled out from the wall. Lillee, who'd never seen a sleeper compartment before, was trying to fit himself into the luggage rack.

Even after a few years' experience, our Dennis was occasionally a bail short of a full set of stumps. During one Test match, he went in as nightwatchman and survived the final few balls of the day. The following morning, his captain Ian Chappell congratulated him and told him to resume his normal place in the batting order. Fine, said Lillee, and didn't hurry back from net practice for the start of play.

The umpires had already gone out onto the field when Chappell realised Lillee had taken him seriously (once you've gone in to bat, of course, you can't simply drop out and wait to bat later on). He had to send someone to fetch Lillee from the nets to continue his innings. 'Boy, was I gullible.'

When Essex slow left-armer Ray East was having trouble with his car, a friendly passing constable got into the vehicle to lend a hand – and succeeded only in ripping the handbrake out. However, the real blunder in this case was made by East, whose sarcasm ('I rather overplayed the part of the indignant innocent') led to the officer smelling his breath, 'and I said goodbye to my driving licence.'

> *Over now to Old John Arlott at Trafford.*
>
> **Rex Alston**

A four-legged fiend ...
It's said that during the knock-up before a match in Bedfordshire in 1955, a player hit the ball so far into a nearby field that it couldn't be retrieved before being investigated by a cow, which liked the shiny red thing so much that it ate it. It was the club's only ball and the match had to be abandoned.

... and some bird brains.
A group of ex-pats who formed a club near Cannes should probably have known better than to site their pitch next to an ostrich farm. The short boundaries didn't help. The leggy omnivores enjoyed the fours and sixes even more than the batsmen.

Needing four to win in a club match in 1991, Ellis Lyppiatt had his shot stopped on the boundary – by a duck.

Batting in a Melbourne club match in 1995, Blair Sellers had one of his drives stopped by a seagull, turning a certain four into a two. He was out for 98.

Who needs friends?

... when you can undo it yourself

If Fred Titmus' bowling was a little below par in one of his Tests in Australia, the flesh-coloured plaster on his right hand might have had something to do with it. He'd injured his thumb falling out of bed. No jokes required; his team-mates have already made them.

Test seamer Eiulf Peter 'Buster' Nupen was regarded as one of the best bowlers ever seen on South African matting. Who knows how much better his Test figures of 50 wickets at 35.76 might have been if he'd had two eyes? He lost one as a young man, while knocking two hammers together. Don't ask.

Derek Randall's career as one of the game's best-loved clowns began early, certainly as soon as he'd made his first major innings in international cricket, 88 in a one-dayer against the West Indies in 1976. Leaving the interview backwards, as if deferring to royalty, he put his foot through a hole in the floor of the stand and had to tug it free, muttering apologies, before limping into the distance with one boot in his hand, giving birth to a legend.

The defeat by India in 1986 won't be among David Gower's treasured memories. It cost him the England captaincy for the first time and kept him out of the following Test, this after he'd injured a shoulder by colliding with a boundary wall.

In a first-class career that lasted 15 seasons, Australian Test batsman Ian Redpath took only 13 wickets – so he could be forgiven for leaping in the air to celebrate taking another in one of Kerry Packer's World Series matches. When he came down to earth, he injured himself so badly he couldn't finish the game.

During the second Test in Australia in 1930–31, West Indian fielder Edward 'Barto' Bartlett caught Alan Kippax at mid-on but crushed a finger against his boot in the process and couldn't bat in the match. The West Indies lost by an innings.

Before the third Test against Pakistan in 1987, off-spinner John Emburey recommended that England play only one spinner on the Headingley wicket. His captain Mike Gatting agreed – and left Emburey out!

Like everyone else, future England captain Percy Chapman knew of CB Fry's all-round sporting exploits (England caps at cricket and football, world long jump record, etc) and looked forward to his first view of the great Renaissance man. This took place at a country house cricket match, during which Fry emerged with a tea tray, hurdled the low wooden fence round the boundary, and fell flat on his face in a flurry of chinaware. 'My first view of the great athlete,' mused Percy amid the porcelain.

After batting for three hours to make a century against Victoria in 1990–91, Allan Lamb decided to run a few miles back to the hotel that evening. Whether this was his own idea or the result of Graham Gooch's love affair with physical preparation isn't clear, but it was probably asking too much of the legs of Lamb: he damaged a calf muscle so badly that he had to miss the second Test. Since he was the team's in-form batsman, this was quite a loss. England went down by eight wickets to fall 2–0 behind in a series they lost 3–0.

Dayle Hadlee had a great deal less success in Test cricket than his younger brother (71 wickets at 33.64 to Sir Richard's 431 at 22.29) but luck played its part in that. He never really recovered from persistent back trouble, for example. Mind you, he brought some of it on himself. In fact, he had a reasonable career for someone who lost part of a toe when he ran over his own foot with a lawnmower!

At the higher levels of sport, Tony Jorden was ocasionally somewhat accident prone. While fielding for Essex, he chased round the boundary, tried to stop the ball with his foot, succeeded only in kicking it over the boundary for four, and twisted his ankle so badly that he could take no further part in the match.

Better known as a rugby union full-back, Jorden made his international debut in Paris in 1970 when England were thrashed 35–13, worth 47–17 today.

Wicked keepers

At Edgbaston in June 1994, Durham wicketkeeper Chris Scott put down a chance so straightforward that the Warwickshire batsman had actually started his walk back to the pavilion. Scott turned to his slips and made one of the great understatements in cricket folklore: 'Jesus Christ, I suppose he'll go on and get a century now.'

Actually he went on to get five in that innings alone: Brian Lara's 501 not out was the first quintuple century in first-class cricket. 'I'm struggling to see the funny side,' said Scott, 'but I suppose in time it'll be good to know I was part of history.' His dropped catch was the most expensive in all first-class cricket, costing 483 runs.

In the first Test of the 1990 series, Kiran More fumbled an easy chance offered by the England opener and captain, who was on 36 at the time. The dropped catch cost India 297 runs and the match. Graham Gooch's 333, the highest ever individual score at Lord's, was joined by his 123 in the second innings to make a personal total of 456, the record for any player in a single Test. Gooch also ended the match by running out Sanjeev Sharma to give England victory by 247 runs. They took the series 1–0.

In the final Test of the 1995 series in the West Indies, Steve Waugh had made 43 when he edged the ball to wicketkeeper Courtney Browne. Although he had to move towards first slip to take it, it was as simple a chance as Test cricket allows, waist-high

and not very wide. Browne was making his Test debut. He dropped the catch.

Waugh went on to make exactly 200, his highest Test score, the bulwark of Australia's 531 which gave them a first-innings lead of 266. They took the match by an innings to become the first side to win a series against West Indies since 1980 (ending a record run of 27 series plus two one-off Tests) and the first to win one in the Caribbean since 1973.

In early 1996 Waugh was dropped when he'd made 37 on the first day of the final Test against Sri Lanka, who regretted the lapse when he went on to make 170, his highest score in a home Test. The Sri Lankans lost all three matches in the series.

Ray Illingworth had little help from his wicketkeepers against Lancashire in 1975, Roger Tolchard missing a chance off David Lloyd, then his replacement Barry Dudleston stumping the same batsman only for the bails to jump up and land back in their sockets. In front of a furious Illingworth, Lloyd made an unbeaten century and Leicestershire were held to a draw.

Jack Russell's been out of the England team almost as often as he's been in. Undeservedly so, too – though he's had his forgettable moments in the past. The worst? Probably against the West Indies in 1989–90.

England built on their surprise win in the first Test by dominating the third (the second had been completely rained off), reducing the hosts to 29–5 in the first innings. They'd barely reached 50 when Devon Malcolm found the edge of Gus Logie's bat and Russell threw himself in front of first slip.

The dropped catch was absolutely critical. Logie, on 17 at the time, made 98, virtually half his side's mediocre total of 199. Needing only 151 in their second innings to win the match, England reached 120–5 before being frustrated by bad light and the delaying tactics of Desmond Haynes, which wouldn't have been of any use if Logie had gone early in the first innings. Russell's miss cost England a 2–0 lead with two matches to go: a definite share of the series and a great chance of winning one against the West Indies for the first time since 1969. Instead, they lost it 2–1.

At Lord's in 1926, England's famous keeper Herbert Strudwick dropped Australian opener Warren Bardsley when he'd made only 6, then gave him two more lives in the same innings. Bardsley's eventual 193 made him (still makes him) the oldest player to score a century for Australia: 43 years 201 days.

A tale of two keepers in the 1896 Ashes series. England won it 2–1 but might have made it a whitewash if one wicketkeeper ('Dick' Lilley) hadn't dropped the other (James J Kelly) off Tom Richardson at the very end of the second Test: *The Times* called it 'an irreparable blunder.' Australia won by three wickets.

England had taken a 1–0 lead in the series at Lord's, where Australia had dropped several catches, 'Kelly proving especially fallible'. In the same match, Australia's captain Harry Trott scored his only Test century after being dropped on 98 – by Lilley off Richardson!

With the 1930 Ashes series level at 1–1, the final Test was played to a finish – and

England seemed to have done enough to win it when they scored 405 in the first innings, only to be undermined by dropped catches off Australia's first three batsmen – all by their vocal and talented little wicketkeeper George Duckworth.

He missed Australia's captain Bill Woodfull on 6 off Maurice Tate, big Bill Ponsford on 45, again off Tate, and – the ultimate horror – Don Bradman on 82 off Wally Hammond. Woodfull made 54, Ponsford 110, Bradman a typical 232 (his 974 runs is still the record for any Test series). Australia scored 695, won by an innings and 39, and regained the Ashes on their captain's 33rd birthday.

Earlier in the series, Duckworth had done Woodfull another favour, missing a stumping chance when he'd scored 52 on his way to 155 in a partnership of 231 with Bradman.

It's said that on the 1928–29 tour of Australia poor George's vision was impaired by the flies who arrived mob-handed to investigate the raw steak he'd inserted in his gloves to protect his hands!

> *Yes, he's a very good cricketer.*
> *Pity he's not a better batter*
> *or bowler.*
>
> **Tom Graveney**

Australia's famous win at Headingley in 1948 (they were set a world record 404 to win) was helped by six dropped catches (*Blunders Vol.1*) and especially two missed stumpings by Godfrey Evans.

Arthur Morris had made 32 when he was stranded by Denis Compton's leg-spin, only for Evans to miss the chance. Don Bradman (here we go again) was on 108 when Godders should have stumped him off Jim Laker. Morris (182) and Bradman (173 not out) made almost all the runs between them as Australia won by seven wickets on their way to taking the series 4–0.

Two winters earlier, Evans had dropped a catch early in Bradman's comeback innings for South Australia against the MCC, allowing the great man to find his form in time for the Test series. Later, in the 1950–51 series, Evans' missed stumping off Ian Johnson allowed Australia to take a lead of 136 in the third Test, win it by an innings, and retain the Ashes.

Evans recovered from all this to become an integral part of many successful England teams, winning 91 caps (a world record at the time) and becoming the first player to make 200 Test dismissals. The last of these were in the second Test of the 1959 home series against India, who were dismissed for 168 and 165 and lost by eight wickets – but Evans also missed four stumping chances in the first innings (he was 38 and not as spectacularly agile as he'd once been) and didn't play for England again.

> *We have just enough time for some more balls from Rex Alston.*
>
> **Brian Johnston**

India, needing to win the last Test to share the 1969–70 home series, reduced Australia to 82–4 in the first innings. Doug Walters had made only four when Bishan Bedi beat him in the flight to give Farokh Engineer an easy stumping chance. He missed it and Walters made 102 to give Australia a first innings lead.

On the third morning, Australia crashed to 24–6 then 57–7, but Ian Redpath was dropped twice by Engineer, top-scored with 63, and helped Australia to a 77-run win that sealed the series 3–1.

Arthur Shrewsbury's name was written on the 1886 Lord's Test. The Australians must have realised it once they'd dropped him at slip when he'd scored only a single, then again at short leg off George Giffen. In between, when he'd made 35, he should have been stumped by Affie Jarvis, again off Giffen. Shrewsbury's eventual 164, an England record at the time, was easily the highest score in a total of 353 that was enough to win the Test by an innings. Australia lost the three-match series 3–0.

Seven years later, against the same country, on the same ground, Shrewsbury made 106 on the way to becoming the first batsman to score 1,000 Test runs – but again he was dropped twice, again the second time off Giffen!

Set 314 to win the first Test of the 1994 home series against Australia, Pakistan still needed 56 with the last pair at the crease. Inzamam-ul-Haq and number 11 Mushtaq Ahmed inched closer to the target until only three were needed, whereupon a ball from Shane Warne went down the leg side and beat not only Inzamam but wicketkeeper Ian Healy, who missed a difficult stumping and let the ball through for four byes.

Pakistan, who haven't lost at home to Australia since 1959, maintained their unbeaten run in Karachi, became the seventh team to win a Test by a single wicket (this improbable partnership of 57 was the highest to win such a match) and drew the next two matches to take the series 1–0.

Much of Len Hutton's 364 for England against Australia in 1938 was compiled at the expense of leg-spinner Leslie O'Brien 'Chuck' Fleetwood-Smith, whose single wicket in the innings cost 298. Hutton's total was a world record at the time, Fleetwood-Smith's still is. Mind you, things would have been rather different if Ben Barnett hadn't missed a chance to stump Hutton off luckless Chuck when he'd made 40.

Rarely can a wicketkeeper have contributed so much to his team's troubles as poor Syed Kirmani in the West Indies in 1976. He'd kept well in New Zealand earlier in the winter, did just as well in Australia in 1977–78 and was still playing for India in 1986 (198 Test dismissals in all) but these were difficult early days. Indeed, *Wisden* claimed that 'hardly a day passed without the Indians wishing that Farokh Engineer was at hand.' Kirmani committed 'the bulk of India's fielding errors,' including important missed stumpings off Roy Fredericks in the first Test and Viv Richards (who made 130) in the second. That wasn't the only time he let the great man off the hook, which wasn't to be recommended. Richards averaged 92.66 in the series (Kirmani only 11.66) to help beat India 2–1.

Arjuna Ranatunga's second Test century for Sri Lanka, against Pakistan in 1986, owed a good deal to dropped catches by Javed Miandad, Salim Malik and wicketkeeper Zulqarnain, who was never capped again. Sri Lanka drew the match and the series.

Even the best don't always get it right. Rodney Marsh's 355 Test victims are still the world record, but in his first series, against England in 1970–71, he dropped so many chances (three in his first Test alone) that he was known as Irongloves.

Marsh took the world record from Alan Knott. Many years earlier, in his very first match for a Kent XI, Knott had been so shocked to be chosen behind the stumps (he was on the books as a spinner) that he dropped the first catch that ever came to him!

Later, playing for England when they needed to win the fifth Test to share the 1972–73 series, he couldn't stop India compiling a first innings of 448. Gundappa

Among the misses were 269 Test dismissals. Alan Knott's laughing

Viswanath had made 39 when he was beaten by Jackie Birkenshaw's off-spin, only for Knott to miss the catch as well as the stumping! Viswanath's 113 helped India draw the match and win the series.

In 1992, after throwing away their chance of beating Australia for the first time (see STRIKING IT POOR), Sri Lanka had a second bite in the following Test. Second, third and fourth, to be exact, two of them by wicket-keeper Romesh Kaluwitharana, who'd

scored a century in the previous Test (his first) but here bungled an easy stumping chance off Dean Jones, then missed the same batsman again off the same bowler, Don Anurasiri.

Jones, who'd also been dropped by Roshan Mahanama when he'd scored only a single in the first innings, and at second slip by Chandika Hathurusinghe in the second, made 77 and 100 not out to help Australia draw the match. They won the series 1–0.

> *You've just missed Barry Richards hitting one of Basil D'Oliveira's balls clean out of the ground.*
>
> **Brian Johnston**

After scoring 228 (a first-innings deficit of 117) in the first Test of the 1986–87 home series against the West Indies, New Zealand sank to 20–2 in their second innings but were saved by a partnership of 241 between their premier batsmen, John Wright and Martin Crowe, who were both given a little help.

When he'd made 17, Crowe was put down at short-leg by Gus Logie off Courtney Walsh. Wright survived a good run-out chance, then wicketkeeper Jeff Dujon dropped him off Walsh on 44 and Joel Garner on 53. Wright made 138, Crowe 119, as New Zealand held out for the draw.

In the third and final Test, New Zealand built on the advantage given to them by Richard Hadlee and Ewen Chatfield, who dismissed West Indies for exactly 100, by declaring at 332–9, a total based on a partnership of 156 between Crowe and his brother Jeff, both of whom were dropped: Martin twice, Jeff by Dujon when he was on 16. New Zealand's win gave them a share of the series.

Replying to the West Indies' meagre 164 in the first Test of the 1989–90 series, England reached 132–3 soon after lunch on the second day – then Dujon dropped Allan Lamb off Ian Bishop. Lamb's 132 was the backbone of a total of 364 that gave England their first win over the Windies since 1974. In the last Test, Dujon dropped Rob Bailey while throwing the ball up in triumph.

England took two uncapped wicketkeepers on the 1907–08 tour of Australia, picking Dick Young for the first Test even though he was commonly considered an inferior keeper to Joe Humphries, who was famous for his skill in taking fast bowling while standing up to the wicket. Opening the batting in each innings, Young scored only 13 and 3 as well as missing 'a couple of critical catches,' which made all the difference: Australia won by only two wickets. Humphries replaced him in the second Test, which England won.

Paul Gibb was a bespectacled introverted wicketkeeper-batsman who was chosen for the trip to Australia just after the Second World War partly because he'd averaged 59.12 in the series in South Africa just before the war, starting with 93 and 106 on his Test debut.

But he'd played purely as an opener in those matches, Les Ames doing the wicketkeeping. In the first match of the 1946–47 Ashes series, Gibb had to do both jobs, and didn't manage either particularly well, scoring 13 and 11 and dropping an easy chance off Colin McCool, who went on to score 95. England lost by an innings and Gibb didn't play Test cricket again.

Playing for Barbados in the vital Shell Shield match against Guyana in 1966, Garry Sobers had scored less than 40 when he went down the pitch to his opposite number as captain, Test off-spinner Lance Gibbs, missed, and carried on walking towards the pavilion – then suddenly realised the wicketkeeper was on the ground groping for the ball.

Gibbs made it plain that he wasn't best pleased with the miscreant, a youngster called Jackman in his first Shield season, especially when Sobers went on to make 204 (before the luckless Jackman caught him at last) and help Barbados win the match by an innings on their way to taking the title.

After drawing the first Test of the 1965–66 series, England took a first-innings lead of exactly 200 in the second, then reduced Australia to 176–4. Soon afterwards, with Australia only four runs ahead, one of Bob Barber's leg-breaks beat Peter Burge, only for Jim Parks to miss the stumping. Burge went on to score 120 and save the game, Australia to eventually draw the series and keep the Ashes.

After losing the first match of the 1992–93 series in the West Indies, Pakistan won the toss before the second and Wasim Akram put the West Indies in, which has often been the done thing in Barbados. The move failed (West Indies made 455) but that had something to do with wicketkeeper Moin Khan dropping opener Phil Simmons twice in the same over, just the kind of start to make heads drop. Simmons scored 87, Pakistan lost the Test and the series.

During the pivotal third Test of the 1932–33 Bodyline series, Australian wicketkeeper Bert Oldfield deflected a ball from Harold Larwood into his face and couldn't take his place behind the stumps in England's second innings.

Meanwhile his opposite number Les Ames had been having trouble justifying his reputation as a wicketkeeper-batsman. Coming in at number 7 this time, he was beaten all ends up by leg-spinner Clarrie Grimmett, only for Oldfield's stand-in Vic Richardson to miss the easy stumping. Ames escaped to make an important 69 and help England take a 2–1 lead in a series they won 4–1.

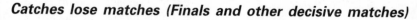

Dropping the Cup

Catches lose matches (Finals and other decisive matches)

Defending a total of 200 in the 1995 NatWest Trophy final, the one thing Northants didn't want to do against Warwickshire was drop catches. In the event, they missed four chances, including at least two which were clear-cut.

Dominic Ostler had scored 11 when he was put down by Alan Fordham at long leg, Roger Twose only 6 when David Capel missed a simple chance at slip. Ostler made 45, Twose 68, the highest scores in the innings, as Warwickshire won (by just four wickets) the only trophy to have eluded them the previous season.

Sad irony for Fordham, man of the match in the 1992 final for his top score of 91 – after being dropped on 18 (*Blunders Vol.1*).

Earlier that season, in the B&H Cup final, Kent's Sri Lankan batsman Aravinda de Silva was made man of the match for his 112, which wasn't enough to stop Lancashire winning by 35 runs – and didn't really make up for his lapse very early in the match: the dropped catch that allowed Mike Atherton to go on and score 93.

> *It's a catch he would have held 99 times out of 1,000.*
>
> **Henry Blofeld**

The 1968 Gillette Cup final brought together the two same finalists as in 1964. This time, replying to a reasonable Sussex total of 214–7, Warwickshire seemed to have left themselves too much to do at 155–6, but then their captain Alan Smith was dropped twice on his way to scoring 39 not out which made him man of the match. Warwickshire got home by four wickets and Sussex, who won the first two Gillette finals (1963 and 1964) didn't lift the trophy again till 1978.

Gloucestershire won the 1973 Gillette Cup, their first major honour since 1877, but were fortunate to reach the final. In the semi, their great South African all-rounder Mike Procter was dropped off the first ball he received from Brian Brain, and again when he'd made 18. His 101 and Sadiq Mohammad's 45 (after he'd also been dropped) were vital in Gloucestershire's win by only five runs.

Ordinarily, dropping a catch off Robin Jackman's bat wouldn't necessarily be a disaster (he was an England seamer not renowned for his strokeplay) but it made all the difference in the 1974 Gillette Cup final. Having scored only 6 when he was reprieved, he went on to make another 30. Surrey's winning margin over Leicestershire was 27 runs.

In the final the following year, Middlesex's last chance of defending a low total of 180 disappeared when Lancashire were 73–2 with 37 overs already gone. Clive Lloyd, whose 73 made him man of the match, hit a ball from Fred Titmus waist-high and straight to mid-on, where Mike J Smith put it down. Middlesex lost by seven wickets.

At the end of the 1978 season, Somerset famously lost both the Gillette Cup final and the Sunday League within 24 hours or so. Needing a tie in their last League match, at home to Essex, they went down by just two runs. Easily the top score in Essex's innings of 190 was the 76 not out of their captain Keith Fletcher, who'd been dropped by wicketkeeper Derek Taylor off Graham Burgess from the first ball he received. Ironically, one of Taylor's middle names was Somerset, who won both titles the following year.

Before that, they had suffered the same frustration in their last Sunday League match of 1976. Needing to beat Glamorgan to take the first title in their history, they lost by a single run after their captain Brian Close, one of the great fielders but now 46 years old, had dropped a catch which allowed Alan Jones (on 21 at the time) to score 70, easily the top score in the match. Close actually held the catch, then let the ball slip out of his hands, the closest he ever came (and they don't come much closer) to picking up a trophy for Somerset.

Kent lost the 1971 Gillette Cup for a number of reasons, not least the famous catch by Lancashire captain Jackie Bond which ended Asif Iqbal's dashing 73. Earlier, Asif had inexplicably changed the ball while he was bowling, which his captain Mike Denness didn't notice: 'It proved to be a vital factor,' the new ball being harder and easier to hit away. Above all, perhaps, Kent's West Indian Test all-rounder Bernard Julien dropped 'a vital catch' then, like Alan Knott, was run out when 'a little bit of panic crept into our later batsmen.' Kent lost by 24 runs.

Ken McEwan had made 16 in the 1985 NatWest final when he was dropped by

Leg stretches for Chris Broad – but it was the hands that needed flexing

Chris Broad off Kevin Saxelby. His eventual 46 not out more than made the difference: Essex beat Nottinghamshire by one run.

Chasing Northants' 228 in the 1987 NatWest final, Notts lost half the side for 84 but were saved by a spectacular innings from their great New Zealand seamer Richard Hadlee, who hit 70 not out but might have been caught three times in the same over from Richard Williams, especially if Allan Lamb hadn't lost sight of the ball as it was crossing the midwicket boundary for six! Hadlee was made man of the match, which Notts won by 3 wickets with three balls to spare.

Northants' attempt to defend a total of only 171 in the 1990 NatWest final ended when

Curtly Ambrose at mid-on missed a chance given by Lancashire's dangerous one-day specialist Neil Fairbrother off Nick Cook. Fairbrother, on only 6 at the time, was far and away his side's top scorer (81 in 68 balls) as Lancashire became the first county to win both Lord's finals in the same year.

In the 1996 Benson & Hedges Cup semi-final, Fairbrother had made only 10 when he was dropped at slip by Yorkshire's captain David Byas. The additional 49 runs Fairbrother went on to make were quite important, to say the least: Lancashire, the Cup holders, won by one wicket off the last ball of the match.

> *It was a good tour to break my teeth in.*
>
> **Bernard Thomas**

Replying to Nottinghamshire's 223 in the 1984 B&H Cup semi-final, Lancashire were indebted to their 21-year-old opener Mark Chadwick, who was called in when Alan Ormrod was injured, and scored 87 after being dropped four times. Lancashire went on to win the final without Chadwick, who was made man of the match in the only B&H Cup match he ever played for the county!

The catch dropped by Giles Ecclestone off the opposition captain Peter Roebuck effectively decided the 1994 Minor Counties Championship final. Roebuck's 33 not out gained the extra bonus point by which Devon beat Cambridgeshire 3–2. That same season, Ecclestone won the *Daily Telegraph*'s national fantasy cricket competition!

Needing to win their final fixture, against Surrey, to win the 1920 County Championship, Middlesex were indebted to a late-order 53 by their England all-rounder Greville Stevens, who was dropped at slip off Bill Hitch when he'd made only 7. Middlesex won the title in their captain Plum Warner's last county match.

Very little grey cells

On the field ...

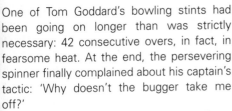

One of Tom Goddard's bowling stints had been going on longer than was strictly necessary: 42 consecutive overs, in fact, in fearsome heat. At the end, the persevering spinner finally complained about his captain's tactic: 'Why doesn't the bugger take me off?'

Let's be kind and blame it on the heat. The Gloucestershire skipper Basil Allen had left the field hours earlier, handing the captaincy to Goddard himself!

When Brian Lara made his world record score against Durham in 1994, everyone associated with him celebrated – except perhaps one of his sponsors, Joe Bloggs Jeans. Lara's total matched the name of a leading rival brand: Levi's 501! As a company spokesman said, 'It would have been better if he'd scored one run more or less.'

Although Lara scored 87 and 145, the fourth Test of the 1995 series in England was Dominic Cork's match, eight wickets (including the first Test hat-trick for England since 1957) following a maiden Test fifty. However, he had a little help.

His first scoring stroke of the third day, an all-run four, should actually have cost him his wicket: he removed a bail while playing the shot. But the West Indies fielders either didn't see it or didn't know what to do with it. They didn't appeal, umpire Cyril Mitchley replaced the bail, Cork (who wasn't yet in double figures) moved on to his 56 not out and his hat-trick, England won by six wickets and went on to share the series.

Matches with a theme were popular last century. One-armed against one-legged, that kind of dubious thing. Smokers v Non-Smokers was a particular crowd-puller; in fact, an 1887 edition produced what was then the highest score in first-class cricket: 803 by the Nons.

During another of these, the suspicion was levelled at the Non-Smokers that they were playing something of a ringer, the giant Australian Test player George Bonnor, who went out to play with a huge cigar in his mouth!

Recalled to the England team for the one-day series against India in 1990, David Gower scored 50 in the first match, then hit six fours in an innings of 25 in the second. When he refused a single, he watched the wicketkeeper throw the ball towards the stumps at his end – then realised that it really would have been better if he'd been standing in his crease instead of well outside it. The run-out was 'incredibly dozy, even by my standards'.

This was the kind of thing that didn't endear Gower to Sgt-Major Gooch – but the latter was capable of similar slips. Gooch had as miserable a time as anyone in India in 1992–93 (*Blunders Vol.1*), setting the tone with his dismissal in the second innings of the first Test, when he played a shot then put his foot back on the line, not behind it. Wicketkeeper Kiran More couldn't believe his luck, Gooch was stumped for 18, England lost every Test on the tour.

During the first one-day international against Australia in 1989, wicketkeeper Ian Healy injured his knee while batting and had to use Dean Jones as a runner. However, when Healy, Jones and the other batsman Tim May all completed a run together, the England captain David Gower politely enquired if Healy's need for a runner was as dire as he'd intimated. The umpires sent Jones back to the pavilion and the red-faced Healy continued his innings, after which he faced the fury of his captain Allan Border, who worried that his first-choice 'keeper might have aggravated the injury just before the Test series.

During a County Championship match in 1982, Middlesex and England wicketkeeper Paul Downton, in pain with a pulled hamstring, forgot he had a runner, and was run out as he hopped to the other end.

> *An interesting morning,*
> *full of interest.*
>
> **Jim Laker**

Jimmy Southerton, the oldest Test debutant of all time (49 in 1877) once walked back to the pavilion even though the umpire had given him not out, and went into the scorebook as 'Retired, thinking he was out, 0.'

A similar fate befell Western Australia opener Graeme Watson in a Sheffield Shield match against Queensland in 1971–72; but at least he'd scored 145.

Cec Parkin was a classy off-spinner who took 32 Test wickets for England, the best-known comedian in county cricket, and something of an outspoken eccentric who was eventually his own worst enemy. His outburst in a newspaper, claiming that he should have been given the new ball in the first Test against South Africa in 1924, put an end to his international career.

Once, while batting during a match in Adelaide, the story goes that Parkin bent to pick a stray piece of grass off the wicket. When it blew back, he picked it up again. And again. And so on until the South Australian fielders eventually took pity and told him that he was wasting his energy: he'd been trying to pick up a grasshopper!

It's said that a cricket teacher at a school in Eastbourne instructed his pupils in the noble art of pinching quick singles by dint of enthusiastic backing-up. Unfortunately, his charges doesn't seem to have been too good at thinking on their feet: in 1956, seven of them were run out in one innings!

It happens at higher levels of the game. During their 1947–48 tour, India played a match (not a Test) against a strong Australian XI at Sydney, during the course of which the famous all-rounder Vinoo Mankad warned Bill Brown that he was constantly backing up too far at the non-striker's end. Brown either forgot or ignored the warning, whereupon Mankad ran him out for 30 as India went on to win the match.

No quick learner, our Bill. In the second Test, also played at the SCG, again he went a-wanderin', again Mankad ran him out, this time for 18. It was the first time this form of dismissal had taken place in a Test match. Even in the 1970s, it was still known as a 'Mankad' in Australia. Brown was dropped for the next two Tests of the series. Recalled for the fifth, he was run out for 99!

Much the same thing happened at Adelaide during the fourth Test in 1968–69, Charlie Griffith, West Indies' controversial fast bowler, running out Australian batsman Ian Redpath with no prior warning. Bad sportsmanship, said some. My own fault, said Redpath: 'Like an idiot, I decided to go walkabout.' Team-mate and future Test captain Ian Chappell agreed: 'He sometimes seemed to be in a daze at the bowler's end, charging down the wicket without watching the bowler's hand.'

Did someone subsequently have a word with big bad Charlie? In the following Test, the last of the series, Redpath again backed up too far, this time more than once – but instead of being run out, he was warned by Wes Hall then by Griffith himself, let-offs which allowed him to reach his first Test century (he'd been out for 0 in the first innings) and help Australia win the match and seal the series.

Although BJT Bosanquet's googlies helped win two Ashes series, he didn't take so many Test wickets (25 in total) that he could afford to turn any down, which is in effect what he did at Sydney in 1904, when his 6–51 would have been 7 if he'd bothered to appeal after trapping Monty Noble lbw.

The same thing happened in 1926, when umpire Frank Chester confirmed that Arthur Mailey would have had the great Jack Hobbs lbw for 0 if he'd appealed. Hobbs went on to make exactly 100 and help England win the match, which regained the Ashes after 14 years.

What was the Nawab of Pataudi playing at when he allowed his slow left-armer 'Bapu' Nadkarni to bowl 32 overs for only five runs against England in 1964? It still ranks as one of the most extraordinary pieces of economy in all first-class cricket: think of it, 27 maiden overs, and only a single off each of the other five. 131 successive balls without a run scored.

But it was precisely what India didn't want. Against a team with several players recovering from illness, they should have been going for wickets. Instead Nadkarni didn't take any in the innings, during which the Noob used six different bowlers (ten in the match), who conceded less than two runs per over but allowed England to escape with a draw.

The same happened in every other match in the series, which were all drawn while Nadkarni was conceding 38 runs in 42 overs, 97 in 57, 6 in 6. He sent down a total of 212 overs for only 278 runs while taking just nine wickets. For pity's sake, why?

Jack Newman took 1,946 wickets for Hampshire (1906–30) but it's said that he would have had many more, and perhaps played for England, but for his habit of blocking the umpire's view with his follow-through!

At Lord's in 1870, JW Dale scored 67 to help Cambridge beat Oxford in the Varsity match, then almost ruined his good work by dropping a simple catch because, as he explained, his eye was on an attractive woman getting out of a carriage.

One or two spectators may have retired hurt after coming onto the pitch to celebrate a century for England against the West Indies in 1966. They tried to chair the batsman who'd made the hundred, not an advisable thing to do with Colin Milburn: he weighed nearly 18 stone.

During the second Test in the West Indies in 1995, Australia's David Boon played a ball back to the bowler, Winston Benjamin, who kicked it away, presumably in disgust, whereupon Boon ran in for the single that brought up his fifty.

Shane Warne's first ball in an Ashes Test, the mighty leg-break that bamboozled Mike Gatting before hitting his off stump, was one of the most famous deliveries in Test history – but poor Gatting shouldn't have been facing it. When Mike Atherton was out, the next man due in, Robin Smith, nowhere near as good a player of spin as Gatting, was still in the toilet! Not to worry. Warne got him too, for the same number of runs (four) as Gatting.

> *He didn't drop the ball.*
> *It fell out of his hand.*
>
> **Ray Illingworth**

At the end of the dramatic second day of the first Test in 1950–51, on a Brisbane wicket turned vicious by rain, England were left with 70 minutes' batting. Before the innings, their captain Freddie Brown ordered the heavy roller, which in those days was still being pulled by a horse called Dobbin. After each trip down the pitch, he had to be unhitched and rehitched, making only four trips in all – but if Brown had insisted on his right to have seven minutes of actual rolling, the process would have taken forever, or at least long enough to save England from batting that evening. With the wicket still doing its worst, the three wickets that went down in that time were crucial in a match they lost by 70 runs. The series soon went with it. Dobbin was retired from active service after the match. Brown wasn't.

During the second innings of the first Test of the 1953 Ashes series, Australia's captain Lindsay Hassett wanted his wicketkeeper Don Tallon to appeal against the light when he went in to bat. 'Give the light a go when you get in, Don.' Because Tallon was slightly hard of hearing, Hassett repeated the instruction as soon as the next wicket fell and Tallon was on his way out of the changing room: 'Don't forget to give it a go.'

Out in the middle, Tallon informed the not out batsman Alan Davidson that the skipper had said to give it a go, which they proceeded to do, throwing the bat at everything. Within minutes, Tallon was caught off an enormous hit. Back in the pavilion, he apologised with 'Sorry, skip. We tried to give it a go, but I couldn't see a thing. The light was terrible!' Davidson confirms that the story's true.

In 1967–68, Natal were outplayed for most of the match by a Transvaal team who eventually needed just 58 from their second innings to win, only for the heavens to open when the scores were level. It was obvious that once the players left the field, there could be no going back on, so the umpires decreed that one more ball would be bowled. If Natal could prevent a run from being scored, the match would be tied.

Aware of the possibility of a leg-bye doing the damage, Berry Versfeld, substituting for regular captain Jackie McGlew, put another fielder just behind square leg. Mike Procter bowled, Eddie Barlow took an almighty swing, his stumps went everywhere – but it wasn't a tie. Down at long leg, Lee Irvine had been shouting at Procter and Versfeld, but to no avail: that extra fielder behind the wicket on the leg side was one too many for the rules. The no-ball cost Natal the match!

Having been dropped behind the wicket off his second ball in Test cricket, against the West Indies in 1966, Basil D'Oliveira might have gone on to make a substantial score if he hadn't deflected a drive by his batting partner Jim Parks onto the stumps at the bowler's end. While he was standing there

ut of his crease, wondering if he was out
he wasn't), Wes Hall picked up a stump and
eld the ball against it. *Now* Dolly was out
I felt a fool, embarrassed and frustrated'),
or 27. 'Sorry, Bas,' said Hall. The match was
rawn.

atsy Hendren was such a notorious
ractical joker that it's surprising how often
ther players kept falling for his little pranks.
an Peebles, for instance, once played
orward and missed, whereupon Hendren,
who was fielding, called out 'He's missed it,'
nticing Peebles to assume that the wicket-
eeper had fumbled. He set off on a run and
eached the far end before he discovered
hat the 'keeper had had the ball in his
loves all along.

On another, much recounted occasion,
lendren was at the non-striker's end when
is Middlesex team-mate Walter Robins was
atting against the Derbyshire spinners,
eeping them out in that familiar way of his,
oing down the wicket to play them
efensively 'on the walk.' If he missed with
is bat, his pads would save him. If he
issed with his pads, nothing would save
im and he would keep walking all the way
o the pavilion.

This was one of those times when he
issed it with everything. As he began the
ong walk, Hendren suddenly called out 'Get
ack, he's dropped it.' Robins turned and
hrew himself into his crease – only to find
he wicketkeeper staring down at him in
vonder. He hadn't dropped it, the stumping
ad been completed, and Robins was out as
vell as down.

In 1928, when Alf Gover was a tearaway
oung fast bowler for Surrey, Hendren asked
im to go easy with the short stuff. 'I'm not
s young as I was.' Naturally, like any red-
looded pace merchant, Gover let him have
lenty of the medicine: his first three balls

Patsy Hendren dreaming up practical jokes off his own bat

were all bouncers, which the ageing
Hendren hooked for four, four and six. Jack
Hobbs had to come over and tell Gover that
Hendren was one of the best players of
quick bowling in the country.

After a particularly long night-before, the
morning-after wasn't being too gentle with
Jack Hearne, who asked Hendren to help
him out to the wicket (they were the two
not-out batsmen overnight). When they
reached the middle, Hearne noticed that
there was no-one else around. Any chance
of a sit-down, Patsy? Why not, said
Hendren, we're the only ones here so far.
Hearne slumped to the grass for a brief rest,
only to discover that the umpire and fielders
were waiting for him with some impatience.
His partner had deposited him 50 yards
away from the action. Another Hendren
patsy.

Very little grey cells (2)

... off the field

Brian Close was a natural all-round sportsman. Highly successful cricket captain, League footballer with Leeds Utd and Arsenal, golfer who played off a 3 handicap with his right hand and 8 with his left. Whenever Yorkshire played a round on their day off, whoever was paired with Closey expected to win.

Occasionally, however, the script went drastically wrong. He once threw his club away in exasperation, and had to climb a tree to get it back. On another occasion, to cap a particularly miserable round, he twice drove into the water at the 12th hole – then tried to use his versatility as a remedy, taking out a left-handed driver. No change; again he found the lake.

Without saying a word (a rare event for DB Close), he carried his golf bag to the water's edge and ceremoniously sent it to follow the last three balls he'd played. Then he stomped back to the clubhouse, leaving the others to finish the round as a threesome.

A few minutes later, he reappeared on the horizon. Fred Trueman thought at first he was coming back to apologise, 'but I should have known Closey better.' Instead, he walked past them and waded into the lake. His keys, including the one to his hotel room, were still in the bag!

During the Nottinghamshire v Yorkshire match at Worksop in 1960, the pavilion clock was showing 1.28 (i.e. two minutes to lunch) with Close on 96 at the non-striker's end – which prompted Len Shackleton, the former England footballer now writing for the *Daily Express*, to comment that it was a pity Closey would miss out on a century before lunch. Oh, I don't know, said Don Mosey, northern cricket correspondent of the *Daily Mail*, I still think he'll do it.

Life was never dull with Brian Close around

A bet was immediately struck. Shackleton watched Vic Wilson play out the rest of the over, then turned to collect his winnings – which Mosey didn't hand over. On the field, Close was preparing to face the next over. What's this, frowned Shackleton, did you know the pavilion clock was wrong? It's not, said Mosey, but lunch at Notts home games is always at two o'clock!

The outfoxed Shack prepared to fume in silence – only for Close to immediately hole out at deep square leg without adding to his score, for which Mosey still hasn't forgiven him!

alking of bets and Brian Close, he knew a
hing or two about the geegees. On one
ccasion, he gave a friend a few tips for the
rand National. Listening to the race on the
adio, Close heard his forecasts come in
rst, second, third and fourth. 'Not only did
not have a bet, but my friend said he hadn't
ither!'

lose once emerged unscathed after
valking through a plate-glass door in a hotel,
ut was probably a greater danger to himself
ehind a wheel. Stories about his driving are
o vivid that the people who tell them may
ven have grown to believe them. His habit
f travelling on a motorway with a road map
n one hand and a cheese sandwich in the
ther, falling asleep at the wheel with Viv
ichards beside him, etc. In one of these,
e accompanied Peter Roebuck's father-in-
aw to a garage to pick up a sponsored car
another version says to have it repaired),
vhich was being given a final polish by the
nechanic when he arrived. Close, it's said,
rove the car out onto the road, round the
rst roundabout, and into the back of a lorry,
hen brought it straight back for the
nechanic to begin repairs.

alking of motorised transport, Percy
Chapman's use of it was as cavalier as his
atting. In the middle of his first Test series,
gainst South Africa in 1924, he was
eturning home from a ball in Henley when
e was thrown off his motorbike, all because
e was wearing a raincoat, whose tail
ecame entangled in the rear wheel. Lucky
o survive at all, let alone with no bones
roken, he nevertheless missed the last
hree matches in the series.

Jo need to go into great detail about David
Gower's flight in that Tiger Moth during the
990–91 tour of Australia; enough's been
vritten about how it affected his England
:areer. But lest we forget: he had a

passenger that day, Derbyshire batsman
John Morris, who volunteered to go up in
the aircraft 'in all innocence'.

Nothing could save him from the guilty
verdict. Neither his century in the match, nor
the 'Gower and Morris are innocent OK'
banner flown from a plane during the next
Test, nor the fact that an England captain,
Tony Lewis, had performed a similar aerial
stunt with impunity during the 1972–73 tour
of India. Morris, who was fined £1,000 for
his £27 plane ride and hasn't played for
England since, later described the event as
'a fairly big own goal'.

David Steele still winces at the memory of
the time he'd been batting for an hour
before realising he'd forgotten to wear a
box. 'I had a quick feel down below to make
sure, and this confirmed the bad news.'

On his way out to bat in his very first Test
innings, at Lord's in 1975, Steele went down
one flight of steps too many and found
himself in the pavilion toilets (*Blunders
Vol.1*), which put him in good company: the
same fate had befallen John Snow on his
first visit to the hallowed place (1963) and
Roger Marshall during the 1973 Gillette Cup
final.

The same sort of thing in reverse, in a way.
After being given out early in the first Test
of the 1979–80 series against England, Allan
Border stormed into the changing room,
flung his bat across the floor, tore off his
gloves, kicked them away, and turned the
air blue with his observations on the lbw
decision. It was only after he'd sat (and
calmed) down that he realised he was in the
opposition changing room. Apologies to the
England manager were followed by some
embarrassing rooting around under chairs to
find the discarded gloves.

When England were still 92 short of making
Australia bat again with only three wickets

Botham cashes in on the Australian bowling, and so does Marsh (right)

left in the third Test of 1981, a firm of bookmakers felt it safe to offer 500–1 against a home win, odds which were snapped up by two of the Australians. Ian Botham's famous 149 not out and Bob Willis' 8–43 made £5,000 for Dennis Lillee and £2,500 for Rodney Marsh.

They were only half-heartedly criticised for betting against their own team (no-one believed they played any less well as a result). The real howler was committed by the man who advised Ladbrokes to quote such enormously long odds in a two-horse race. It's said that when he was asked to name a figure, he thought England's chances were so remote that he plucked a number out of the air: 'Oh, 500–1.' The red-faced man was Ladbrokes expert in matters cricketing: former England wicketkeeper Godfrey Evans!

Actually, on second thoughts, the biggest blunder in all this was committed by Marsh, who persuaded Lillee to bet just that £10 instead of the £50 he originally had in mind, because he wanted to stop his mate wasting his money. His solicitude cost Lillee £20,000!

Before the fourth Test against the West Indies in 1988, bets were being laid as to who'd be chosen as England's third captain of the series. One journalist quoted Chris Cowdrey, last capped more than three years earlier, at 100–1. You've guessed it.

The great Sunil Gavaskar was born to play cricket: his father was a good club cricketer and his uncle Madhav Mantri had kept wicket for India. But he himself was nearly lost to the game from the very start. When he was born, one of his relatives noticed a small hole in his ear-lobe. The following day, it had disappeared. The babies had been switched. After a frantic search, the newborn Sunil was found in a cot beside another woman. But for that hole in his ear, India would have been 10,122 Test runs worse off and Gavaskar would have been brought up as a fisherman.

Surrey batsman David Ward was once offered odds of 40–1 against Chelsea losing the 1994 FA Cup Final 4–0, but didn't take the bet.

Dr Roy Park really should have arranged for a locum to take over his duties on the night of 30 December 1920. Instead, he was called out to attend a difficult birth that turned into an all-night vigil. The following day, batting for Australia against England, he

was bowled by the only ball he ever faced in Test cricket!

Arthur Mailey, Australia's talented and quixotic leg-spinner of the 1920s, also earned a living as a caricaturist and writer on the game – despite an unpromising start. Sent to report on the funeral of a Mayor of Melbourne. he returned with a very detailed piece. Did he know, queried his editor, how many mourners he'd mentioned by name?

As if he would …

Three hundred and eighteen. And three hundred and seventeen are right. The only one you've got wrong is the name of the corpse!'

Equally typical of Mailey is the tale of how he once provided the *Evening Standard* with his forecast of an Australian touring team, and forgot to include a wicketkeeper.

> *And he's got the guts to score runs when the crunch is down.*
>
> **John Murray**

During the 1956–57 tour to South Africa, England pace bowler Peter Loader was dozing in the sun on a fishing boat when the crew woke him to tell him a huge tuna had caught hold of his line. For the best part of an hour, Loader fought to land this giant fish, encouraged and advised by everyone on board, and apparently never stopping to wonder why the leviathan's head or fins never broke the surface. Only when he was suitably exhausted did the mighty beast show itself to be a metal bucket.

Big-hitting Gilbert Jessop attributed his poor form in 1905 to having spent the previous winter 'studying the intricacies of those vexatious problems which ever beset the path of the tyro at the Royal and Ancient game.' Translated: he'd played too much golf.

In the first Test against Australia, he got himself out with a shot he described as 'more reminiscent of a spared iron shot than any stroke known to careful students of batsmanship'. It was his only Test innings of the summer. He was out for 0!

When Ray East and John Lever met two attractive women in a Berlin nightclub, they were excited at the prospects and exchanged notes when their conquests went to answer calls of nature. The Essex men's anticipation turned to something else altogether when they saw their new-found friends disappear through a door marked *Herren*. As a spinner, East felt he should have been able to spot a wrong 'un.

> *The black cloud is coming from the direction the wind is blowing. Now the wind is coming from where the black cloud is.*
>
> **Ray Illingworth**

Is this why some of Ray Illingworth's selections as England team manager raised a few eyebrows? During the second Test against India in 1996, he was caught on camera turning his binoculars in his hands and looking through both ends.

During the 1972–73 tour of India, new England captain Tony Lewis signed an autograph for a local security guard – and was surprised to find the same man sitting at an exclusive table before the first Test. On the card in front of him, signed by AR Lewis, was the request 'Please admit bearer to the VIP area.'

Another Indian got the better of Australian batsman Kim Hughes in 1979–80, a shopkeeper called Suffering Moses who rarely did any suffering at all if his success in this instance is anything to go by. Having convinced Hughes that he'd turned down a huge offer from Nelson Rockefeller for a chess set in which the pawns were carved into the shape of elephants, he sold the item to his prey for £500. Back at the team hotel, after Hughes had shown off his prize, one of the elephant's tusks fell out. The chess set was worth £12 at most.

During a stint on BBC Radio's *Test Match Special*, the late Alan McGilvray fell for one of Brian Johnston's oldest practical jokes, accepting a piece of one of those famous chocolate cakes sent in by listeners, then biting off such a large chunk that he could only splutter a reply when Johnners asked him a question.

On another occasion in the same commentary box, Johnston asked McGilvray's opinion again, only to find the venerable Aussie fast asleep behind him.

Although he was relatively new to the *TMS* team in 1991, Jonathan Agnew probably should have known better than to describe Ian Botham's hit-wicket dismissal against the West Indies in the way that he did with Johnners alongside him in the commentary box.

BJ was predictably reduced to a helpless on-air fit of giggles when Agnew, recalling Botham's efforts to avoid treading on his stumps, remarked: 'He just didn't quite get his leg over.'

During a match between Greywell and Old Optimists in 1935, a local umpire caused some ill feeling in giving seven Optimists out. One of them, Syd Levey, was feeling decidedly vengeful when he engaged the rogue official in conversation during the interval. Indicating the nearby parish church, he opined that the spire must be two hundred feet high. Nonsense, replied the umpire, it's no more than a hundred.

The conversation reached an impasse that went on long enough for a wager to be struck. It was no more than five shillings, but enough to have the umpire replaced immediately: Law 51 of the revised rules of cricket forbade any betting by umpires during a match!

In 1995 Rick Sidwell won two free tickets to the B&H final. The tickets would have cost a total of £40. The cigarettes he had to smoke to win them (12,800, no less) cost £1,700. If you don't believe it, don't shoot this humble messenger: the story was in the *Daily Telegraph*.

Alderman knows he's either going to get a wicket or he isn't.

Steve Brenkley

When Colin Cowdrey heard on the radio that his son Chris had taken Kapil Dev's wicket with his fourth ball in Test cricket (1984), he drove the wrong way down a one-way street.

Well, it *was* a rare event ...

Beyond all recognition

Arthur Chipperfield, Ernie McCormick, Bill O'Reilly – and
Don Bradman, looking happy to be recognised

When Tony Greig and Hylton Ackerman flew into Adelaide to play for a Rest of the World team, they were welcomed by a small figure in dark glasses and cardigan, who welcomed them to Australia and invited them to join him for a coffee. Tired after a long flight, the last thing the two South Africans wanted was an ear-bashing by local bigwigs, so they gave the little fellow their luggage and beat a retreat to the washroom to plan their escape.

But there was no way out, so they went into the coffee bar, were introduced to two other officials, and sat through a surprisingly painless chat about the game ('the trio certainly seemed to know a thing or two'). Greig, allowed to do most of the talking (no great surprise there), asked the little man in the cardigan if he had any connection with cricket in the area. Sort of, was the reply. We help run things around here – which Greig took to mean that perhaps he organised the airport cricket team.

Before long, the swing doors parted to reveal Garry Sobers, the Rest of the World captain, who made straight for their new host. How are you, Sir Donald? Greig: 'I don't think I've ever felt more foolish in my life.' He'd failed to recognise Bradman.

He can take heart from knowing that he wasn't the first. On their way to England in 1938, Australia played their traditional match in Ceylon. Having been told that the Don was the next man in, the local crowd applauded loudly when the batsman scored 116. Some may even have told their grandchildren of the day they saw the great man bat. There was just one thing. Bradman wasn't playing. The century was scored by the similarly diminutive Lindsay Hassett.

It wasn't just foreigners who got it wrong. Before the first Test of the 1950–51 Ashes series, Bradman had gone out to inspect the wicket, and no-one in the Brisbane crowd recognised him, even though he was the country's biggest sporting name and his 19-year Test career had ended less than three years earlier.

During the first Test of the England v West Indies series in 1995, journalist and broadcaster Jack Bannister was flattered to be told that there was no need to show his new TCCB press pass at Headingley. So you know who I am, then?

Oh yes sir, said the gateman. You're Peter May.

Fred Trueman was often in trouble of one sort or another during his first England tour, to the West Indies in 1953–54, culminating in an incident in which an Englishwoman complained to team captain Len Hutton that she'd been jostled in a lift by two of his players, Trueman and Tony Lock. They were ordered to report to the hotel lounge, where the woman gave them a prolonged telling-off, which the two endured in untypical silence.

After they'd made their apologies and the woman had swept out of the room, Hutton expressed some surprise. 'I thought you took that very well.'

So do I, said Fred, considering it wasn't us!

Sussex's lack of success in the County Championship, especially in the late '60s and early '70s, might have had something to do with the committee, or at least some of its members, who didn't always know a good thing when they saw one. One such worthy, sitting with John Snow, Tony Greig and Ken Suttle at a dinner, is said to have been able to tell them apart only because Snow had been on TV, Greig was 6ft 7in, and 'that means you must be Suttle because the three of you were coming.' Suttle had just played 423 consecutive matches for the county!

These committee men seemed to be forever guessing where he was concerned. Another of the breed, watching some actual play, was told that Sussex were batting at the time. How do you know that? Because Oakman and Suttle are in. Oh yes, said the man responsible for running the club. By the way, which one's Oakman? Alan Oakman was not only a former England player, he stood 6ft 5in alongside Suttle's 5ft 7in!

There's more. After Sussex batsman Mike Buss had been bowled, a committee member asked, 'What happened there, Mike?' but the player didn't know: he wasn't Mike Buss but his brother Tony.

It gets even worse. The club's president, the Duke of Norfolk, was with the Kent captain Colin Cowdrey when another cricketer came past. Who's your player, Colin? Peter Graves, your Grace. And he's one of yours. What a way to run a railroad.

And I suppose, per head of population, a really tremendous ovation from this crowd.

Tom Graveney

During the 1932–33 Bodyline tour, two Australian boys were comparing notes on the autographs they'd just collected from the England party on a train. One was decidedly unimpressed with one of the signatures, which he rubbed out, saying he only wanted the names of the cricketers themselves, not the accompanying journalists.

Unfortunately for him, that particular reporter had recently played a bit of Test cricket himself. The boy had deleted the autograph of Jack Hobbs!

Perhaps it takes one to know one? Well, not always. When Len Hutton arrived in Australia in 1950–51, he was approached by a middle-aged gent in an Adelaide hotel. Sorry, said Len, but we meet a lot of people on a tour like this and I can't quite place you.

Well, said the other, who'd kept his accent despite settling in Australia, last time we met I clean bowled you at Sheffield. It was Harold Larwood.

During the 1972–73 series in Pakistan, while Mike Denness was waiting for a call from his wife back in England, the telephone operator congratulated him on his hundreds in consecutive Tests, saying they were two of the best he'd ever seen. This was forever happening to Denness on that tour. Not the successive centuries (far from it) but people confusing his name with that of Dennis Amiss.

The same thing happened at Wimbledon, where Centre Court tickets for Amiss and Tony Greig were left at the gate in Denness's name.

In 1995 the Indian Communications Department refused to connect Sunil Gavaskar's telephone until he could provide a certificate proving that he was a well-known sportsman!

Grounds for complaint

After winning the second Test to level the 1995 series against the West Indies, England were entitled to their optimism going into the third, at Edgbaston – only to run into the wicket from hell.

England manager Ray Illingworth had asked for a pitch with even bounce, with the ends shaved to help his spinners. What he got was a mixture of Surrey and Ongar loam which produced a rock-hard surface under an uneven layer of grass: tailor-made for the West Indies' tall fast bowlers, whose eyes must have lit up when the very first ball, Curtly Ambrose's loosener, sailed over wicketkeeper Junior Murray for four wides.

Two players had fingers broken as England were dismissed for 147 and 89 in only 74.2 overs, losing by an innings. They hadn't been bowled out twice in fewer balls since facing Australia on a similarly shocking pitch in 1888.

Warwickshire's chief executive Dennis Amiss (ironically a former England opening bat) and head groundsman Steve Rouse had prepared a wicket (their first in Test cricket) that Geoff Boycott called one of the worst he'd ever seen at this level. Mike Atherton thought it 'a diabolical pitch,' Clive Lloyd described it as a slagheap, and Robin Smith, who top-scored in each innings, 'wondered at times if I had enough life assurance'.

Everyone lost out: the TCCB more than a quarter of a million pounds in refunds and cut-price tickets, England their very real chance of winning a series against the West Indies for the first time since 1969 (they did well to recover and draw 2–2).

The following year, in the Test series against India, the wicket played slightly better in that the match ended in four days not three, but two more fingers were broken.

For the third Test against Pakistan in 1987, Headingley groundsman Keith Boyce elected to use a brand new wicket, a decision which made the match something of a national lottery, which England didn't win. After an hour of the first morning, they were 31–5, going on to make only 136. It was the first time they'd ever lost by an innings to Pakistan, who took the series by that one match to nil, the first time they'd won a rubber in England.

Back in 1984, the wickets for all five Tests provided such uneven bounce that they were bound to favour West Indian pace rather than English swing and seam. Don't take this word for it; ask Ian Botham, who described them as 'bloody awful ... I can't understand why we played on such dangerous pitches.' England suffered their first 'blackwash,' losing the series 5–0.

Essex lost the 1989 County Championship because they had 25 points deducted for a substandard pitch (*Blunders Vol.1*), a fate they were perhaps lucky to be spared back in 1976. After winning the toss at Westcliff in July, Northamptonshire were all out for 115 on what their captain Mushtaq Mohammad called the worst wicket he'd seen all season. They lost the match by eight wickets and the Championship (which they've never won) by 16 points.

While preparing the Wanderers wicket in Johannesburg before the first Test against New Zealand in 1994, head groundsman Chris Scott used less water than the South African seamers would have liked, leaving a surface that crumbled just enough for the gentle left-arm spin of Matthew Hart to take eight wickets and win the match for New Zealand by 137 runs.

The third Test of the 1954-55 Ashes series was played on a Melbourne pitch that had long been prone to breaking up. England, naturally apprehensive before their second innings, were relieved to find that the surface was suddenly holding together very well – this despite hot weather and a drying wind on the rest day. Just below the topsoil, the wicket was surprisingly damp...

Although the groundstaff always denied any surreptitious watering, the secretary of Melbourne CC, former Test batsman Vernon Ransford, admitted that there had been a chat about giving the pitch 'a little fizz'.

It turned out disastrously for the home side. After England had made 279, the highest score of the match, Australia had to face Frank Tyson on a crumbling pitch. He took 7–27 to fizz them out for 111, the deadly Nelson, and put England 2–1 up in a series they won 3–1 to retain the Ashes.

A group of English cricketers arriving to play a charity match in Prague (yes, that's right) left instructions at the rugby stadium to cut them the customary pitch 22 yards wide, then returned the following day to find a perfectly mown pitch – but only four inches wide and 50 yards across the pitch. The groundsman had marked out a rugby 22-metre line.

Both captains criticised the Headingley pitch before the 1975 World Cup semi-final, but Ian Chappell benefited more than Mike Denness, putting England in and giving the new ball to left-arm seamer Gary Gilmour, who took 6–14 in 12 overs to dismiss England for 93. Australia in turn slumped to 39–6 before recovering to win by four wickets (Gilmour 28 not out). It had been a famously hot summer (483 runs had been scored by Australia and Pakistan on the same wicket ten days earlier) and some watering was due – but it was somewhat over-enthusiastic. Jim Laker took the view that 'nobody could successfully defend the action of the groundsman for a fixture as important as this one.' It was all over in 65 overs.

In the 1920 season, the pitch at Leicester had a reputation for being something of a terror – and didn't do the home players much good. For instance, although Surrey scored no more than 309, Leicester lost by an innings, thanks partly to having to bat with three men short in the second innings – all injured by balls rearing up from their own wicket.

Batting for Hampshire against Notts in 1968, Barry Richards chased a wide delivery from Carlton Forbes and edged it onto his stumps, from where it went to the boundary. Instead of being bowled, Richards collected four more runs: although the stumps had been hit hard by the ball, the bails hadn't come off. The Portsmouth pitch was so hard that the stumps had had to be hammered into the ground. A new set appeared from the pavilion, but it was too late for Notts: Richards went on to score 206!

New Zealand relished their hosts' choice of pitch in 1985–86. With the three-match series in Australia level at 1–1, they were made a present of a Perth wicket which had been laid only a few months earlier, ideally suited to their great fast-medium opening bowler Richard Hadlee, who took 11 wickets to help New Zealand to their first series win against Australia, whose captain Allan Border believed the pitch was used 'about three months too early' and that groundsman John Maley 'would agree it was simply not ready for a Test match'.

When the West Indies invited New Zealand to make a full tour in 1971–72, it was probably with a view to winning a Test series for the first time since 1966–67, after which they'd lost to Australia, England (twice) and India, and drawn with New Zealand, who were now expected to provide easier meat – but the West Indian groundsmen served up a sequence of pitches that were so flat and easy that the visitors were able to draw all 12 of their matches despite losing the toss in all five Tests. Afterwards, the West Indies captain Garry Sobers bemoaned the lack of genuinely fast bowlers in the islands (yes, you read that right) and blamed the pitches for not giving them more encouragement. There was no shortage of pace, or pacey pitches, when West Indies next won a home series, in 1975–76.

At the end of that 1971–72 series, New Zealand played a friendly match in Bermuda, where the pitch had been prepared with, shall we say, a view to a result. The whole thing rather backfired on the locals, who dismissed the visitors for 249 in their first innings but still lost with a day to spare.

> *He's trying to exercise with some kind of pyrotechnics.*
>
> **Simon Hughes**

Even the worst of the modern wickets, however, can't compare with the minefields that batsmen had to put up with before the First World War. WG Grace's first-class career average of 39.55 could only have been much higher if he'd been spared the shooters and lifters that menaced him and every other batsmen from pitches that were under-prepared and left open to the English elements. Even the MCC wrongly believed that a few hours' work was enough to prepare any wicket.

Typical of these treacherous strips of sod was the one on which the Australians had to play against Wembley Park in 1896. 'Not yet sufficiently matured for first-class cricket', it reduced Australia to 106 and 131 – but they won by 135 runs! The hosts, hoist by their own petard, managed only 65 and 37.

We all make mistakes — and that's officials

When the famous medium-pacer Alfred Shaw died in 1907, he was buried according to his wishes: the length of a cricket pitch from the grave of his equally celebrated Notts and England team mate Arthur Shrewsbury. Some time after the interment, someone discovered that the distance between the two tombs wasn't 22 yards but 27: shock horror. Luckily for someone's arithmetical reputation, the county secretary remembered that Shaw always took a five-yard run-up!

With England needing to win the fifth and final Test to draw the 1930–31 series, Percy Chapman won the toss and put South Africa in to bat — but an hour's postponement robbed England of the advantage of putting the opposition in on a pitch which dried quickly enough to allow the hosts to score 252 and hold out for the draw that won them the series and ended Chapman's Test career. Reason for the delay? The bails were the wrong size.

Whose brainwave was it to bring in a law allowing a new ball to be taken after only 55 overs? This when England's seam bowlers in the immediate post-war period were mainly pre-war veterans, and only fast-medium at that.

It played straight into the hands of the 1948 Australians, who had one of the great fast-bowling double acts in Ray Lindwall and Keith Miller. Cutting a swathe through the country, they won the series 4–0 and bowled England out for 52 in the last Test.

The 55-over rule was scrapped the following year.

In 1990, callers ringing a television phone-in on the future of Yorkshire county cricket found themselves being put through to a helpline dealing with the problem of premature ejaculation. No comment. BT blamed it on their engineers.

When the Sabina Park crowd began throwing bottles during the second Test against England in 1967–68, one of the police chiefs ordered tear gas to be used — but instead of subduing the unruly element caused all kinds of havoc in the posh seats and the England changing room, where Geoff Boycott hid his face in the sink to escape the fumes. The police had aimed the gas into the wind!

The age-old charge that English players play too much cricket has something to do with the schedule imposed on them at county level. Take these as just two of a great many examples. In the middle of a three-day match with Notts, Essex had to drive back to Chelmsford to play a Sunday League game — against Notts. The two teams travelled 300 miles to play each other. Another time, Essex had to leave their championship fixture in Derby to go to Cardiff for a Sunday match, this while Middlesex were playing in Glamorgan but had to travel to Derby for the Sunday tie!

Small wonder that when he was asked where they were playing next, John Lever once replied 'Canterbury, I think.' Close enough, given the fixture list. It was Cardiff.

Towards the end of the 1968 season, Ray Illingworth asked Yorkshire for a three-year contract. The county, who'd always dealt only in one-year arrangements, refused. Just to make sure the message went out loud and clear, chairman Brian Sellers let it be known that he could go 'and any other bugger with him'.

So while Yorkshire won the County Championship for the third consecutive time that season but haven't done it even once since, Illingworth moved on to lead Leicestershire to the first titles in their history: the B&H Cup in 1972 (beating Yorkshire in the final) and 1975, the Sunday League in 1974 and 1977 and above all the Championship itself in 1975 (Yorkshire finished second!). He was also a very successful England captain from 1969 to 1973.

Sellers himself had been one of the best county captains, and one of his successors, Ronnie Burnet, called him the most dynamic chairman Yorkshire ever had – 'but he made some terrible mistakes'.

The England squad that went to Australia in 1962–63 was managed by Bernard, Duke of Norfolk – the result, it was said, of a casual joke. It certainly turned out to be. At least one of the players confirmed that 'his qualifications for the job just did not exist.' He just happened to be the England captain Ted Dexter's club president and horse-racing partner, though it was said that he actually accepted the post because it gave him the chance to organise the Queen's next trip to Australia! During the tour, he had to return home to help arrange Winston Churchill's funeral (which didn't take place till 1965). Australia retained the Ashes.

David Clark went to Australia as England's manager in 1970–71, but didn't gel with captain Ray Illingworth, who called him 'an amiable but somewhat ineffectual man'. Nor did he endear himself to the rest of the team when, asked if he'd rather see every one of the remaining four Tests drawn or Australia win the series 3–1, he replied that he'd rather see four results.

> *He's a very dangerous bowler. Innocuous, if you like.*
>
> **David Lloyd**

In the final of the 1995 World Masters Cup, West Indies beat India thanks partly to an innings of 56 from 53 balls by Gus Logie. The tournament was for players aged 35 and over. Logie was 34.

The organisers of the Croydon indoor school where Tony Lock learned to bowl were partly to blame for his suspect action. The ceiling was so low that he had to bend his arm to avoid the beams!

In 1969–70, Australia originally intended playing Tests in Pakistan as well as India. When the Pakistani leg of the tour had to be cancelled, the Australian authorities agreed to send a team to South Africa instead. Ian Chappell: 'I hope the board never makes the same mistake again.'

The slow spinners' wickets of the subcontinent (where Australia won the series 3–1) were precisely the wrong preparation for the subsequent series on South African wickets that favoured pace and bounce. Traumatised by the fast bowling of Mike Procter and Peter Pollock, batted out of it by Graeme Pollock and Barry Richards, Australia lost all four Tests, the last three by the widest margins South Africa had achieved till then.

Gatemen at a number of Test grounds have earned a reputation for jobsworthiness, among them the obdurate guardian of the Lord's pavilion during the Test against South Africa in 1994, who refused entry to an elderly gent who turned out to be Archbishop Desmond Tutu.

Calcutta is celebrating the assassination of Mahatma Gandhi.

Henry Blofeld

Devon won the 1994 Minor Counties title by drawing the Championship final against Cambridgeshire, thanks to the unsatisfactory rule whereby bonus points were decisive in the event of a draw, allowing the side which took such a lead to shut up shop on the second day, which Devon duly did, helped by four hours of rain. The loophole was closed the following year, too late for Cambridgeshire, who lost by three bonus points to two.

The 1993–94 series between South Africa and Australia wasn't the sweetest-tempered of all time (Merv Hughes and Shane Warne were both fined for attacks of the verbals) but things might have been a little more cordial if the arrangements had been better. The TV umpires, made responsible for deciding whether fielders had crossed the boundary ropes before stopping the ball, had no direct link with the umpires in the middle,

and several of these decisions turned out to be wrong. Worse, a number of run-outs couldn't be adjudicated on because fielders kept obstructing the camera! The broadcasting authorities refused to pay for the installation of additional cameras, which led to such unsatisfactory incidents as South African opener Andrew Hudson being given not out in the third Test after completing his run well wide of the crease. The series, thankfully enough, was drawn.

Although the West Indies didn't raise any official objections against Simpson 'Sammy' Guillen winning his first caps for New Zealand against them in 1955–56, someone somewhere might have plugged a few loopholes: his appearances were, strictly speaking, illegal: he hadn't lived in New Zealand for four years as the rules demanded – and he'd played in five Tests for the West Indies!

Security wasn't exactly airtight at Headingley in 1909. During the third Test against Australia, all-rounder Gilbert Jessop injured his back. While he was lying down in the pavilion, a doctor came in and manipulated his back, then told him he'd be able to play again within half an hour.

He wasn't. After the physician had finished with him, he could hardly move a muscle, not only unable to bat in either innings but unfit for the rest of the season. England's defeat eventually cost them the series. As for the intruder, no Test cricketer was ever treated by him again, which isn't surprising: he wasn't a doctor!

Those players of Rejects CC who received prizes at their annual dinner and dance scratched their heads when taking possession of the actual trophies. The leading batsman was presented with a statuette of a fisherman, the top fielder with a gilt couple performing a ballroom dance, the wicketkeeper with a splendid comb inscribed with Hairdresser Grade One. The club captain had raided the houses of the previous year's winners, picking up whichever trophy came to hand without examining the inscriptions.

After winning a series in England for the first time (1950), the West Indies accepted an invitation to tour Australia in 1951–52, to decide the unofficial world title. The former Australian Test batsman Alan Kippax, who'd made 146 against the Windies in 1930, advised against the trip. 'Make them come to you and you'll win for sure. Go there and you'll be murdered.'

It must have made as much sense at the time as it does in retrospect. For a start, the West Indies had a right to be at home (they hadn't played there for four seasons) and their board should have insisted on the Australians doing the visiting. But Kippax wasn't the only antipodean who knew the score: on Caribbean wickets, the spin bowling of Ramadhin and Valentine would have been favoured to repeat its success in England, but was unlikely to do similar damage on Australian pitches.

So it proved. Although Valentine bravely took 24 wickets at 28.79, he got little support from the other end, Ramadhin's 14 costing 49.64 each. Meanwhile the West Indian batsmen were overwhelmed by fast bowling on wickets designed for its use in a hostile manner, passing 300 in only one innings out of ten. The series was lost 4–1.

The trustees of the Sydney Cricket Ground who postponed the first Test of the 1897–98 series without informing the two captains (!)

did their own team no favours. The extra three days allowed Ranjitsinhji to recover from illness and score 175 as England won by nine wickets.

Harry Makepeace, who played cricket and football for England, seemed to have made his first century for Lancashire against Middlesex in 1907, reaching exactly 100 by lunch before his captain Archie MacLaren declared. Unfortunately, the scoreboard had been showing the wrong total, and Makepeace finished on 99 not out. He had to wait another four seasons to make that debut hundred.

When George Canning (Lord Harris) was an England selector, the name of Arthur Carr came up at a selection meeting in the 1920s. 'Rather old,' pronounced the peer, 'but he's from Kent, so we can't go far wrong.'

The others in the room were perplexed by this: Carr played for Nottinghamshire. It transpired that Harris was thinking of Douglas Carr, a Kent leg-spinner who'd won his only cap in 1909 when he was already 37.

In a group match at Lahore in 1996, World Cup newcomers Kenya gave themselves a good chance of beating a Test-playing country for the first time when they reduced Zimbabwe to 45–3 before bad light followed by rain forced the teams to leave the field.

The authorities brought in a helicopter to dry the playing area – but it succeeded only in blowing the covers away, spilling water onto the wicket and forcing the match to be abandoned. It was replayed the following day, when Kenya lost by 5 wickets.

Oh lord, Ted

'If you're going to lose, you might as well lose good and proper and try to sneak a win.'
TED DEXTER

In Richie Benaud's opinion, among others, Ted Dexter was one of the two best England batsmen since the War. Many of his 4,502 Test runs at 47.89 were the result of attacking strokeplay that looked genuinely imperious ('Lord Ted'). Fearless as well as immensely talented, he took the battle to Hall and Griffith at Lord's in 1963, producing one of the great cameo innings (70) in Test cricket. In a comeback match for Sussex, against Kent in 1968, he made a double century against Derek Underwood at his most Deadly. Class all the way through.

But he was something of a cavalier captain at Test and county level, liable to be seen practising his (excellent) golf shots during an opposition batting partnership or arranging the longest drinks break in County Championship history to coincide with a radio broadcast of the Derby. By his own admission, he broke David Allen's confidence in Australia in 1962–63 'and I deprived the side of a great bowler for much of the tour' – and he allowed Fred Trueman to send down all that rubbish which lost the 1964 Ashes series (see BOWLING THEM IN). Several contemporaries referred to his 'genuine vagueness' – so, all in all, when he was made chairman of the England selectors in 1989, there were some who wondered which way the whimsy would take him, and the team.

They didn't have long to wait. At the very start of his tenure, the Ashes series of 1989,

Dexter ignored the Headingley groundsman's advice and persuaded David Gower to field first when he won the toss before the first Test. Something to do with a weather forecast that went wrong. Australia declared at 601–7 and won by 210 runs.

When England also lost the next match, Lord Ted decided that some decisive leadership was called for. Before the third Test, he began the usual pre-match meal by handing out song sheets, on which was emblazoned his own version of *Onward Christian Soldiers*, five verses and chorus of *Onward Gower's Soldiers*, complete with such stirring battle cries as 'At the shout Howzat, Brothers lift your voices, Knock the kangaroos (*sic*) flat,' and 'Indulgence we emplore (*sic*), Don't despair too early, The lion soon will roar,' not to mention the unforgettable 'To David G the King, Just this once, and hell why not, Let us his praises sing.' (The *sics* are his, not mine.) When you get in the bath, lads, he urged, sing this at the top of your voices.

Unfortunately for him, this is the kind of thing his reign's remembered for, which is nothing like the whole truth but somehow inevitable. And he did make a rod for his own back by referring to England's new pace bowler as Malcolm Devon and employing a team chaplain (Andrew Wingfield Digby), which prompted Ian Botham to snort that 'once again the lunatics had taken over the asylum.' It's also true that he was rather too emote from the England team (Graham Gooch said he wanted him to come into the changing room more often).

Ultimately, though, what brought him down was a lack of dexterity in dealing with the press, especially a string of utterances which they played up out of all proportion and used to ridicule him. Perhaps Dexter thought that his years in journalism would protect him, but his biggest mistake was in not recognising that the pack was out for blood.

If he had, perhaps he would have thought twice before speaking out, after the disastrous tour of India and Sri Lanka in 1992–93, against the designer stubble adopted by some England players. He hadn't been interested in discussing this daft red herring, but gave in when the press pushed the question at him. Similarly, when asked yet again about the team's lack of success, he might have avoided the trap of saying something along the lines of Venus being in the wrong juxtaposition. This was a joke of course, but by then he should have realised that it would be deliberately misrepresented as a serious remark.

He was unfortunate in a number of things. His first choice as captain, Mike Gatting, was vetoed by Ossie Wheatley (who he?), thereby undermining his authority right at the start. He couldn't have known that when he compared some comments made by

Gooch to being hit in the face by a dead fish, he'd later have to choose him as captain.

And he did some good work behind the scenes. Benaud had no doubt that the structures he put in place 'will be of great benefit to English cricket in years to come. Equally, I'm in no doubt that others will take the credit for it.'

Nevertheless Lord Ted really should have thought harder before saying, after his first series in charge had ended in a 4–0 defeat by the Australians, that he couldn't remember any actual mistakes he'd made.

By the time he resigned, after another mauling at home by Australia (4–1 in 1993) which also ended Gooch's captaincy, he'd been generally portrayed as a buffoon, someone on another planet, by a press who treated him without mercy even though he'd been one of them for years.

Gower and Dexter, the daydream team

Misc. misses

The last bowler to take all ten wickets in a County Championship innings was Richard Johnson of Middlesex in 1994 – but should have been Dominic Cork a year later. During his explosive first season of Test cricket, he took a career best 9–43 for Derbyshire against Northamptonshire, which would have been all ten if Colin Wells hadn't dropped Russell Warren.

Playing for Kearsley in the Bolton League, Steve Dublin was dropped when he'd made 13, which predictably turned out to be unlucky for opposition team Heaton: he was dropped again, by the wicketkeeper, in an over from Rob Slater which included three no-balls and from which Dublin hit eight sixes! He made 120 not out from only 46 balls to win the match off the very last.

In England in 1961, Australian opener Bill Lawry, one of the most obdurate of the species, scored 420 runs at an average of 52.50 in his first ever Test series, which Australia won 2–1. He drove England bowlers to distraction for a decade, making them curse his doggedness – and the luck he enjoyed before that 1961 team was picked. By his own reckoning, his place 'hung precariously in the balance' before Victoria's match against New South Wales. When he'd made 12, he edged Ray Flockton to Peter Philpott. 'The catch was simple enough, waist high to second slip.' Philpott dropped it, Lawry went on to make 266 and book his place on the tour.

While Jim Laker was taking his 19 wickets for England against Australia in 1956, his famous spin twin Tony Lock was perhaps unlucky to pick up only one at the other end – and was definitely unfortunate not to stop Laker taking all ten against the tourists while playing for Surrey. He'd taken the first nine when Keith Miller was dropped at extra cover off Lock. It was that kind of summer for both of them.

Fred Trueman's match for the Combined Services against the touring Australians in 1953 wasn't a complete success. Despite being England's opening bowler, he wasn't given the first over, and his usual place at short leg went to an officer, who promptly dropped a catch off him. The lucky batsman, Keith Miller again, who wasn't off the mark at the time, went on to score 262 not out, the highest score of his first-class career, as Australia notched up 592–4 declared and won by an innings. Trueman's 14 overs cost 95 runs and he was told that he'd never play for the Services again. Not that he was exactly heartbroken: the letter arrived two days after he'd been demobbed!

In the early part of the 1973 summer, New Zealand opener Glenn Turner was dropped by Norman Graham of Kent, Alan Ormrod of Worcestershire, and John Dye of Northamptonshire. He went on to score 1,018 runs between April 24 and May 31, the last batsman to reach a thousand by the end of May.

Wally Hammond also scored 1,000 runs before the end of May (1927) and was also helped by a few dropped catches, five in his penultimate innings alone, against Hampshire.

Similarly, when CB Fry set the world record of a century in each of six consecutive first-class innings (1901), he was dropped in the fourth (on 14 and 52) and fifth (on 45 and 80). When Don Bradman equalled the record in 1938–39, he was dropped when he'd scored only 6 in his fourth innings.

Hampshire were all out for 15 against Warwickshire in 1922, but if a ball from Harry Howell hadn't gone for four byes when former England wicketkeeper 'Tiger' Smith was unsighted, and Lionel Tennyson hadn't been dropped off his only scoring stroke, Hampshire would have made a world record lowest score of 7!

When Ian Botham joined Queensland in 1988–89, it was widely expected that the state might at last win the Sheffield Shield for the first time in its history. Things went well until the penultimate match, in Tasmania, whose leading batsman David Boon scored a century in each innings, but only after being dropped by Allan Border off the third ball of the match. Queensland lost the game and didn't win the Shield for the first time till 1994–95, by which time Botham was long gone.

In 1893 CM Wells took the wickets of Maurice Read and William Attewell with successive balls, and was denied a hat-trick by a missed catch. 'Bad luck, young fellow,' said his captain, a certain WG Grace, 'not to get a hat-trick in your first Gentlemen v Players match, and at Lord's too.'

Wells' reply isn't recorded, but his thoughts might have been worth a few pence: it was Grace who dropped the catch!

> *The Queen's Park Oval.*
> *Exactly as its name suggests:*
> *absolutely round.*
>
> **Tony Cozier**

When Archie MacLaren was dropped at mid-on against Somerset in 1895, he'd already scored 262, but the missed chance still cost the opposition dear. MacLaren went on to amass 424, until 1994 the record for an individual first-class innings in England.

Somerset were probably used to it by then. Their captain, the cricket and rugby international Sammy Woods, remembered that in the previous match they'd lost by an innings and 317 to Kent, who scored 692. Now they went down by an innings and 450 as Lancashire made 801. 'A nice week's work,' said a rueful Woods.

In 1906 a teenaged left-hander made his debut for Kent, against Lancashire at Old Trafford. Although he already had something of a reputation as a slip fielder, he was posted at third man. Before long, a cut by Johnny Tyldesley winged its way towards him and, when his hands missed it, hit him in the chest.

The new boy was moved to mid-on, where Tyldesley picked him out again. Again

he put the chance down. This time he was sent across to mid-off, but the ball persisted in following him, another skier from Tyldesley hitting him on the foot. Later, when his turn came to bowl, Tyldesley smote him so hard and so often that his 26 overs cost 103 runs for just a single wicket. When he batted, he was bowled third ball for a duck.

No-one watching could have guessed that the gangling youth would go on to take 1,018 catches in first-class cricket, still far and away the world record, play 64 times for England, and be remembered as one of the greatest all-rounders of all time. It had simply been a bad first day at the office for Frank Woolley.

On the 1982–83 tour of Pakistan, some of the Australian players took a boat trip from Karachi harbour, during which batsman Greg Ritchie decided on a quick dip. Taking out his false front tooth, he tossed it to Jeff Thomson, who dropped it overboard and couldn't relocate it when he dived in after it.

A few days later, Ritchie was fitted with a replacement, which he broke by treading on it while answering a nocturnal call of nature. He eventually had the dental gap properly bridged.

After being dismissed for 78 in their first innings of the 1842 match, the Gentlemen were saved in their second by easily the highest score in the match (88, out of a total of 206) by Nicholas Wanostrocht, known as Felix – but only after he'd been dropped at slip off his very first ball (he'd made a duck in the first innings). Handicap matches aside, it was the Gentlemen's first win in the series for 20 years.

The 1866 match was also decided by a single innings, Tom Hearne's 122 not out for

After that bad first day, Frank wore the woolly with distinction

the Players, who won by just 38 runs – but he had even more help than Felix. Plum Warner's history of the matches records that 'He was missed at least six times.'

The Players didn't win again till 1874, this time thanks to Ted Pooley's 39 not out, the highest score in their second innings, after he'd been dropped while still in single figures. The winning margin was only two wickets.

In 1894, the Players won by an innings, thanks to Bobby Abel's 168, helped by two dropped catches before he'd reached 50.

In 1904, the Gentlemen were set an unlikely 412 to win, which they made with two wickets to spare, thanks partly to an innings of 80 by Stanley Jackson, who was dropped, each time at slip, on 0 and 53.

Three years later, again the Players' turn, this time John Gunn and Albert Trott top-scoring with 75 and 49 after both being dropped at slip. The Players won by 54 runs.

The Gentlemen lost one and drew two of the 1932 matches, but would surely have won the second if they'd taken the slip catch offered by Jack Hobbs off Gubby Allen in the second innings. The Players were only about 30 runs ahead at the time, with four of their best batsmen out: Herbert Sutcliffe, Frank Woolley, Wally Hammond and Patsy Hendren. Hobbs made 161 not out and the match was drawn.

Now a blunder that may have been anything but. In 1922, Kent bowler George Collins, who'd taken the first nine Notts wickets to fall, was fielding at slip when a ball from Tich Freeman found the edge of the last batsman's bat and sailed straight to him. Collins dropped it, then went on to take all ten wickets in the innings!

Finally, two missed catches that didn't cost anyone anything, not even their freedom. In 1947–48, Natal's captain Dudley Nourse came in to silly mid-off to put pressure on Border batsman Cyril White. Leg-spinner Ian Smith bowled, White went for the big hit to dissuade Nourse from such close proximity, the fielder flung up a desperate hand and held on.

He didn't drop the catch but White wasn't out. Nourse had caught a swallow! Having played its part in cricket folklore, the bird was released unharmed and followed the ball over the boundary.

Joe Hulme, very fast Arsenal and England winger and equally speedy Middlesex fielder, once dived for a ball in the deep, only to find that he'd thrown himself at a low-flying blackbird. The ball had gone over the boundary before he moved.

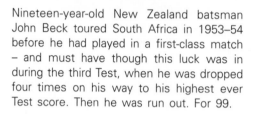

Running out losers

In Tests

Nineteen-year-old New Zealand batsman John Beck toured South Africa in 1953–54 before he had played in a first-class match – and must have though this luck was in during the third Test, when he was dropped four times on his way to his highest ever Test score. Then he was run out. For 99.

During the first Test of the home series against England in 1991–92, another New Zealander, Dipak Patel, pulled Chris Lewis to midwicket, ran two, hesitated over the third, and was run out by Derek Pringle. In more than 50 Test innings, it was the closest Patel's ever come to a century. Like Beck, he was on 99.

Graham Gooch scored 20 centuries in Test cricket, but the first didn't arrive for virtually five years. In the 35 innings before that, the most galling miss came during the third Test in Australia in 1980, when he called for a risky single to mid-off (Geoff Boycott called it 'a silly thing to do,' Gooch himself said 'I got that wrong, didn't I?') and was run out by a yard for 99.

Of course, Boycott's part in this sphere of the game was usually that of a main protagonist, not to say culprit. It's said that Colin Cowdrey once appeared at a function wearing a tie with the number 75 printed on it, representing the number of players GB had run out while playing for England.

Although his reputation is rather more folkloric than it deserves to be (at least he thinks so), he was certainly responsible for a number of hiccups, including a few in Ashes matches, notably those of Bob Barber

in 1966, John Edrich in 1971, and Derek Randall in 1977 (*Blunders Vol.1*).

However, the tide didn't flow all one way. Dennis Amiss ran him out against New Zealand in 1973 ('I was furious, done like a dinner') and Ian Botham endeared himself to a few people by running out Boycott (England captain at the time) when the skipper seemed to be scoring too slowly against New Zealand. Sir Geoffrey had his revenge in a Test against India two seasons later (1979): Botham run out 0. Ironically, Boycs' last first-class innings, 61 against Northants in 1986, ended in a run-out after a mix-up with Jim Love.

He played a part in opposition run-outs too. Set only 226 to win the last Test and therefore take the 1973–74 series 2–0, the West Indies were 65–2 when opener Roy Fredericks pushed a ball from Jackie Birkenshaw behind Boycott at square leg, ran the easy single, then turned for the difficult second. Clive Lloyd let him get halfway up the pitch, then stopped, as did Fredericks. Then Lloyd carried on, leaving his partner to try again from a standing start. Fredericks' run out was the crucial dismissal: his 36 was the highest score in the innings, which subsided to 199, leaving England the winners by just 26 runs. It was the last time they beat the West Indies till 1989–90.

All those years later, it was again a West Indian opener who caused the landslide. England, very much the underdogs, found themselves, immediately and familiarly, under the cosh, the mighty opening combination of Gordon Greenidge and

Boycott run out in 1971. The Australians are *not* hitching a lift back to the pavilion

Desmond Haynes putting on 62 in the very first innings of the series.

Then, after turning the ball to fine leg, and seeing it so badly fumbled by Devon Malcolm that it hit his leg, they came back for an extra run. This despite the fact that the world's most prolific opening partnership (it was their 79th Test together) knew the old maxim about never running on a misfield.

Admittedly, Malcolm still provides some unintentional comedy in the deep, but he's always had a strong arm, which now fired the ball back over the stumps to run out a surprised Greenidge for 32.

That single dismissal changed the shape of the match. The West Indies collapsed to 164 all out (their lowest total against England since 1969) and lost by nine wickets, ending a sequence of 29 Tests without defeat against England going back to 1976.

Denis Compton and run-outs. A book in itself. One of his miniature masterpieces was put together in a Test against Pakistan in 1954, when he called Trevor Bailey for a run, then told him to wait, then sent him back, all this while wandering down the pitch to check the lie of the land, with the result that the batsmen were level in the middle of the pitch by the time poor Bailey tried to return home. Run out for 42, he was another victim of Compton's famous 'three-call trick.'

Bill Edrich, Compton's partner for Middlesex and England, blamed it on simple forgetfulness (Denis was once sitting in a traffic jam as England were about to start a Test, having forgotten that play started half an hour earlier on the last day). 'He'd play one straight to Neil Harvey,' recalled Edrich, 'then call for a run because it slipped his mind that Harvey was one of the great cover fielders.' Perhaps his most memorable lapse was the run-out of his brother, an England football international – in big Leslie's own testimonial match!

Dashing Den repaid the debt from time to time. Was Vijay Merchant overconfident by the time he chanced a risky run in the third Test against England in 1946 (he'd scored 128), or did he misjudge the fielder? Compton had won 12 wartime caps at football and went on to pick up an FA Cup winner's medal in 1950. He ran Merchant out by kicking the ball onto the stumps.

Australian opener Graeme Wood was in the Compton and Boycott class at this kind of thing. The horrors of the 1978–79 Ashes series, for instance, have been thoroughly documented (in *Blunders Vol.1*, for instance). When he arrived in England for the 1981 series, the habit was still with him. By the time the fifth Test came round, the England captain Mike Brearley felt that 'It was not

Denis Compton about to call yes, no, wait, or all three

entirely due to impeccable judgment that Wood had so far run out only himself.' Now he sent back his opening partner John Dyson too late, David Gower threw in, Dyson was run out (and dropped from the next Test!), Australia lost the match and the series.

England captain Mike (MJK) Smith was up there with the worst of 'em. It's said that a typical exchange while he was batting with Alan (AC) Smith for Warwickshire ran something like this: 'No, AC.' 'Yes, Mike.' 'Wait, AC.' 'Damn it, Mike.' 'Sorry, AC.'

Australian batsman Jack Moroney had faced only five balls in Test cricket, in the first Test of the 1949–50 series in South Africa, when he pushed one from John Watkins behind point and set off, only for Keith Miller to send him back. Moroney slipped, and was run out for 0 in his first Test innings.

Easton McMorris was also dismissed for 0 in his first Test knock – without having knocked at all: run out at the non-striker's end, off a no-ball!

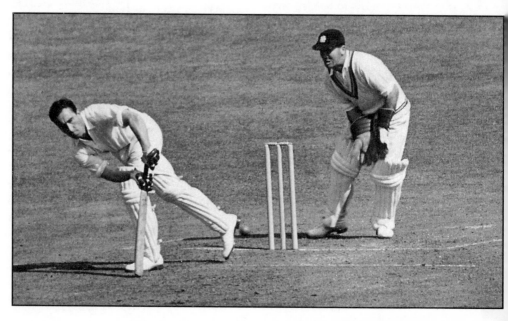

During the Test in Sri Lanka in 1993, John Emburey insisted on a third run to third man. It was his call, but he was 40 at the time and his partner Chris Lewis didn't expect the extra trip down the wicket. Lewis, who was looking good on 22, was run out (Emburey not out 1), England lost a Test to Sri Lanka for the first time.

When Everton Weekes was controversially run out (for 90) in India in 1948–49, it didn't affect the outcome – West Indies won this fourth Test by an innings to take the series 1–0 – but it made a difference to him personally, putting an end to his run of a century in each of five consecutive Test innings, still the world record.

After the 1950–51 series, journalist and former Australian batsman Jack Fingleton wrote that England wicketkeeper Godfrey Evans 'unhesitatingly gets my vote as the worst runner I have seen in Test cricket.' During the third Test, he sent Doug Wright back, then called him for the run. Not only was Wright run out, he pulled a groin muscle and couldn't bowl in the match! England lost it by an innings, their last chance to regain the Ashes.

Set 444 to win the second Test and win the 1958–59 home series against West Indies, India were set on the way by an opening partnership of 99 between Pankaj Roy and Nari Contractor, only to have the good work undone by two bad calls from Pahelam 'Polly' Umrigar.

First he changed his mind after calling for a run; Roy's crêpe soles couldn't cope with the twist and turn and he was run out by Rohan Kanhai. Then, after helping Vijay Manjrekar take the score to 173–2, Umrigar

called for an impossible single and ran Manjrekar out. India subsided to 240 all out to lose the match and eventually the series.

India's performance against England in 1967 was perhaps best summed up early in their first innings of the series, at Headingley, when Ajit Wadekar was allowed to come halfway up the pitch before being sent back by his captain Mansur Ali Khan, the Nawab of Pataudi junior. Wadekar slipped, fell flat on his back, and was run out for 0. India, now 59–4, lost all three Tests, this one by six wickets.

In the first Test of the 1973–74 series in the Caribbean, England put their dismal first innings behind them (131 all out, to trail by 261) with an opening partnership of 209 between Geoff Boycott and Dennis Amiss in the second. England were very well placed for the draw at 328–1 when Amiss pushed the ball into the covers and set off. There were definitely two runs in it (there was a long boundary on that side) and probably a third, but Amiss hesitated when his captain Mike Denness called for it. By the time Amiss decided to go, Denness was stranded. His run out for 44 started the collapse ('my dismissal was crucial') that led to the last nine wickets going down for 64 runs to give the West Indies their first win over England at home since 1954 and end their own run of 22 home Tests without a win.

Chasing 193 to win the first Test of the 1950–51 Ashes series, a tough target on a rain-affected pitch, England lost half the side in reaching 30, but had Hutton and Compton to come. If Godfrey Evans and Arthur McIntyre could stay in while the wicket calmed down ...

They were both wicketkeepers, McIntyre picked for his batting. After hitting Jack

Iverson for four square on the leg-side, he flicked him in much the same direction and set off for an easy run.

In fact an easy run or three, which should have been quite enough to be getting on with. Then, out of keeping with the team's needs at that stage of the match, McIntyre called for a fourth run. Evans, far more experienced internationally, should have sent him back but didn't. There was enough time for Bill Johnston to throw wide of wicketkeeper Don Tallon and for the latter to toss the ball eight yards onto the stumps. McIntyre was run out for 7 and didn't play another Test till 1955. England's defeat by 70 runs set them on the way to losing the series.

Even this, however, couldn't match the run-out incident earlier in the same match. It didn't affect the outcome, but stands as a classic of its kind.

Australia's last-wicket pair were batting at the end of the first innings. Bill Johnston edged Alec Bedser over the slips and was so sure it was four all the way that he stopped halfway down the pitch for a natter with the bowler! 'You know, Alec, that's one of my best shots. I get most of my runs with it.'

While this friendly little interlude was going on, Johnston's partner Iverson had reached the far end and was haring back to the bowler's end. In due course it dawned on big Bill that far from reaching the boundary, the ball was now on its way from fielder Reg Simpson to wicketkeeper Evans. Alarmed, Johnston set off in that direction too, in company with Iverson, who'd completed his second run.

Running neck and neck, they made a magnificent sight: Johnston tall and famously inelegant ('he somewhat resembles a duck taking off from water'), Iverson weighing 15 stone. The pitch wasn't big enough for the both of them – so Iverson turned and ran back to Bedser's end, pursued by the ball, which Evans had thrown with a gloved hand.

No-one was run out, but no-one scored any runs, even though Iverson had run almost four. You beauty. Johnston was out next ball!

Running out losers (2)

In Cup finals and the like

The 1973 Gillette Cup final was virtually decided by the dismissal of the Sussex captain, the big-hitting England all-rounder Tony Greig. His top score of 61 had effectively won the semi-final against Middlesex. Now he went to steal a single off the last ball of an over, tried to get back, and was run out by Jim Foat without scoring. Gloucestershire won their first major title since 1877.

Clive Lloyd was Lancashire's most dangerous batsman in every one-day game they played. Man of the match in the 1975 Gillette Cup final, for instance (see DROPPING THE CUP). In the final the previous year, he'd again been the team's top scorer – but with only 25! It would probably have been considerably more if he hadn't been run out after calling for a run that wasn't there and being sent back by Andrew Kennedy. Kent won by four wickets.

Needing to win their last qualifying match to reach the 1992 World Cup semi-finals, the West Indies held Australia to 216–6 but slumped to 99–5 in reply, and their last chance disappeared when Brian Lara, who'd made 70, called for a sharp single and his partner Winston Benjamin stayed where he was.

Yorkshire won the 1965 Gillette Cup final in a welter of runs, but were rather lucky to reach it. Replying to their modest 177 in the semi, Warwickshire reached 64–1 at tea, then slumped to 97–5 after four consecutive run-outs 'of amazing stupidity.' It was said that they ran like 'a lot of little prep-school boys'.

Replying to Oxford's first innings total of 365 in the 1892 University Match, Cambridge made only 160, mainly because Gerry Weigall ran out two of his partners – 'He clearly was responsible for Jackson (34), who looked all over like making a century, and for Wells' – and arguably a third, Hill. Cambridge, forced to follow on, lost by five wickets.

Surely a unique occurrence, this. In a Melbourne club final, Test all-rounder Bob McLeod was run out in each innings without facing a ball!

Running out losers (3)

In other matches

Spin twins Tom Goddard and Cecil 'Sam' Cook both bowled for England, but their batsmanship was such that they came in at numbers 10 and 11 for Gloucestershire – and their running between the wickets was legendary. In one match, so the story goes, they were both injured and provided with a runner; inevitably, all four batsmen ended up at the same end, then ran back together like a team of horses in harness. It's said that their captain George Emmett suspended Goddard and Cook for two matches apiece. It's also said that the incident involved Cook and 'Bomber' Wells, but let that pass!

> *The rain has now stopped. Only a heavy drizzle now.*
>
> **Richie Benaud**

Talking of running like horses ... while batting together for Oxford University against Surrey in 1922, Tom Raikes and 'Crusoe' Robertson-Glasgow became so confused (and presumably kept their eyes on the ball rather than each other) that they ran in the same direction – not once but four times, 'as if attached to a harness'. When one of them was eventually run out, the umpires had to decide who it was by tossing a coin!

With only one ball left of their match against the 1961 Australians, Northamptonshire were level with wickets in hand. Obviously, whatever happened, the batsmen would have to run, or so everyone thought.

The striker swung at Alan Davidson's final ball, missed, set off like a hare for the other end, and was easily run out by Bobby Simpson to give Australia a rather fortunate draw. Meanwhile, the other batsman had 'stood gravely at the other end refusing to budge'. His name? Lightfoot!

The Players would have beaten the Gentlemen in 1846 but for the run-outs of their top scorers in the second innings, W Martingell and the famous defensive batsman Joe Guy. They lost by just one wicket. With the scores level, Guy was moved in closer to the batsman, who hit a very gentle catch – to where Guy had been standing the ball before!

In the equivalent match of 1899, Jack Mason shared a partnership of 120 for the Gentlemen's seventh wicket, which was ended when he called for a very sharp single and his partner was run out.

The error didn't affect the result (the Gents won by an innings) but nevertheless Mason wasn't a popular man: his partner was none other than WG Grace, who'd made 78 before the run-out, thereby missing a century on his last appearance at Lord's. It really had been a sharp single for a man of his girth and age: he was very nearly 51!

The Gentlemen might have won the third match against the Players in 1934 if Bob Wyatt hadn't been dismissed 'when attempting an impossible run' in the second innings. They finished 20 runs short. Wyatt was run out for 99.

of his partner, who boasted of once having scored 5 not out in two and half hours against Notts.

The Monkey also captained England at rugby, but (unlike Barlow) was a distinct failure in Test cricket (despite taking a wicket without conceding a run!). In his three matches, two of which were lost and the other drawn, he was captain twice, including the famous defeat in 1882 that gave birth to the Ashes, a match in which he batted at number 10 in the first innings despite being a supposedly recognised batsman. His Test scores were 2, 4, 2, 9, 0 and 4! He was bowled by Fred Spofforth in each of his first four innings and stumped in the last two, so at least he escaped being run out.

Albert Knight, who played for England in 1904, had the unnerving habit of forgetting his batting partner's name, which led to all kinds of confusion. One of these unfortunates, playing for Leicestershire, was asked by Yorkshire's George Hirst, 'Won't you tell him your name, sir? Then we'll all be happy.'

Finding themselves a player short before a match in 1982, Douai School drafted in one Rob Booth, who had no pretensions to cricketing prowess. Going in last, he was faced with a no-win-but-every-chance-of-a-draw situation, needing only to keep out the last ball of the match. Having managed that with surprising aplomb, he then set off on a run, then another, then a fatal third. The run-out cost Douai the match.

Hard to imagine exactly what Booth and his partner were thinking of. Before that last delivery, Douai were approximately 50 runs behind! After it, school coach John Shaw announced his retirement from all forms of cricket!

Monkey businessman? Albert Neilson Hornby

Albert Neilson 'Monkey' Hornby was so bad between the wickets that his Lancashire opening partner Dick Barlow said that 'First he runs you out of breath. Then he runs you out. Then he gives you a sovereign for running you out. Then he runs out of sovereigns.' He once ran Barlow out by calling for an impossible single off the first ball of a match. Mind you, Hornby may sometimes have been glad to see the back

Not running out anyone

Missing the chance to hit

Needing only 104 to win the low-scoring first Test of the 1979–80 home series against the West Indies, New Zealand made terribly heavy weather of it, losing wickets so regularly and cheaply that they were still 30 behind with only two left. The target then shrank to four with the last pair at the crease, Gary Troup and Stephen Boock.

The latter, who batted at 11 because there was no 12, somehow kept out five consecutive balls from Michael Holding, was almost run out when running a bye, survived an lbw shout immediately afterwards, managed to score two runs to bring the scores level, then dashed for a leg-bye when the ball went off his pads backward of square leg.

Off-spinner Derick Parry, a rather peripheral character in an age of all-out pace (23 Test wickets at 40.69 each) picked up, threw in, and missed by a wide margin. West Indies' defeat by one wicket eventually cost them the series 1–0, the last they lost before 1995. Parry's last moment in Test cricket was as dismal as his first: in 1978 he'd been bowled by the first ball he faced!

One of the 1981 NatWest Trophy semi-finals wasn't decided till the very last ball, off which Derbyshire needed one run to bring the scores level and beat Essex by virtue of having lost fewer wickets.

Batsman Paul Newman hit the ball back to bowler Norbert Phillip, who took aim, fired, and missed. Phillip had taken three wickets as well as top-scoring with 42 in the Essex innings, but Derbyshire went through. In the final, they scored a single off the last ball to beat Northamptonshire on the fewer-wickets rule!

A famous last-wicket stand of 70 between Allan Border and Jeff Thomson almost won Australia the fourth Test against England in 1982–83. Thomson's excellent supporting role was worth 21 runs before he was dramatically caught at slip, but his team mates nevertheless soaked him in the dressing room after the match – for having conceded four overthrows when missing a run out. Australia lost by three runs!

In the second Test of the 1907–08 series Australia recovered from a first innings deficit of 116, set England 282 to win, reduced them to 209–8 and were still favourites when the ninth wicket fell at 243.

Sydney Barnes, many experts' choice as the greatest bowler of all time, who'd taken 5–72 in Australia's second innings, now made 38 with the bat, supported by number 11 Arthur Fielder, who hit an on-drive off Warwick Armstrong and set off for a single.

Jack Saunders got the ball in accurately enough, but wicketkeeper Hanson Carter fell over and England levelled the scores. Australia had every chance of forcing the first tie in Test cricket when Barnes pushed the ball to cover point. Gerry Hazlitt picked up, 'took a wild shy at the stumps, missed by yards, and we had won. If he had thrown in an underhand one ...'

Australia's defeat by one wicket cost them a clean sweep of the five-match series.

After drawing the first four Tests in 1953 England were pleased to dismiss Australia or 275 in the first innings of the fifth, then built on this by passing 100 with only one wicket down. Soon afterwards, Peter May pushed a ball from Ron Archer to midwicket.

Although it was May's call and he stayed where he was, his partner and captain Len Hutton took several strides down the pitch. Still May didn't move – so Hutton screeched to a halt and turned back. Too late. His opposite number Lindsay Hassett threw in to Archer, who knocked the bails off with Hutton well out of his ground. Australia seemed to be back in the game.

Not quite. In his eagerness, the fielder had broken the wicket without the ball, which he'd dropped. While Archer's 'head and shoulders drooped with utter mortification,' Hutton escaped to make 82, enough to give England a first-innings lead in a match they won to regain the Ashes after a record gap of 19 seasons.

Another close run thing for Hutton against Australia in 1953

On the first day of the first Test of the 1956 Ashes series, Keith Miller bowled to Colin Cowdrey, who pushed the ball towards cover point for an easy single but unlikely two.

The other England batsman Peter Richardson turned for the second run, was sent back by Cowdrey, skidded, fell over, and looked up to see his opening partner rushing towards the other end, having apparently decided to sacrifice himself. The run out would have been a formality if wicketkeeper Gil Langley hadn't fumbled the return from fielder Alan Davidson.

Seeing this, Richardson got up, left his bat where it was, and hared off to the bowler's end – whereupon Langley threw the ball to Miller, who didn't take it cleanly and went sprawling into the stumps just as Richardson rushed in. To the delight of the crowd, he was given not out, went on to score 81 (vital in an total of 217) and help England draw the match. They won the series 2–1.

Some of Australia's fielding in the 1977–78 series in the Caribbean was enough to make grown men fume. Grown men like Jeff Thomson, for instance. In the second Test, Bruce Yardley only had to toss the ball in underarm 'and the guy was run out by miles'. Instead he threw it miles over Thommo's head, aggrieving the fast bowler so much that he kicked the stumps down. When the crowd remonstrated with him in their usual gentle manner, 'There was a photo of me with my hand raised, apparently waving to two people.'

Fielding at mid-on against Kent, Surrey seamer Alf Gover strolled after the ball, intending to catch batsman Les Ames napping as he went for a second run. Gover reached the ball, picked it up with feigned indifference – then turned sharply to throw it in, only to find Ames standing safely in his crease, grinning. Gover had taken it so unhurriedly that he'd allowed the batsman to run three!

Two into one shouldn't go

The 1960–61 series between Australia and West Indies was one of the most vivid, starting with the first tied Test in history and ending with a narrow 2–1 win for the hosts – yet the West Indies had their chances to win it, and dropped quite a few of them, especially in that famous first Test, including four off Norm O'Neill when he made 181, his highest ever Test score.

In the very last over of the match, one of the most dramatic of all time, West Indies took a flurry of wickets to force the tie – and might have won it but for two more missed opportunities, both by fast bowler Wes Hall. He started well enough, having Richie Benaud caught off a bouncer, but then failed to run out Ian Meckiff, and dropped a catch he had no right to go for, completing his follow-through by putting down Wally Grout at square-leg where Rohan Kanhai had been waiting to take an easy catch. Hall apparently brushed him out of the way before dropping the catch! The extra run arguably made the difference between winning the match and tying it, between drawing the series and losing it.

Australia's 462–8 declared, their very first innings against New Zealand in 1973–74, was built on Keith Stackpole's 122, achieved thanks to no fewer than four dropped catches before he'd reached 50, starting with a collision between Mike Shrimpton and Brian Hastings while trying to catch him off the sixth ball of the match. Australia won by an innings and took the series 2–0.

India lost 2–1 in the West Indies in 1975–76 but would have drawn the series had it not been for 'innumerable missed chances' in the second Test. One of these was a stumping bungled by Syed Kirmani (see WICKED KEEPERS) but the rest were mainly catches, especially on the last day.

Deryck Murray batted for more than an hour after being dropped early on by Bishan Bedi, Bernard Julien was missed at short leg, and Viv Richards survived a run-out chance. Worst of all, West Indies captain Clive Lloyd made 70, easily the top score in a total of 215–8, but only after mistiming a drive straight to mid-off, where substitute fielder Eknath Solkar, one of the best in the business, would have caught it comfortably if Brijesh Patel hadn't sprinted across and collided with him. The match was drawn.

Having made only 147 in the 1978 B&H Cup final, Derbyshire needed to field well and above all hold their catches. Instead, they dropped Kent opener Bob Woolmer off successive balls. Each time the culprit was a world-class fielder: first their South African captain and former Test all-rounder Eddie Barlow missed a chance at first slip; then England wicketkeeper Bob Taylor moved across and knocked the ball away from Barlow. Woolmer's 79 accounted for more than half of Kent's 151–4 and Derbyshire had to wait another 15 years to win the Cup for the first time.

The Adelaide Oval was something of a jinx ground for Jeff Thomson, at least in Test matches. Against England in 1974–75 he injured his shoulder while playing tennis on the rest day (*Blunders Vol.1*), and against India in 1977–78 he was injured after bowling only 27 balls.

Above all, in the first Test against Pakistan in 1976–77, he bowled a bouncer at Zaheer Abbas, who mistimed a hook almost straight up in the air. Thomson looked, couldn't see anyone coming, and went for the catch himself. Just as he began his dive, he was hit by team-mate Alan Turner, going for the ball late. The collision tore ligaments in Thommo's shoulder (his shirt had to be cut open to see to the injury), and not only kept him out of the rest of the series but almost ended his career. He was never quite the same force again.

While he was in the changing room after the collision, someone he didn't recognise came in and asked if he could look at the injury, then pronounced that it would probably need an operation to pin the shoulder.

His reaction was typical Thommo: 'Pig's arse – and anyway, mate, who are you? What would you know about it? I'm waiting for the doctor to come in.' You've guessed it: he was the doctor.

During the second Test of the 1971–72 series in the West Indies, New Zealand fielder Geoff Howarth was set to make a run out (Vanburn Holder and Inshan Ali were taking risky singles) but as he dashed to take the throw at the bowler's end, a 'very good chance was lost' when he collided with umpire Ralph Gosein!

Pretend it's Sunday, Reverend

(and keep your hands together)

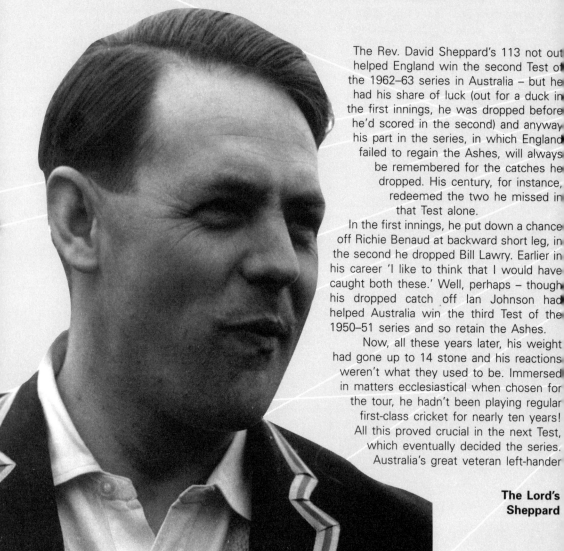

The Rev. David Sheppard's 113 not out helped England win the second Test of the 1962–63 series in Australia – but he had his share of luck (out for a duck in the first innings, he was dropped before he'd scored in the second) and anyway his part in the series, in which England failed to regain the Ashes, will always be remembered for the catches he dropped. His century, for instance, redeemed the two he missed in that Test alone.

In the first innings, he put down a chance off Richie Benaud at backward short leg, in the second he dropped Bill Lawry. Earlier in his career 'I like to think that I would have caught both these.' Well, perhaps – though his dropped catch off Ian Johnson had helped Australia win the third Test of the 1950–51 series and so retain the Ashes.

Now, all these years later, his weight had gone up to 14 stone and his reactions weren't what they used to be. Immersed in matters ecclesiastical when chosen for the tour, he hadn't been playing regular first-class cricket for nearly ten years! All this proved crucial in the next Test, which eventually decided the series. Australia's great veteran left-hander

The Lord's Sheppard

The Rev. David preaching the virtues of forgiveness

Neil Harvey seemed to have lost his touch and nerve, scoring 0 and 10 in the second Test. Here in the third, he came in with Australia 14–1 in their first innings and soon lofted a gentle catch straight to Sheppard at extra cover. Australian batsman Norm O'Neill called it a sitter.

The reverend himself 'saw it all the way into my hands – and out of them. If ever I have wanted that secret trap-door and underground route to the pavilion it was then.' Brian Statham shouted 'bad luck', though Fred Trueman's thoughts had probably less to do with the forgiveness of sins. Harvey went on to make 64 and help Australia win a low-scoring match and square the series.

For the vicar, the torments of the damned didn't stop there, and again Harvey was the sinner given a second chance. In the fourth Test, he swung the ball head-high to square leg, where Sheppard, who confessed that his confidence was hellishly low by now, dropped it. Harvey's 154 effectively drew the match.

Oddly enough, the man of the cloth had taken some good catches during the tour, including a skier that fell from the heavens in that fourth Test – but 'the ones that I dropped were at such vital moments.' The faith of his superiors was largely unaffected (he went on to become Bishop of Liverpool), unlike that of the more earthly powers (this was his last season in Test cricket).

During the tour, it's said that an English couple in Australia suggested to Sheppard's wife that her husband might be just the man to christen their new baby. Oh no, she replied, he'd be bound to drop it.

Many unhappy returns

Comeback trials

The daftest of all? Probably George Headley's in 1954. One of the greatest batsmen of all time, the pillar of the West Indies throughout the 1930s, the first black player to captain them, he averaged 60.83 in 22 Tests. His genius, obvious from the start, was probably best expressed on his first trip to Australia (1930–31). Predominately an off-side player at the start of the tour, he was bogged down when the Australians, especially Clarrie Grimmett, attacked his leg stump. Dismissed by his first ball of the series, by the end of it he'd scored two famous centuries and Grimmett was calling him the best leg-side player in the world. Other Australians called him the black Bradman. West Indians called Bradman the white Headley, and they weren't joking.

By 1954, however, he was 44 (the oldest West Indian ever to appear in Tests) and had been out of international cricket for five years after playing only two Tests since before the War – none of which stopped Jamaicans from organising a public subscription to bring him home from England after which the selectors didn't dare leave him out of the Kingston Test.

In each of his two previous Test innings on the ground, he'd scored a double century. But those had been 19 and 24 years earlier; now he took an hour to make 16 in the first innings and scored only a single in the second before being bowled by Tony Lock's controversial faster ball. Thankfully it wasn't enough to dilute the memory of what had once been, but Headley didn't play for the West Indies again.

After taking only 1–109 and being run out for 2 against England in 1964, South African off-spinner Dr 'Kelly' Seymour was dropped until the first Test of the 1969–70 series against Australia. In the second innings, he was fielding at mid-wicket when Ian Chappell hit a long hop straight at him.

Not only did Seymour drop it, thereby depriving part-time bowler Barry Richards of his first Test wicket, he broke his finger in the attempt. Physician heal thyself indeed. He made a duck in each innings and didn't play Test cricket again.

When Wally Hammond scored his imperious 240 against Australia in 1938, he gave only one chance, a caught-and-bowled dropped by Arthur Chipperfield, who broke his finger in the process, couldn't finish the over, took no further part in the match, and wasn't capped again.

George 'Gubby' Allen was a fast bowler who took 81 Test wickets while refusing to bowl Bodyline for Jardine, and a batsman good enough to score a Test century. For much of his later life, he was also one of the most influential figures behind the scenes at Lord's (some say his input was for the good of the game, others agree with Fred Trueman!), which may explain his choice as captain of the England team to the West Indies in 1947–48.

Allen hadn't been a bad skipper in the 1936–37 Ashes series, beaten only by Don Bradman's resurgence in the last three Tests – but the fact remains that England were the only side ever to lose a series after taking a 2–0 lead, and those had been Allen's last Test appearances. Now, 11 years on, he was 45 and, according to John Arlott, among others, 'not even remotely match fit'. Indeed, he had to miss the first Test and bowled less than three overs after breaking down in the third. He took only five wickets in the series at 41.00 each. England didn't win a single first-class match on the tour, lost the series 2–0, and Gubby, later inevitably Sir George, didn't play Test cricket again.

One of his later pronouncements as an England selector was that cricketers shouldn't train to the highest possible level of physical fitness!

Another who was recalled as captain after more than a decade out of Test cricket, as much for reasons of social class as playing ability, was Iftikhar Ali, the Nawab of Pataudi, who'd won three caps for England in 1932–34, scoring a century against Australia in his first Test innings. In the first season after the war, after an international absence of 12 years, he was invited to captain India in England.

His decision to accept the job was widely criticised as much then as now: he'd never played for India before, knew next to nothing about the players under him, and was known to be in poor health. He averaged only 11.00 in the Tests and according to *Wisden* 'seemed too ready to switch his batting order and too conservative in the deployment of his field.' India lost the series and Pataudi wasn't capped again.

Frank Woolley was a much loved left-hander who played first-class cricket for 32 years and brightened most of them with his batting ('There was all summer in a stroke by Woolley'), slow left-armers and ability in the field.

His Test averages, perhaps a fraction disappointing (36.07 with the bat, 33.91 as a bowler) are nevertheless those of a quality all-rounder – and he could be a genuine matchwinner: against Australia in 1912 he scored 62 and took 5–29 and 5–20 to decide the entire Triangular Tournament. Against the all-conquering pace of McDonald and

Gregory in 1921 he scored 95 (out of 187) and 93 at Lord's. He averaged 128.00 against the 1929 South Africans 17 years after taking 5–41 against their predecessors.

India's first official Test, at Lord's in 1932, seemed to be his swansong. England won, but Woolley was 45, scored only 9 and 21, didn't bowl, and was left out of the Bodyline tour of Australia.

Then, with the 1934 Ashes series in the balance, he was surprisingly recalled for the fifth Test, in which England trailed by 380 on first innings and lost wicketkeeper Les Ames to an injury.

As well as scoring five centuries and taking 83 wickets in Tests, Woolley had picked up 63 catches, a world record at the time. The only player to take more than 900 catches in first class cricket, his total of 1,018 looks certain to survive deep into the next century. At one stage, despite having had no previous experience of the job, he would have been the obvious substitute for Ames.

Now, at 47, he was having trouble bending down. He took a catch in Australia's second innings, but conceded 37 byes, still the Test record (Ames had given away only four in a first innings of 701). England lost by 562 runs and didn't regain the Ashes for another 19 years. Woolley made only 4 and 0 with the bat and that really was the end.

Although Tim O'Brien was apparently held in high esteem by WG Grace, this may have had something to do with his becoming Sir Timothy Carew O'Brien, 3rd Baronet. As a batsman, he was supposedly 'a master on sticky wickets', but he obviously didn't meet many of those in his representative career. He went to Oxford University, for instance, specifically to pick up a cricket blue, only to be clean bowled for 0 in each innings of his first match against Cambridge!

Naturally, this feat led to an almost immediate elevation to Test cricket, the second match of the 1884 series against Australia at Old Trafford, where he followed those ducks in the University Match with another, bowled yet again. The 20 runs he scored in the second innings weren't enough to save him from being dropped for the next match, which England won.

He had to wait four years for a second cap, when he was 'put in as hitter' against Australia at Lord's, but 'failed in his mission,' scoring 0 and 4 as Australia won by 61 runs.

Recalled again more than seven years later – as captain, no less, probably for no other reason than his knighthood in the interim – for the trip to South Africa in 1895–96, TC scored only 35 runs in the three Tests (against woefully weak opposition) as well as raising a few eyebrows by taking George Lohmann in with him as opening bat in the first two. As a bowler, Lohmann found the matting wickets very much to his liking (35 wickets at a preposterous 5.8 each) but wasn't in the same class as a batsman: he made a pair in the first match and only two in the second, when O'Brien was out for yet another 0. Sir Tim played in five Tests in all, averaging only 7.37 with the bat and making a duck in three of his eight innings.

---

*His feet were a long way
away from his body.*

Ravi Shastri

In 1895, 22-year-old forward Frank Mitchell was thrown into an England rugby team with nine other new caps who confounded everyone by beating Wales 14–6. Mitchell, who converted the last of England's four tries, was there to stay.

He played in all of England's matches that year and the next, scoring a try against Wales in 1896. He wasn't capped again after that year, but there were other strings to his bow.

In the winter of 1898–99 he opened the batting in two Tests for England in South Africa. After fighting in the Boer War, he

moved to that country, returning to England as captain of the team that toured in 1904 without playing any Tests.

That should have been that. A shortish, distinguished international career in two sports. However, when South Africa were invited back to England in 1912 to play in the only triangular tournament ever held, playing against Australia as well as the hosts, big Frank couldn't resist. Although he was now 39 and hadn't played Test cricket for 13 years, he accepted the captaincy.

In the first match of the tournament, Mitchell made a duck. In the next, he scored only a single in each innings. He averaged just 4.66 in the tournament (South Africa lost five matches and drew the other) and bowed out for good. He was captain in his last international in each sport.

In the same 1912 tournament, Australia were without the services of several regulars, including such all-time greats as Trumper, Armstrong and Clem Hill, all because of a dispute with the Australian board, who found themselves in need of a new captain, for which they went back to Syd Gregory, a short whiskery batsman who'd once (for a single day) held the world record for most runs in Test cricket.

But that had been ten years earlier, and Gregory was now 42. He scored 32 and 40 in the first Test, but England won it by 70 runs, and after that his form fell away: he made only a single in each innings of the decisive last Test, Australia lost it (and the tourna-ment) by 244 runs, and Gregory went back into international retirement. He was the first player to span 20 years in Test cricket.

In 1932 medium-pacer Don Cleverley played in his first Test, against the touring South Africans, bowled 22 expensive overs, and was dropped after New Zealand lost by an innings.

Dropped for good, it seemed. Certainly till the Second World War. Then, in the first Test played by any country after it, he was drafted in against Australia at Wellington: a gap of 14 years 28 days.

Although he made only a single in each innings, he was the only batsman Lindwall, O'Reilly and Co didn't get out as they dismissed New Zealand for 42 and 54 and didn't deign to play them again till 1973. Don, who hadn't bowled too cleverly in his two distant Tests (0–130), didn't play in another. No great surprise in that, perhaps: in a first-class career that lasted from 1930 to 1953, he averaged less than four wickets a year!

Teddy Wynyard was one of the leading all-round sportsmen of his day, scorer of a goal in the 1881 FA Cup final, Test cricketer for almost a decade – though he should really have been a one-cap wonder.

After making only 10 and 3 against Australia in 1896, he was dropped, apparently for good. When he heard of his call-up for the trip to South Africa in 1905–06, he could have been forgiven for thinking there was some leg-pulling going on (his birthday was April Fool's Day): he was 44 and well past his peak.

In the first Test, he started well enough with 29 in a low-scoring match, but his failure to score in the second innings was crucial: England lost by only one wicket to give the hosts their first ever Test win after 17 years of trying. Wynyard made another duck in his next Test innings and didn't play international cricket again.

If Walter Keeton didn't set much on fire in his first Test for England, against Australia in 1934, he wasn't a completely damp squib either (25 and 12 in a drawn match) but was left out for five years, perhaps because he suffered in comparison with Don Bradman's typically monumental 304.

On his return, against the West Indies in 1939, Keeton was bowled by Tyrell Johnson's first ball in Test cricket, made only

20 in the second innings, and (like Johnson) wasn't capped again. Meanwhile, the player he replaced, little Eddie Paynter, who averaged 59.23 in his 20 Tests, was scoring 154 for Lancashire.

Bill Voce was one of the leading participants in the 1932–33 tour, Harold Larwood's main henchman in the Bodyline controversy and an international class left-arm fast bowler in his own right, his 27 wickets on his return to Australia in 1936–37 ensuring that England made a fight of the series; indeed his 10–57 in the match effectively won the first Test.

By 1946, however, he was 36, past his prime and overweight, recalled to the England team only because the War had stunted the development of any new pace-bowling talent. After a single comeback match against India, he went on the 1946–47 tour to Australia, where he played in only two Tests, taking 0–161, and wasn't picked again after England lost the series 3–0. In three Tests after the War, Voce took only a single wicket.

Because Brian Luckhurst had done so well in Australia in 1970–71 (455 runs at 56.87), the England selectors must have thought they were making an inspired choice rather than a simple gamble when they took him back Down Under four years later. But he'd been out of Test cricket since 1973 (after scoring 1 and 12 as the West Indies won by an innings and 226) and was now 35, lacking the reactions to counter the assault by Lillee and Thomson. After averaging only 13.50 in the first two Tests, both of which England lost heavily, he was dropped for good.

Manny Martindale bowled in much the same way as he was: short and fast. In 1933 he helped inflict a form of Bodyline on its

perpetrator, the England captain Douglas Jardine, and took 14 wickets in only three innings. At home, he took 19 at only 12.58 each to help beat England in 1934–35, his 7–84 in the fourth Test contributing to the West Indies taking a winning 2–1 lead.

After that, he was out of international cricket until the 1939 series back in England, where he found that his speed and accuracy had deserted him. In the three Tests, his four wickets cost 78.50 each and he conceded well over four runs per over. If he'd been in any kind of form, the West Indies might have won the three-match series instead of losing it 1–0. He didn't play Test cricket again.

> *Chris Lewis didn't bowl, then came in and scored 30 – a top all-round effort.*
>
> **Alec Stewart**

In 1978, when Stewart Storey was captain of the Sussex 2nd XI, he was recalled to add some experience to the team against Middlesex in a B&H Cup match. The first ball he received, from fearsome West Indian fast bowler Wayne Daniel, reared up, hit Storey's elbow, chin and shoulder, shot across to cover point more than 20 yards away, and ended up in Graham Barlow's hands. 'That,' said Mike Gatting dryly, 'was the end of his comeback.'

John Dunning was one of the very inexperienced bowlers against whom Wally Hammond made his world record 336 not out in Auckland in 1933 (Dunning 2–156). In New Zealand's next Test, in England more than four years later, Dunning took 0–64 and 0–60, finishing with an international career of five wickets at an average of 98.60.

John Lever had one of the most explosive debuts in Test cricket, taking 7–46 and 3–24 and scoring 53 to help England win in Delhi in 1976–77. Five years later, his Test career seemed to have ended in the same stadium after taking 2–104 and scoring 2 – but he was recalled against the same country after another four years, for the second Test in 1986.

It didn't work out. Although he took six wickets in the match, they cost 166 runs and he bowled too many half-volleys early in India's first innings, allowing openers Sunil Gavaskar and Kris Srikkanth to make a flying start. No great surprise perhaps, given that Lever was now 37 and had been visibly nervous before the match. England lost by 279 runs and he didn't play Test cricket again.

Cricket bloomers

(and other items of clothing)

After the trip to England in 1995, West Indies seam bowler Kenny Benjamin was fined 10% of his tour fee for breaching dress-code regulations. He protested his innocence, claiming that he hadn't been issued with the required accoutrements. He came to England, he said, wearing Ian Bishop's blazer, Junior Murray's shirt and Winston Benjamin's trousers!

In the first Test of the 1933–34 home series against England, the respected all-rounder Amar Singh scored 0 and 1 and took 0–134, poor figures but none too surprising for a big man playing in tennis shoes! India lost by nine wickets.

All out for 120 in reply to England's 429 in the second Test of 1978, New Zealand's chances of a second-innings recovery were wrecked by two unnecessary run-outs. First, opener Robert Anderson tried to get off the mark with a single to David Gower, of all fielders, then John Parker's important 38 was ended when he slipped, the result of playing in shoes without spikes despite a recent shower of rain.

Roy Fredericks' dismissal in the 1975 World Cup final didn't affect the result, but ended his chance of participating fully in the victory. He slipped in the act of hooking Dennis Lillee for six, trod on his stumps, and was out hit wicket for 7, having decided to bat in boots without studs.

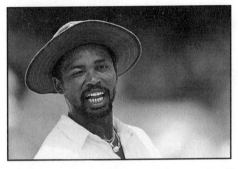

Kenny Benjamin (wearing his own hat?)

When Louis Powell went out to play his first innings for Somerset, against Lancashire in 1927, he put on a pair of extra-strong pads to face the pace of Ted McDonald – but forgot to wear a box. He lived to be 92.

It's reported that New Zealand seamer Chris Pringle once went in to bat against Pakistan while wearing two right-handed gloves.

In 1991, while batting in a match in Norfolk, Terry Sutherland was hit on the thigh by a ball which set fire to his trousers. He'd forgotten to take a box of matches out of his pocket.

Robert Poore was a very big man, a prodigious hitter (301 against Somerset, an average of 116.58 for Hampshire in 1899, three Tests for South Africa) and something of an eccentric. In his later years, by now a major-general, he took to wearing a solar topee (a heavy colonial sun hat) while fielding in warm weather. In one match for the MCC, he was fielding in the covers while watching leg-spinner Jim Powell bamboozle one of the local batsmen. Mark my words, he said to team-mate George Fenner, there's going to be a catch soon.

The very next ball, launched into the wild blue yonder by the exasperated batsman, descended alarmingly fast in the general direction of cover point. Poore did his best to locate the missile, but was hampered by his cranial accessory: the topee's brim was so wide and stiff that he couldn't see a thing.

After circling the outfield for an eternity, the major-general had to admit defeat: it's no good, Fenner, I can't see the wretched thing. Quite understandable, replied George: extra cover caught it ten seconds ago.

In the first Test of the 1977–78 series in Australia, India's leading middle-order batsman Dilip Vengsarkar top-scored in their first innings and might have led them to a reasonable total if he hadn't used his head too quickly. He'd reached 48 in the first innings before jerking away from a Jeff Thomson bouncer. This was all quite normal, both the Thomson bumper and Vengarkar's method of playing it, but this time he jerked too hard and his cap fell off onto his wicket. India lost the match by just 16 runs and the series 3–2.

What a sight Wes Hall made as he charged in on his long run, gold chain swinging round his neck as he bowled very fast and often all afternoon for the West Indies. What pain and embarrassment he must have felt in Australia ('caused a hold-up for running repairs') and while playing for the MCC,

when he damaged an eye. Each time, he'd hit himself in the face with the cross on the end of the chain!

Wes Hall and the cross he had to bear

CA Smith, later Sir Aubrey, the only player to captain England in his only Test (in 1889, the first ever played by South Africa), later became a well-known actor in Hollywood, where he ran his own cricket team well into middle age, by which time his eyesight wasn't what it used to be. On one occasion, after dropping a slip catch, he stopped the game and called for his butler, who strode across the sward and bowed. My spectacles, demanded Sir CA. When they had been brought out, in a case on a silver salver, he graciously allowed the umpires to continue the game.

Inevitably, the first ball after the resumption found the edge and thence the hands of the cricketing knight, who peered at it on the ground after he dropped it. 'Egad,' he's said to have said, 'the damned fool brought my reading glasses.'

Rodney Redmond toured England in 1973 but trouble with new contact lenses kept him out of the Tests. In fact his eyesight problems led to an early retirement from first-class cricket, which was unfortunate for New Zealand as well as for him: in his only Test, against Pakistan in 1972–73, he'd scored 107 and 56.

Getting ready for one of his stints on BBC Radio's *Test Match Special*, Christopher Martin-Jenkins got up just before dawn in his hotel, washed, dressed, and made his way to the Trent Bridge commentary box, where he discovered the perils of dressing in the dark: he was wearing one black leather shoe and one brown suede shoe. A small matter, but Brian Johnston and company made a big thing of it for weeks afterwards.

In the pitch invasion at the end the 1975 World Cup final, umpire Dickie Bird had one of his trademark white caps taken without his express permission. A few days later, a London bus conductor of West Indian descent was complimented on the very similar piece of apparel he was sporting. Not similar, the very same. Yes, he said proudly, Dickie Bird gave it to me. The passenger was rather sceptical about this, which was understandable given that he was Bird himself!

Vernon Royle was one of the great fielders, a terror at cover point – but less fearsome as a batsman (18 and 3 in his only Test, an average of 15.66 for Lancashire), something he proved in his very first county match. Picked against the old rivals Yorkshire in

1873, he forgot his shirt and had to play in a multicoloured Harlequin top, which is said to have embarrassed him so much in front of a large crowd that he was bowled first ball in each innings by England seamer Allen Hill.

Playing in a colts match in Wales, James Didcote was twice no-balled because his wicketkeeper Gareth Jones allowed the peak of his cap to protrude in front of the stumps!

One for the believe-this-and-you'll-believe-anything slot. Fielding for Kent in a county championship match, Les Todd ran to cut off a shot, sliding into it with both feet, only to pull up in sudden pain. It was only then, so they say, that he realised he was playing in bedroom slippers.

You seem to be batting into sticky water.

Mike Scott

And one item of clothing that didn't hinder the wearer too much. During the fourth Test in the Caribbean in 1929–30, England opener Andy Sandham had to use his captain Freddie Calthorpe's bat after breaking or selling all of his own and to wear Patsy Hendren's boots while batting (surely he hadn't sold all of his?). The bat was too long and the boots were too big, Sandham slithered and struggled in the heat, and several times during the innings wished himself back in the coolness of Surrey. It took all of Joe Hardstaff's persuasion to stop him giving his wicket away. Sandham scored 325, the first triple century in Test history!

Eating disorders

(so does drinking)

On the fourth evening of the 1982 Lord's Test against Pakistan, with England needing only one run to avoid the follow-on but their last man Robin Jackman at the crease, three of their players dined together at a French hostelry: Jackman himself, David Gower and Allan Lamb. The following day, Jackman was out for 0, condemning England to follow on and lose by 10 wickets. In their second innings, Gower and Lamb were also out without scoring. The night before, all three had ignored an old superstition by ordering duck!

The night before their one-day match against Ireland in 1969, the West Indies accepted some typically generous local hospitality, quite possibly including some of the black liquid kind. The following day, their team of well-known Test players was dismissed for 25.

Ted Dexter once broke his leg after being run over by his own car (don't ask), and Chris Lewis had Devon Malcolm shave his head at the start of the 1993–94 West Indies tour then missed the first match because he was suffering from sunstroke! But these were mere novices compared with the great Australian master of this kind of thing.

If ever a man was a danger to himself it was Ashley Mallett. It's surprising that he survived to take 132 Test wickets (1968–80) with his off-spin, given that when he wasn't setting fire to newspapers on airliners or falling over sets of stumps, he was spraining his ankle by treading on a ball or flooding an entire hotel suite by leaving the bath running

while he engaged in a wrestling match with Rod Marsh. Even for someone nicknamed Rowdy because he wasn't, he once batted remarkably soporifically, having taken sleeping tablets instead of salt pills.

Umpire Dickie Bird, the greatest worrier in cricket, naturally shared the traditional English mistrust of Indian food (see WITH FRIENDS LIKE THESE). During the 1987 World Cup in Calcutta and the rest, he was quite seriously ill and had to spend time in bed. Small wonder, given that his daily diet consisted of two boiled eggs at breakfast, two more for lunch, and 'I relaxed a little at dinner and had two boiled eggs with chips.'

Derek Underwood and journalist Chris Lander should have known better than to accompany Ian Botham on some of his excursions to the restaurant at the top of the team hotel during the 1981–82 tour of India. One of these resulted in Deadly Derek providing the evening cabaret by mistaking another table for the dance floor (to placate the couple dining at it, Botham sent them tickets for the Test). Lander later performed his own party piece by singing to the guests in the penthouse bar then falling into the audience, hence his nickname Crash.

During the match against Western Australia in 1986–87, Botham himself had such a good night-before that on the morning-after he was on his way out to bat when the England 12th man tapped him on the shoulder and suggested that he 'might need this' then handed him his bat.

The liquorice allsort tooth and a boiled egg in the pocket? Dickie Bird ponders the problems of modern umpiring

Similarly, Bob Willis (who had a higher opinion of his ability than this) once walked to the wicket at Edgbaston without his bat.

When Paul Gascoigne accepted an invitation to appear on *A Question of Sport*, he laid himself open to Ian Botham's still youthful sense of humour. Having been convinced by Both that advocaat was a non-alcoholic drink, he imbibed a fair quantity thereof, with the result that he was barely able to speak when the programme was shot. Asked if he wanted a home or away question, he simply grinned before eventually holding up a card saying 'home'.

The laugh, though, was on Botham, who'd inveigled him into drinking the insidious brew because he thought Gazza was on Bill Beaumont's team. He wasn't, and 'we came a good second that evening.'

In another edition of the programme, Graham Gooch was shown an array of faces and asked what their common link was. No idea, he said. Answer: they'd all opened the England innings with him.

Yorkshire 232 all out, Hutton ill. No, I'm sorry: Hutton 111.

John Snagge

England's win in the first Test of the 1930 series was the ninth match in which they'd been captained by Percy Chapman, the sixth against Australia. They'd won them all. But even then Chapman was showing signs of physical decline. True, even in England's first defeat under his leadership, the very next in the series, he was still good enough to score his only Test century and take a brilliant catch at gully to dismiss Don Bradman – but

he was no longer the splendid athlete he used to be (rugby triallist at Cambridge) having to field much closer to the wicket because his weight had ballooned to well over 15 stone, three heavier than when he regained the Ashes in 1926. After winning those first nine Tests, he didn't win one of his last eight.

Much of this was down to a well documented fondness for the demon drink which owed something to his job with a whisky company. Before the 1930 series, he made a speech advocating the reduction of duty on scotch! By the end of it, England had lost the Ashes and Chapman had been dropped as captain in favour of Bob Wyatt which former captain Arthur Gilligan called 'one of the biggest cricket blunders ever made.' Certainly England's innings defeat cost them the series 2–1.

Chapman's batting, based on physical gifts rather than sound technique or temperament, fell away dramatically, proof of the folly of drinking and driving, or hooking, or hitting any other kind of shot. He led England to South Africa the following winter but averaged just 10.71 in the series (the only one he lost as captain) and didn't play Test cricket again. His subsequent decline was well documented and much mourned. He once declared the Kent innings closed because he was shaking at the thought of having to bat, and when he shared half a pint with Les Ames and 'Hopper' Levett, they were pleased to see him drinking so little, only to be informed that it wasn't beer in the glass but whisky

In 1995 Wayne Radcliffe was banned for five years by Wakefield District Union for relieving himself on the pitch, even though he'd 'turned towards some trees' and 'hardly anybody saw.'

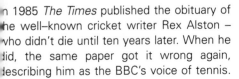

Writing wrongs

'I'll decide when I write my obituary.' **IAN BOTHAM**

In 1985 *The Times* published the obituary of the well–known cricket writer Rex Alston – who didn't die until ten years later. When he did, the same paper got it wrong again, describing him as the BBC's voice of tennis.

In 1971 the doyen of all writers, Neville Cardus, read his own obit in a local paper. 'I have no wish to challenge the authority of the press. They must have their sources.'

Back in 1896, news came through of the death of Charles Coventry, a former England player. At the funeral service in Worcestershire, the assembled mourners were suddenly informed that he'd survived the latest skirmish in the Boer War. He didn't die till 1929.

Just how good was the wicketkeeping during England's 1989–90 Test series in the Caribbean? Vic Marks in *The Observer*: 'Russell set the highest possible standard behind the stumps.' Robin Marlar in the *Sunday Times*: 'The keeping in this series was abysmal.'

After veteran openers Brian Close and John Edrich had been subjected to a brutal bombardment by Andy Roberts and Michael Holding in the third Test of 1976, Marlar wrote that umpire Dickie Bird 'stood like a pillar at square leg and did nothing about it.'

Hard to know what he could have done, given that he wasn't officiating in the match. The umpire in question was Lloyd Budd.

When Reg Simpson won his first cap, in 1948, his local Nottingham paper mentioned

that he'd been 'a detective in the local police farce'. After spotting the misprint, they added a correction, telling their readers that the sentence should have read 'Simpson has been a defective in the local police force.'

After off-spinner Fred Titmus had taken nine wickets in the first Test in India in 1963–64, a leading Indian writer referred to the 'England fast bowler Titmus'.

These Freds, fast or slow, were obviously hard to tell apart. FS Trueman may not have attained his full speed and fire in his first season (1949) but even so *Wisden* were risking the great man's ire when they wrote that Yorkshire had given a trial to 'Trueman, a spin bowler'!

Not that Fred himself always got it completely right. Years later, he wrote that his county team mate Jimmy Binks was 'the greatest uncapped wicketkeeper who ever played cricket.' Binks played twice for England against India in 1964.

Nor was Binks particularly impressed when the Fiery one ran him out at Lord's in 1963. Binks, on 88 at the time, played 412 consecutive Championship matches without ever scoring a first-class century. His mood wasn't improved when Trueman scored his own maiden hundred soon afterwards!

Every Monday, the *Daily Telegraph* used to run a Commentary section by Jim Swanton, featuring details of remarkable cricketing feats achieved that week, especially in public school matches 'which Swanton could never resist'. Many of them were sent in by the Kent and England batsman Peter

Richardson – and were purely fictitious. Richardson was one of the great practical jokers of his day.

Eventually Swanton's secretary (who later married Richie Benaud) realised what was going on and began checking postmarks to see which astounding tale had arrived from where Kent were playing their latest match, whereupon Richardson simply arranged for the opposition team to send it from their next destination. It's said that 'everyone in cricket knew about this, except EW Swanton.'

Not that he was the only one to be duped by the incorrigible Richardson. When Brian Johnston was short of information on Mike Denness, he made the mistake of contacting the latter's Kent team-mate, with the result that Johnners was soon revealing, on air, that Denness' father was a Banff sheep farmer whose son had to travel 250 miles by scooter to play cricket every weekend. Actually, Denness senior was a district sales manager for a cigarette company.

> *Too many players attempt to play the ball with their pants.*
>
> **Garry Sobers in *The Sunday Telegraph***

Soon after becoming a separate country (1948), Pakistan entertained a Commonwealth team, whose blazers were embossed with the word 'PARKISTAN' in gilt lettering.

Abdul Kardar played Test cricket for both India and Pakistan. While he was at Oxford University (1947–49), it's said that his bowling induced one writer to describe him

as 'an Indian mystic', which appeared in print as 'an Indian mistake'. Kardar, later the despotic president of the Pakistan board, was not amused.

Bill Frindall, the BBC's scorer on *Test Match Special*, once received a telegram from his mother addressed to 'Chestnut Special, Edgbaston.'

And pictures that didn't tell the story

A photo of wicketkeeper Lisa Nye appeared on the cover of the official programme for the 1993 Women's World Cup tournament – even though she'd been dropped from the England squad.

During the 1970–71 Ashes tour, an Australian newspaper ran a series of photos showing England's John Snow apparently picking the seam of the ball. Shock horror, Poms up to their tricks.

Well, not quite. Snow, playing up the image of the big bad fast bowler, had seen the photographer coming and pretended to do the dirty deed, knowing that it was impossible to pick the seam on a Kookaburra ball: it didn't have one! Someone in the picture editor's office should have sussed that one: after all, it was an Australian ball.

In an Australian drama series based on the 1932–33 Bodyline tour, its makers' attitude to historical accuracy was exemplified by the sequence which showed wicketkeeper Les Ames making a stumping off Harold Larwood!

Extras

Too early birds

In 1938 a trophy was presented to the scorer of the fastest half-century at Hove. In the penultimate match of the season, Hugh Bartlett made a century in 57 minutes, including a very quick fifty. He couldn't play in the last match, so the trophy was presented to him during the tea interval on the first day – after which George Cox scored a hundred in an hour, including a fifty that was faster than Bartlett's. The trophy had to be handed over.

At Sydney in January 1980, Australia played England in a one-day game, in which a panel of journalists made Dennis Lillee man of the match for taking four wickets while conceding only 12 runs from ten overs – but again the award was made too soon. Not only did Graham Stevenson, in his first international match of any kind, take 4–33 and run out Geoff Dymock, he came in at number 10 and hit 28 not out in 18 balls to win the match for England by two wickets.

You've got to be in it to win it

In 1994, Chinmay Gupte travelled to Blackheath in Kent to play for the MCC, only to find that the match was being held in Blackheath in Surrey. The following year he turned up in Blackheath in Surrey when (you've guessed it) the match was in Blackheath in Kent.

During the 1988–89 Australian season, Mafi Khan arrived late from Pakistan because his travel agent had arranged for him to travel to Obock, Tanzania instead of Hobart, Tasmania.

During the match against Surrey at the Oval in 1926, Leicestershire wicketkeeper Tom Sidwell was recorded as 'absent, lost on the Northern Line'!

When Feltonfleet failed to arrive at Belmont to fulfil a school fixture, their cricket teacher realised what must have happened and drove the team to Belmont. On the way, they were involved in a minor collision with another school bus: Belmont travelling to Feltonfleet!

When Australian Test bowler Jack Saunders left the ground briefly during Victoria's match against the touring MCC in 1903–04, he expected to be able to return in plenty of time to bat. Unfortunately for him and the team, they had to face Wilfred Rhodes while he was away, and Saunders couldn't get back in time to help out. Victoria, batting with only ten men, were dismissed for 15!

When Lord Ward 'failed to be present when his turn came to bat,' Oxford lost the 1841 University Match by eight runs.

In 1969, Peter Ellis planned to parachute onto the field during a club match. At the

King Viv didn't obey the Order of the British Empire

end of his descent from 3,000 feet, he missed the playing arena and landed instead on a 11,000 volt cable, stampeding a herd of cattle and cutting off the electricity supply to seven surrounding villages. Ellis, unaffected by the shocking experience, walked to the wicket still wearing his crash helmet and made a single before being dismissed.

Viv Richards, awarded the OBE in 1994, wasn't at Buckingham Palace to collect it. Hard to believe that he forgot, but that's what they say ...

Sounded out

Following on 314 runs behind in the first Test of the 1897–98 Ashes series, Australia did well to score 408 in their second innings, but it was only enough to set England a target of 95, which would surely have been more if Charlie McLeod hadn't been slightly deaf.

The handicap didn't stop him scoring a century in the second Test, but it proved decisive here. Unable to hear the call of no-ball when Tom Richardson bowled him, he set off for the pavilion, whereupon wicketkeeper Bill Storer rather unsportingly ran him out. Since he'd been well set on 26 (he'd made 50 not out in the first innings), his was obviously an important dismissal. Australia lost by nine wickets.

Garry never had a nickname.
He was always called Garry
or the King.

Pat Pocock

Against New Zealand in 1978–79, Pakistan opener Talat Ali was dismissed by Richard Hadlee in each of his five innings in the series, including the second Test, in which he was bowled for 13 in the second innings when he mistook Hadlee's grunt for the umpire's call of no-ball, something that county batsmen were forever doing against that famous grunter Allan Jones, of Somerset, Sussex, Middlesex and Glamorgan.

Index

Acknowledgments for Illustrations

Allsport UK Ltd
Simon Bruty 127
Mike Hewitt 58, 115
Clive Mason 64-5, 109
Adrian Murrell 13, 43, 49, 51, 78, 98, 151, 179
Ben Radford 12, 175
Historical Collection 176

Hulton Getty Library 10, 16, 28, 46, 59, 66-7, 68, 96, 103, 157, 165, 168, 169

Popperfoto 18, 24, 27, 33, 37, 72, 82, 87, 89, 91, 107, 123, 133, 134, 136, 140, 154, 158, 163, 184